A HISTORY OF
THE ROYAL HAMPSHIRE COUNTY HOSPITAL

Alured Clarke (1696-1742) from the portrait by Willis. He was Canon of Winchester, and founder of the Hampshire County Hospital in 1736.

A HISTORY OF
THE ROYAL HAMPSHIRE
COUNTY HOSPITAL

Barbara Carpenter Turner

Phillimore

1986

Published by
PHILLIMORE & CO. LTD.
Shopwyke Hall, Chichester, Sussex

ISBN 0 85033 606 6

Printed and bound in Great Britain by
BIDDLES LTD.
Guildford and King's Lynn

Contents

List of Illustrations

Acknowledgements

I have to thank many people for their help and constructive advice in the years when I have been writing this book. At first I was able to discuss it with my husband and his sister, Doctor E.M. Rix. They had both been frequent visitors to the Hospital in the days of their aunt, Emily Carpenter Turner, and had come to know many of the people in whom I began to be interested and some of whom I met, and I had many discussions, too, with the late Miss M.E. Gould, of St Thomas' Hospital. I owe a particular debt to Mr W.E. Boorman, M.P.S., for his detailed work on early apothecaries and his study of smallpox, both marked by the two great virtues of modesty and thoroughness. Some people I have thanked within the text, but I want to thank the staff of the library at the Wellcome Institute for the History of Medicine, the librarian E.J. Freeman, the archivist Miss J.G.H. Sheppard and the assistant archivist Ms L.A. Hall. For information about the origin of the Littlehales family, I have to thank the archivist of Shropshire County Council and in particular Mr M.T. Halford's assistant, Miss Ruth Bagley, and also the staff in the Wiltshire County Record Office. Two successive librarians of the Royal College of Physicians, Mr. L.M. Payne and Mr H. Davenport, so helpful about doctors and surgeons, and also Mr Harry Haysom, F.R.C.S. and others whose professional task it is to assist historians in Hampshire, all of whom have helped so generously. The staff of the Hampshire County Record Office, past and present, headed by Miss R. Dunhill; Miss Gill Rushton the Winchester City Archivist; Mr M. McGrave and Mrs P. Stevens of the Hampshire Central Reference Library, and all the staff of the Winchester City District Library, and Mr D. Dyme there; Doctor John Harvey and Doctor Roger Custance, archivists to Winchester College, and in the Bursary there I thank Mrs M. Wilks, that expert on Kingsgate Street and St Michael-in-the-Soke.

I want to thank those kind people who have been at the heart of the matter during the last two years and who know so much about the Hospital since the apppointed day; Miss Margaret Skellern, S.R.N.; Mrs C. Dobson, the librarian of the R.H.C.H., who has produced many of the book's illustrations, and who has always supplied me with anything I wanted to read; that experienced administrator Mr T. Perkins; Mr R. Urquhart (Deputy-Chairman of the Winchester Health Authority); and all those members of the present medical staff whose advice has been so invaluable, and who have been so kind in explaining and describing the technical advances of the post-War years.

Finally, I do indeed thank my publisher Noel Osborne of Phillimore; the Authority's General Manager, Howard Nattrass, for his efficient and seemingly endless capacity in supplying all kinds of help; and of course the Chairman, Lord Northbrook, for his great support and encouragement. May the Royal Hampshire County Hospital continue to be what the first chairman deemed it might become – a general blessing to our country.

Preface

The work of Alured Clarke, his foundation of the Hampshire County Hospital in Winchester in 1736, has sometimes been called the creation of a pioneer hospital. So perhaps it may not be thought inappropriate to describe this book as its pioneer history, a first attempt to give some account of the 250 years of the Hospital's existence. The account is derived chiefly from the Hospital's own archives, the series of Minutes of the Court of Governors, of Minutes of the Weekly (Management) Committee, and from the Annual Reports. It is a substantial archive, beginning in 1736, though the Annual Reports have not survived in their entirety, and there are gaps in both sets of Minutes. The result is essentially a narrative history, based on the two sets of Minutes. Where other material has been used, the sources are indicated in the footnotes at the end. Much can be discovered, or is known about the Governors of the Hospital and medical staff, some of them national personalities, but just because Clarke's Hospital was intended for the Poor Sick and the Poor Lame, and 'the Poor', historically speaking, leave little behind them in the way of a personal record unless they have come to the notice of the law, not so much is known about the individuals who were the Hospital's patients. Generalisations about patients have been avoided, especially descriptions of treatment elsewhere in other hospitals which does not necessarily find a parallel in Winchester. There is clearly room for much future research into many aspects of the Hospital's story.

The Hospital's history poses some interesting problems, of which the most fundamental is the mere fact of its survival over 250 years, and the second is the extent of its success in achieving a high reputation surpassing that of other similar institutions. It survived because it was needed, because it could change sufficiently to meet the needs of successive generations, and always, at critical moments, there was some strong minded individual at hand willing to devote time and energy, and sometimes money, to produce the solution to some crisis. Richard Taunton, John Hoadly, Sir Thomas Baring, Sir William Heathcote, Leonard Keyser and Sir George Cooper are the obvious examples. Yet it was not they who gave the Hospital its medical reputation which made young doctors and surgeons so anxious to serve in Winchester. Despite the difficulties of the early years, there was soon never a shortage of physicians and surgeons. Surgeons came to Winchester once it was apparent that in the famous Charles Lyford (d.1805) and his son and grandson, there was associated with the Hospital a dynasty of very able men, and this tradition of excellence in surgery was paralleled by the career of Charles Mayo. It was the Hospital's great good fortune that this high standard of surgery was accompanied by the work of equally able physicians, John Makkitrick and the Littlehales, father and son. These were the men who set the Hospital's standards. It must be added that the essential feature of much of this success was the availability for dissection and anatomising the bodies of criminals hung after sentence at Assizes, not an easily recognised advantage of Winchester's standing as an Assize town.

The Founder himself had set the standard required from his Matrons and the nursing staff; Florence Nightingale not only enhanced this standard; she also turned an occupation into a highly valued profession. Her own connections with Hampshire, her local friendships, her considerable knowledge of the Winchester Hospital were undoubtedly factors in its continued success. One final historical factor can be suggested which helps to explain the Hospital's success and its endurance. Not only had Winchester been an Assize town, it had been a military city with a garrison and a large Barrack area. So it was natural that its Hospital should have played its particular part in the care of the wounded in both the two World Wars. At a dreadful moment in 1916, Canon Vaughan, the historian of Winchester Cathedral, preached the St Luke's Day Sermon for the Hospital's Anniversary. To him, the Hospital was an oasis of light and of tender care in a darkening world of death and destruction and 'it would be interesting to trace the history of our Hospital'. He must have known that the story of the Royal Hampshire County Hospital would be a story of hope.

Introduction: Before The Foundation

i) *Some Early Winchester Hospitals*

Long before 1736 when Alured Clarke founded what he hoped would be that 'general blessing to our country', the County Hospital, there had been men and women in Winchester who had devoted themselves to the care of the poor and the needy, the sick and the dying. It would have been surprising if this had not been the case in a town which became one of the great centres of Christendom, some two hundred years after St Birinus converted the West Saxons to Christianity in AD 634. The traditional credit of founding Winchester's first hospital, dedicated to St John the Baptist and still a flourishing charity, belongs to an early Bishop of Winchester, St Brinstan (c.AD 934). Leland recorded the tradition, a statue of the Bishop stood in the Chapel, and the monks of Hyde Abbey in their calendar remembered Brinstan each year as a local saint and the founder of the Hospital.[1] Throughout the Middle Ages, Winchester men and women were cared for in St John's; it was not only a hospital building with a chapel attached to it, but also the meeting place of the Corporation of the City, and a headquarters for the Winchester craft gilds. It was here that the greatest of all Winchester's annual celebrations, the Corpus Christi day procession, assembled year after year, and that the Mayor was elected each Michaelmas. Benefactors of all kinds left their money and real estate to the Hospital, making it what it remains, a very wealthy charity. In the medieval Hospital, the functions of nursing hospital and almshouse appear to have been combined; there were apparently male and female nurses, and there is some evidence to suggest that entry was a matter of influence, of knowing members of the Corporation. St John's stood within the wall, but the so-called Winchester Domesday Surveys of c.1110 and 1148 record another apparently Anglo-Saxon foundation outside Westgate, where there was what has been called a cottage hospital, referred to in the text as a hospital 'on the ditch', 'built for the love of God' and near a group of five shanties (*bordelli*) 'to shelter poor folk', both apparently private foundations.[2] This hospital in the ditch did not long survive the Norman Conquest, but on the hill at the eastern end of the town, the Hospital of St Mary Magdalene, a foundation which dates from at least 1155, served generations of men and women who were considered to be suffering from leprosy; it is represented today by a group of almshouses on the Weirs. The original Hospital, '*juxta Winton*', stood on the down still known as Morn or Magdalene Hill, and its ruins were finally pulled down in c.1798, when Bishop Milner, the Roman Catholic historian of Winchester, saved its Norman western door, now incorporated in the modern Catholic Church in Jewry Street.[3] Other parts of the building were used by the builder in charge of the demolition to make his own house, The Hermitage, a 'Gothic' structure, recently demolished in Middle Brook Street.[3] The diagnosis of 'leprosy' in the Middle Ages undoubtedly included other diseases, but the need to isolate its probable victims was widely accepted; leper hospitals were common in medieval England, and usually dedicated to the same saint. St Mary

Magdalene on the hill in Winchester was under royal patronage, and the Sheriff of the county of Hampshire made regular payments to it on behalf of the King, but apart from one late medieval document, a manuscript probably compiled for the benefit of William of Wykeham, there is little documentary evidence about this particular hospital.[5]

Winchester's most famous medieval hospital was and is undoubtedly that of St Cross, founded by Bishop Henry de Blois in the village of Sparkford, immediately south of the city, in c.1136, and eventually a nursing hospital, a refuge for poor wayfarers, a place where the poor could be fed, and where free school meals were given to the poor scholars of the Winchester High School, years before William of Wykeham founded Winchester College. Though de Blois' foundation seems to have been intended originally for old men who were so feeble that they could not stand without help, this Hospital eventually became an almshouse rather than a nursing institution, rather like St John's and St Mary Magdalene, though there seems always to have been some measure of professional nursing, and even occasionally a Hospital doctor. Moreover, at St Cross, the original foundation was reinforced by Bishop Waynflete's addition of a second original group of 'brothers', derived from an intention of Cardinal Beaufort. The 'red' brothers, of Beaufort's Almshouse of Noble Poverty, joined the 'black' brothers of de Blois' later foundation, and add in no small measure to Winchester's reputation as a picturesque and historical city.

That reputation is very largely a legacy from the years when the city contained three great monastic establishments, the Priory of St Swithun (Winchester Cathedral), St Mary's Abbey for nuns, and St Grimbald's Abbey (alias St Peter's) for monks at Hyde, a third Benedictine House.[6] All three of these great churches had infirmaries for their own members, but it is not always realised that they also had nursing hospitals for the poor and needy, foundations which were essentially intended to look after the families, in particular the aged parents, of nuns and monks whose very calling prevented them from carrying out that duty in any other way. The 'Sisterne Spital' of St Mary's stood in the middle of the present Broadway, roughly where King Alfred stands today, and the nuns who worked in it until 1539 were much beloved, for their particular hospital answered a real need in this east end of Winchester. The building survived the dissolution, passed into the hands of the Corporation, became a notorious Tudor slum, and then the Bridewell of the City until its demolition in c.1790, when the Broadway was created.[7]

The 'sistern spytal' which belonged to the Cathedral also survived the dissolution of that monastery. It stood in what is now College Street, on its southern side, and consisted of a chapel on the street frontage with a hospial building behind it where, as the Cathedral archives record, the 'poor sisters' were maintained and nursed until they died. In 1419, when there were 16 sisters there, a lay physician had to be employed to attend them, at a cost of 10 shillings for a year's work, including his supply of medicine. After the Dissolution, the Sisterne Chapel was let by the newly formed Dean and Chapter to a baker from the Soke who made it into a private house, and the Hospital itself was occupied by a series of tenants, most of whom were naturally connected with Winchester College.[8] Little is known about the third monastic hospital, that of Hyde, a monastery whose archives have been almost completely lost.[9] The preliminary point has been perhaps sufficiently made, that

Winchester had a tradition of hospitals long before the 18th century, and that in the Middle Ages there were six foundations where the old, the poor and the sick might hope to find some measure of experienced nursing.

ii) *Early Medical Practitioners*

There can be no doubt that the three monasteries helped the sick and the poor who came to their gates, nor that there were individual monks and nuns skilled in the arts of medicine and of nursing. Dom David Knowles has described Anglo-Saxon medicine as a tripartite mixture of traditional practice, herbal knowledge, and popular magic. It is a description which could be applied to an early manuscript from St Mary's Abbey, a book written for Winchester nuns.[10] Though all three Winchester monasteries remained much under the influence of Fleury and Cluny, houses 'not interested in medicine', the practices of the great European medical schools at Salerno and, later, Montpellier, were very important, and were brought to England by the new Abbots after the Norman Conquest. Edward the Confessor's physician, Baldwin of St Denys, did not die until 1098, and had been rewarded with the Abbey of Bury. Abbot Faricius of Abingdon was *accoucheur* to Matilda, Henry I's wife. His contemporaries included Hugh, a monk of St Swithun's Priory, who became Abbot of Chertsey in 1107. The successful practice of medicine sometimes proved a bar to monastic promotion, however, for grateful patients offered money or land and, in any case, female patients were not, strictly speaking, acceptable. The teaching of medicine by monks was forbidden by Pope Alexander III in 1136, just at the time when Bishop Henry of Winchester (de Blois) was apparently considering the founding of St Cross Hospital. In c.1200, the Cathedral Priory granted its marsh land at Houghton to a neighbouring land owner, William Briwere, in exchange for an annual rent of 20 shillings, half of which was to be spent on the medicinal needs of the Priory's Infirmary.[11] Some Priory tenants were under an obligation to provide large quantities of wild strawberries at mid-summer, as a delicacy for the Infirmary, but the surviving Infirmary rolls throw little light on medical practice, and in 1320 the Priory appointed an outsider, Master Thomas of Shaftesbury, clerk, as the Chapter physician. His agreement with Prior Richard and the rest of the convent has survived and is dated 18 February 1319. He was probably an old man, looking forward to a peaceful old age in the Priory, for it was he who had paid the Prior a lump sum, 50 pounds sterling, not vice-versa, in return for a daily allowance of bread and beer, two dishes from the Prior's kitchen, a yearly suit of livery, and a room in the Priory kept in good repair. He undertook to serve as 'Physician according to their need', but the food promised was not to be supplied 'as long as he stands at the Prior's table'.[12]

The belief that illness was the result of sin remained widespread, and can still be found today. The remedies prescribed by Bishop Edington in 1348 to ward off the Black Death were non-medicinal, including much walking in processions and the recital of the penitential psalms.[13] It does seem probable, however, that the existence of the monastic communities in Winchester, of these early hospitals, and of Winchester College, encouraged the demand for medical care, and after the Reformation and the Dissolution of the monasteries that care had to be provided by laymen. Other important factors which made for change included the foundation of the Royal College of Physicians in 1518, a body given the right, in 1522, to license all physicians in England, except graduates of Oxford and Cambridge, whose permission to practise continued to be granted by diocesan bishops. The ancient divisions of surgeons, physicians, as well as alchemists and priests remained. The company of Barber-Surgeons of London, an amalgamation, was founded in 1540.

iii) *After the Dissolution*

The whole practice of medicine in Winchester must have received some encouragement in October 1559, just after the death of Mary I, when John Warner was appointed Dean of the Cathedral, for here was a priest who was also a doctor. An Oxford graduate, he had been appointed first Regius Professor of Medicine at that University of 1546, and became a Fellow of the College of Physicians after taking up his Winchester appointment;[14] two of his books survive in the Cathedral Library.

After his death in 1565, two names stand out as physicians of distinction. Thomas Bassett, who died in February 1575/6, described in the inventory of his goods made after his death as 'In Physicke Doctor', was a very successful and wealthy Winchester doctor. His house contained a hall, a large parlour, a study, a kitchen, with separate buttery and 'backehouse', two first floor bedrooms, and some valuable plate, a goblet and a beer pot of parcel gilt, two large salt cellars, each with a cover, and a set of six spoons. Bassett was still a Catholic, these were difficult times, and he kept a small collection of weapons in his bedroom, a rapier and three daggers. He had perhaps become too old to go any distance in visiting his patients and, indeed, it was more usual for patients to come to their doctor, not vice-versa. He had no stable, no nag, though he had kept his riding boots and his spurs. He certainly must have looked prosperous and his clientèle would surely have considered that their doctor was successful when they saw him at home in his gown 'guarded with velvet', or wearing his doublet of tawny satin, his jacket of black satin, his coat of grosgrain silk, or his jerkin of damask, and he owned six shirts, a large number indeed for a man of his time. It seems clear that, like his contemporaries, he was a doctor who made up his own medicines, using the still (Stillitorie) in the 'backehouse', and that, in advance of his time, he used a microscope, since 'a glasse for a student' was also amongst his effects. When he died, he had just negotiated a lease of the Charnel Chapel in the churchyard of St Mary's Abbey, but why he wanted this particular property must remain a problem. It would be tempting to suggest that its contents would have provided him with a supply of bones sufficient for any student of anatomy, and that Thomas Bassett was one of the most advanced doctors of his time.[15]

Simon Tripp(e), who died in 1596, and who had been appointed physician to the Dean and Chapter in 1581 at an annual fee of ten pounds a year, was another successful medical man, a true Renaissance doctor who had studied at Oxford, Cambridge and Padua.[16] From a Devonshire family, he had eventually settled in the city, taking a long lease of what is now Colebrook House, a property which he virtually rebuilt. His practice soon gave him enough money to invest in other property, and he bought the lease of Barton Mills from the Bishop of Winchester and of Winnal parsonage, and sent his son as a scholar to Winchester College. Most of the rooms in his house had wainscott, and in a closet leading out of what is now the main bedroom, Trippe kept his dispensary – glasses, bottles, and a 'stilliterie' – and in the study he had what must have been one of the largest private libraries in Winchester, 'books of all sorts' valued at 50 pounds. Medical books were usually expensive, and rare. It is to another Winchester doctor, Ralph Hulton, who died in 1618, that the Cathedral Library owes its copy of the beautiful *Herbal* by Gerald Fuchs.

It must also be remembered that Winchester College, during the 16th century, produced many distinguished men of medicine, including Walter Bailey (Scholar 1544), Regius Professor of Medicine at Oxford from 1561-82, and Physician to Elizabeth I. The Headmaster of Winchester from 1560-71, Christopher Johnson (Scholar 1549), subsequently became Treasurer of the Royal College in 1594; Anthony Alyworth (Scholar 1559) also held the Regius Professorship of Medicine, and was Physician to Queen Elizabeth, whose Commissioners removed and imprisoned another Wykehamist, Edward Alslowe (September 1547) from his Fellowship at New College, for allegedly plotting the escape of Mary, Queen of Scots. These few names certainly do not exhaust the list of Wykehamists who practised medicine in the 16th century.[17]

iv) *Plague in Winchester, 1603-c.1720*

Warner, Bassett and Trippe were physicians at a time when Winchester suffered greatly from outbreaks of the Plague. Indeed, in certain respects, the city had still only partly recovered from the great outbreak of the middle of the 14th century, the Black Death, alleged to have left Winchester with 11 streets in ruins and nearly one thousand houses empty. There were intermittent outbreaks of 'plague' throughout the 15th and 16th centuries; they were far beyond the control of any group of private individuals, however skilful in medicine they might be, and the city Corporation took steps to prevent 'nuisances', to keep Winchester's water supply clean, and to arrange for the nursing of the sick and the poor. The Craft Gilds were flourishing in the Middle Ages, but the kind of help they could offer to a sick member was limited; medieval 'welfare agencies' could not cope with widespread outbreaks of disease, and it was natural enough for the Corporation to take on the burden. In comparison with some medieval cities, Winchester had a good water supply, that fundamental for good health. There were many wells, and many open streams, but wells and open streams were easily contaminated. Nevertheless, there was a common latrine at the west end of Colebrook Street, off Paternoster Row, and a public lavatory, the Maiden's Chamber, at the western entrance to Middle Brook Street. The Cathedral, Winchester College, St Mary's Abbey, and Hyde, had reasonably efficient water sewers, and a supply of drinking water came into the Close from the Conduit House at Easton, *via* Water Lane – pure water from chalk and still the source of most of the water drunk in the city.

Yet the very nature of Winchester, its close-packed community, its brooks which were lethal when contaminated as they often were, its site in a river valley, were only a few of the factors which encouraged the spread of 'plague' when some casual visitor or merchant brought in the infection. In September 1553, the Mayor (old and frail), had to be elected in his house because a boy had been brought into St John's Hospital, 'two pestilent sores upon him'. The usual 'stopping up' of the Brooks, to clean them, had to be delayed in 1559 because of 'the great sickness in the city', and in 1564, the annual Supper, to be kept after the feast of St John the Baptist, was cancelled on 16 June 'for avoiding the danger of the Plague now remaininge'. In May 1583, a general order required that all inhabitants 'should rid, make clean, and carry away, all the filthe before every one of their doors' – they were then to wash out the gutters with five buckets of water, and every man was 'to pave before his door'. Moreover, '... if any house within this city shall happen to be infected with the Plague ...', dogs were to be kept indoors, on penalty of being killed by the Beadle. As part of the same general regulations, eight women were appointed as vergers and nurses of such houses 'as be suspected of infections ... a convenient place for such women to be provided for by Mr. Mayor and his brethren'.[18]

These regulations were followed by the appointment of a paid Town Scavenger in September 1601. Much more stringent rules had to be enforced in 1603 when there was plague in London, and the new King, James I, brought his Queen and his court to Winchester for safety, and brought the plague with them. The intermittent evidence of Hampshire parish registers from 1535 onwards, and of a few town records like those of Andover and Southampton, reveal how rare it was for any kind of outbreak to be an isolated instance.

The outbreak of 1603 in Winchester was severe and the County Magistrates eventually sent out a general warning. A special watch was kept at the city gates and the keys of Durngate, a postern, were handed over to the Mayor. Suspected cases were isolated from the community. When there was a further outbreak, at least one house was burnt down to prevent its remaining a source of infection, a precautionary measure well known in Hampshire. Once again, the election of the Mayor had to be held in the Court House on the corner of St Thomas Street and not at St John's. Some small towns and villages were particularly at risk from infection in time of war. After the Earl of Warwick's troops surrendered at Le Havre on 29 July 1563, the plague-ridden remnant of his unfortunate army arrived in Portsmouth. Ninety-eight people died there in August, 82 in September. Some men went on to Petersfield, where there were 44 burials in September, 39 in October, including six on one day. Parish registers tell the story of other, more isolated outbreaks. Forty burials, including that of the Vicar, had to be held in Hurstborne Tarrant in 1593; the reason for this death rate is not clear, but the outbreaks of plague of 1625 and 1626 were much more widespread, and connected with the passage of troops to the continent. Perhaps it might be said, at this point, that Winchester's situation as a garrison town, and as a town for civil and military prisoners, provided several reasons for concern about the health of the civilian population; not only was the risk of plague increased, but when in time that disappeared, there appeared smallpox; and there were always the venereal diseases. In 1625 and 1626, Southampton suffered from plague, and in Winchester, the scholars of the College were sent out to Hursley for seven months.

All these experiences proved of little value in 1665 when the plague came to Winchester again, followed by further outbreaks in 1666 and 1667, and there were major outbreaks elsewhere, notably in Sparsholt, Alton, Basingstoke and Petersfield. On 4 April 1667, Pepys, from a safe distance, wrote 'One at table ... told me that ...

one side of the street (in Petersfield) had almost every house infected through the town, and on the other, not one shut up'. The outbreak at Sparsholt began about 20 June, with the arrival of one Humphrey Bishop, 'an inhabitant of Winchester'. A major outbreak in Andover followed, where an innkeeper in Lower London Street had maintained that his suspicious swelling was only a common boil, and had allowed 25 members of different families to enter his house.[19] Nine separate pest houses had to be set up and there were even burials in gardens and in fields. Forty-six people died in Basingstoke.

The outbreak of 1666 in Winchester apparently began at Whitsuntide, in the Soke; Winchester College was closed, and the boys were sent out to Crawley. 'Plague accounts' for the two Winchester parishes most affected have survived, those for St John-in-the-Soke and for St Peter Chesil.[20] Financial relief for sufferers came in from all sides; money was sent from as far away as the Isle of Wight; Southampton and Romsey helped, as did the neighbouring villages of Easton and Chilcombe. A pest house, thatched with sedge, was filled with beds lined with straw, in St Peter Chesil parish. Householders were removed by order of the churchwardens to this primitive Hospital, and their own houses were boarded up. The burden of all relief fell, in fact, on the parish churches and their parishioners, whose wardens also shut up some infected families in their own houses, relieved travellers and apprenticed orphan children with money raised from the parish rates. Despite all the precautions, the plague was back again in the summer of 1667; Winchester College was closed from August until the end of December and the dead were buried in what became known as 'Plague Pits Valley', between Twyford Down and St Catherine's Hill. The fortunate (and ambitious) result of these experiences was the foundation of the Charitable Society of Natives and Citizens, a Society which originated at the feast held on 29 August 1669, and whose object was to apprentice those orphaned children whose parents had died of plague.[21] This Society, founded originally for 'natives', Wintonians born and bred, was followed in 1720 by that of the Society of Aliens, residents not born Wintonians; both these groups remained in active and friendly rivalry until the end of the 19th century, and are commemorated by Winchester's only obelisk, the so-called Plague Monument outside Westgate. In general terms, it would be true to say that, by the end of the 17th century, the plague had begun to give way as a general scourge, and was slowly being replaced in Winchester as a major illness by the venereal diseases and smallpox. It may have been significant, too, that the patriotic local historian, John Trussel (d. 1648) believed that, though Winchester was a healthy city, newcomers were frequently affected, 'entertained by a short but sharp fever' and 'Throats' had become a feature of life in the Cathedral Close by the late 18th century.

v) *Practitioners, 1600-1736*

The second half of the 17th century produced a high measure of medical skill in Winchester, amongst physicians, surgeons and apothecaries. There is no doubt that some men were attracted by the visits of the Royal Court, and the presence of Charles II, but not all practitioners were wealthy. Doctor Thomas Grent, who died in 1661, was a physician who lived in Winchester College as the scholars' resident doctor. He received an allowance of 25 shillings a quarter, and carried on his surgery from his rooms, with modest equipment, two white flagons, a brass mortar, and iron 'pessell', a stone mortar and a wooden pestle, and 'gallipots, glasses, boxes, medicines, and other materials', worth 30 shillings. Grent had only 52 shillings in ready money, but his 'hopeful debts' (presumably owed by Wykehamists) amounted to three hundred and twenty pounds.[22] In considerable contrast to Doctor Grent, Doctor Arthur Taylor, who was buried in the Cathedral on 10 August 1674, was a very wealthy and successful man. Born in Longparish, he had a large house, three horses, and a coach, probably acted as physician to the Dean and Chapter, and was certainly physician to St Cross Hospital.[23] When Taylor died, his debts, assets and gold and silver totalled £1,666 11s. 0d.

There can be no doubt that physicians were acceptable members of Hampshire society, and that the connection between the established church in Winchester and leading physicians already existed before 1700, and was to prove an important factor in the foundation of the County Hospital. Doctor William Coker, who was buried in the Cathedral in 1704, had practised for 26 years, and may have attended Isaac Walton. Doctor Nicolas Stanley, described as *'nulli secondus'*, and buried in the Cathedral in 1687, was a London physician and the son of the Headmaster of Winchester College. Doctor William Over, a physician who practised in the city, was also concerned with education and, when he died in 1701, he left a large sum to found a Free School for poor boys; the school, set up eventually in the then disused chapel of St John's Hospital, was to have a headmaster who was not to be Irish, Welsh or Scotch, or a north countryman, lest his accent should corrupt the soft Wessex voices of his Winchester pupils.

Of course, not everyone in 16th- or 17th-century Winchester consulted a doctor. Apothecaries still had notable practices. William Bath (d. 1599) was such a one, and his son Thomas (d. 1613) was described as 'Pharmacopola'. Another family of apothecaries were the Lynes. Richard (d. 1656) and Shadrack, buried in the Cathedral in 1701, had a house in the Pentice.[24] There is not much evidence about 17th-century surgeons, but again the profession was often a family one, and there were connections with ironmongery; the two 'trades' were not infrequently connected. Leonard Cropp, who died in 1656, was a 'chirugion' who practised in the Soke, and had a brother who was an ironmonger. The Winters, who lived in the 'corner tenement' at the entrance to Canon Street (now the *Wykeham Arms*), and whose trade tokens then bore a fleur de lis, were ironmongers and inn keepers, and may have practised a certain amount of pharmacy as well.[25] The apothecaries were much in the front line of medicine as far as patients were concerned.

Not all Hampshire practitioners were successful. In 1709, at a time when the Bishop's licence was necessary in order to practise, the episcopal office issued a *Caveat* against John Tutte, an apothecary, on the grounds that his patients had been made worse.[26] Wealthy clients frequently ran up large bills, but the responsibility for caring for the sick or disabled fell on the parish overseers, who could only raise money by imposing rates as they were required to do by law. Alured Clarke's first appeal was based not only on Christian principles but also on the grounds that the founding of a Winchester Infirmary (*sic*) would save money, and keep the rates down.

I The Founder And The Foundation, 1736-1737

At the beginning of the 18th century, Winchester was a small market town with a static or perhaps even declining population unlikely to have numbered more than 6,000 souls. The hope which had encouraged its citizens in 1683, when Charles II had begun to build a palace on the western hill, had been cruelly dashed by George I, who left the great, gaunt building unfinished, and gave away some of the materials. Winchester was not again to be 'royal' and some members of the community were not even loyal. The College was tainted with Jacobitism and the number of commoner boys declined; Whig fathers did not care to entrust their sons to the care of a High Tory Headmaster.[1] The Corporation was cautious, and not very inspiring; its members could recall only too easily the dangerous days of James II's reign, when political activity had produced a reign of terror, Alice Lisle had been executed, and Thomas Wavell, a linen-draper, and his friends had been virtually ruined for opposing what they called tyranny. In the time of the first two Georges, much of Winchester was more or less asleep, dulled with a degree of political ineptitude in which political corruption could and did easily develop from political influence. Central government was soon in the hands of Walpole and the Whig party; local politics followed suit; the Bishops and the Cathedral clergy were inevitably Whig nominees, and very influential in city affairs. It is true that there was a basic political rivalry in central Hampshire which affected Winchester, a rivalry of the Paulets of Hackwood and Abbotstone versus the Brydges of Avington Park, but, as long as the city returned two Members of Parliament, both families could be satisfied, provided that each had a successful nominee.[2] There were difficulties sometimes, for the right to vote was restricted to freemen, members of the Corporation, a self-perpetuating, self-electing body. Votes had to be secured, and there was undoubtedly a measure of bribery and corruption. Money changed hands, influence was very important.[3] There were all kinds of complications; local tradesmen wanted the Itchen navigation improved, but the Bishop of Winchester was the riparian owner and Southampton did not want a rival port, as long as Robert Walpole remained Prime Minister. Many of the most important Winchester properties were leasehold, belonging to the Corporation or to St John's Hospital. A man could not hope to gain a lease if he did not have friends with the right connections in the right places. Society in Winchester was restricted, contained within certain exclusive and limited circles, and lacking the degree of robust middle-class prosperity which achieved so much in Victorian Winchester. There was charity; Doctor Over's Free School for boys, Christes' Hospital for old men, were probably the most vigorous of the foundations. Defoe, writing just before 1724, had noted that St Cross was in a measure of scandalous decline; St John's was little better, St Mary Magdalene had remained an empty wreck since the Civil War, though a few almspeople of the foundation remained in one or two humble cottages. There were physicians, surgeons and apothecaries in practice in the town but the care of the poor and of the unemployed was a burden placed by law on each and every parish. The overseers of the poor levied a parish poor rate and did what they could.[4] Yet a thinking man, looking at Winchester and its neighbourhood for the first time, and with the eyes of a stranger, could not but be aware of the extremes of wealth and of poverty, and of the scarcity of institutional medical care for the normally able-bodied and active men, women and children, who formed the poorer and larger part of Hampshire society.

Such a man was Alured Clarke, the Founder of the County Hospital in Winchester. Born in 1696 into a large and long-established Huntingdonshire family, both his parents lived to a great age; his father, also Alured, died on 28 October 1744, aged 86, his mother, Anne (née Trimmell) on 26 May 1755, when she was eighty-eight. His father was greatly loved, as the words of his memorial suggest:

'He was an active, useful, upright magistrate in this town above sixty years, a lover of justice and friend to the publick. His earnestness to reconcile differences amongst neighbours; his zeal to do good both to his friends and foes; his constant industry and incessant care of his family; his generous, open, cheerful temper; his humanity, good nature, and universal benevolence, (through a long life spent without guile) rendered him beloved, respected, and honoured by all who knew him.
Reader! His example is worthy your imitation, for he was a truly honest, virtuous, good man.'

Alured Clarke obviously grew up in a caring and loving family. He seems to have been a delicate child, but he was a clever boy, and won an exhibition to St Paul's School. Thence he was able to proceed to Cambridge, and at Corpus Christi made a wide circle of friends with whom he corresponded for many years, and, as a Fellow, was able to tutor his brilliant younger brother, Charles, who was called to the Bar in 1723, the very year that Alured gained his first preferment in Hampshire. At Corpus, he had joined a Corresponding Club, whose members included Samuel Kerrick and Edmund Pyle, the latter a future Canon of Winchester. The editor of Pyle's letters has described Alured as probably the most loved member of this informal society. Amongst his brothers and sisters, it was probably Charles with whom he had most contact; for that brother married a Winchester girl as his second wife, and had Hampshire contacts which allowed him to become Member of Parliament for Whitchurch in 1742-3, just a few months before Alured died.[6]

The brothers had the additional advantage of a mother, one of whose own brothers eventually became a Whig bishop of Winchester, and who quickly secured the Deanery of Winchester for another of Clarke's Trimnell uncles.[7] Alured himself was a delicate child, but a scholar, with an easy, persuasive manner of speaking, whose family's political influence gained him the position of Chaplain-in-ordinary to the first two Hanoverian kings, though he failed to obtain the Professorship of Rhetoric at Gresham College. In May 1723, he accepted the living of Chilbolton in Hampshire; a canonry in Winchester Cathedral almost inevitably went with that living, and Clarke left London, temporarily. He was probably already in the first stages of that wasting disease which eventually killed him, and was to think more than once of applying for employment of some kind which would take him to a warmer climate. There is evidence that some members of his mother's family were not robust. Hardly had Alured arrived in Winchester in May 1723, when his bishop uncle died in August, aged only 60, and in 1729, his other uncle, the Dean, was buried close to the Bishop, both near Wykeham's Chantry in the Cathedral.[8] Two years after the Hospital was founded, Dean Trimnell's successor, Naylor, died 1739, aged only forty-seven. Canon Soley, a great supporter of the Hospital Scheme, died in the year of its opening. The new, young Canon certainly had a good deal of experience of sickness amongst his Winchester contemporaries, though his health did not prevent him from accepting a prebendal stall in Westminster Abbey in 1731, and the Deanery of Exeter in January 1741, both of which he held with his Winchester canonry until he died in 1742. The man who founded the County Hospital in Winchester was thus a pluralist and a man who owed much of his own advancement to his family's political influence, and a man anxious for preferment in the church. One of his most valued correspondents was Mrs Claymond in London, who was very influential, and who had the Queen's ear, and was a member of the Household.[9]

What was remarkable about him was the single-mindedness with which he was able to devote himself to a particular purpose, a purpose which he was able to persuade other people was also their purpose, whatever their other differences. Moreover, since he never married, he was able to give much of his income to charity. His achievement in founding a County Hospital in Winchester was remarkable, its initial success due almost entirely to Clarke's own capacity and enthusiasm, and his assembling together of a very mixed group of people who became a group with one united objective and this, too, in a poor town, a poorish county, 'thin of people', and with 'no settled manufacture'.[10] In the words which Clarke used to describe his great enterprise, 'the Gentlemen who engaged in it, had long observed the fruitless experiences which attached to the care of the poor-sick in every parish; they saw with great concern, that even the private charities were wasted and rendered ineffectual by the various sorts of ill management' ... and 'it appeared to us [that] a hospital would be of more use in the country than even in London'.

Just when he first began to consider founding a County Hospital in Winchester is not exactly certain. He was well aware of other, London, hospitals, and was a frequent correspondent of a few men and women concerned with the social problems of the age, but many years were to pass in Winchester before he concerned himself actively with what became the great Winchester project. Most of the information about his plans is derived from his own writing, the Sermon which he preached in Winchester Cathedral on Opening Day, the Rules which he thought out, and the appeals he sent to potential supporters. He had certainly begun to organise the first appeal by the early summer of 1736, an appeal for what he sometimes called at this stage an Infirmary in Winchester.[11] Before this appeal was made, and there was no Winchester newspaper which could give it publicity, he had to secure the support of as many influential people in the county as possible, and this meant the Bishop of Winchester, the nobility, and the Members of Parliament. The Winchester Members of Parliament were particularly important; they controlled the Corporation, and therefore the business and professional life of the City, the men who were going to be called on as volunteers to do so much work for the new Hospital, men who were effectively going to provide much of its life blood in the years to come.

It was probably the Bishop of Winchester to whom Clarke made his first approach. His Uncle Trimmell had been succeeded for a short time by Bishop Willis, who died in 1734, and then came Bishop Hoadly, who has not always had a good press, but he and his family proved to be loyal and generous supporters of the Hospital, perhaps in the first place because the Bishop's eldest son and namesake, Doctor Benjamin Hoadly (born 1706), was a distinguished Fellow of the Royal College of Physicians, elected when very young to the Royal Society, and who, in the year of the Hospital's foundation, had been appointed Gulstonian Physician and was lecturing on the respiratory organs. Doctor Benjamin died in his father's lifetime in 1759, but his younger brother, John, Chancellor of the Diocese and Master of St Cross, came to the Hospital's help on more than one occasion, and the Bishop's name heads that of Clarke's first list of subscribers, dated 5 August 1736, with a gift of 20 pounds, the largest sum given at this stage. Most of the Cathedral Chapter and many of the clergy followed his example.[12] No-one gave more than or as much as Bishop Hoadly, but the subscriptions follow a definite pattern according to the donor's status in society. Ten guineas was the sum expected of all Members of Parliament, even from the young Lord Lymington who, with his wife, was to be numbered amongst Clarke's personal friends. It was clear that, once one Member of Parliament subscribed, the others had to do so too, but of the two Winchester Members, George Brydges of Avington House was also the employer of William Pescod, his Steward, an able lawyer who was very influential in Winchester. Brydges's successor at Avington, his cousin, the first Duke of Chandos, soon came to be a controlling influence in city affairs, working through Pescod and through the Waldrons, a family of varied social standing who were always being Mayors of Winchester. Robert Waldron the younger became the first Hospital Treasurer, and William Pescod and his mother provided the first Hospital building.[13] To begin with, Clarke had to collect as large an amount of money as possible. The decision to found a County Hospital, as distinct from a mere Winchester Hospital, needs little explanation. Winchester alone could not have sustained a city hospital; county supporters would come from a wide area. Above all, the arrangement would recognise the relationship between the City and its rural surroundings, and would recognise too the decay of medieval hospitals in smaller Hampshire towns. Winchester was the rational centre for a County Hospital, and, though many of its patients came from the city, its financial supporters came and continued to come from every part of the county during its long history as a voluntary establishment. There is no record of Clarke's early discussions with William Pescod or Robert Waldron, but it is clear that the Founder discussed the practical steps to be taken with those two influential Winchester men, and that James Crosse, the Recorder of Winchester, was another member of this group. Pescod eventually succeeded Crosse as Recorder; both were talented lawyers, with much legal experience to offer in the service of the new Hospital.

The first list of subscribers survives only in a thin volume found in 1984 amongst the archives of the Dean and Chapter, bound with a subscription list for quite another purpose.[14] There are 198 subscribers on this list, including many women; the smallest subscription was four shillings, but the total sum cannot be settled with any firm accuracy for it is clear that many of the entries are promises rather than actual payments. Members of Parliament gave 10 pounds, county gentlemen usually two guineas, professional men like Loving Wavell, the surgeon, and Charles Barton, the Chapter Clerk, offered one guinea, and shopkeepers and tradesmen gave four or five shillings. The total actually received may have been between three and four hundred pounds, but this must only be deemed a guess as far as this list is concerned. There are other lists in the Hospital Minutes. In any case, the preamble promised endless administrative problems, since even the small sums were to be, or could be, paid in quarterly instalments. 'Subscribers' Arrears' were to prove amongst the most tiresome of the Hospital's financial problems, especially when the only stated regulation, concerning finance, was 'obedience to the rules of our Holy Religion'. However, in 1736, some money did come in, sufficient for a start, and Clarke had next to find a suitable building, and to call together all those whose financial support was sufficiently substantial to qualify them as Governors, and who shared his ideals and his belief in the need for a county hospital.

The First Hospital Building: Colebrook Street

In terms of the official records, the Hospital in Colebrook Street was opened after two meetings of Governor/Subscribers and three meetings of 'The Committee', with additional short meetings of both bodies on Opening Day.[15] Clarke's Sermon was published almost immediately in what has become known from its frontispiece as *A Collection of Papers Relating to the County Hospital for Sick and Lame, etc, at Winchester*.[16] It is this *Collection* which, with the minute books of the Governors' meetings and those of 'The Committee', provides most of the information about the early years of the Hospital, and reveals much about the Founder's ideas and ideals.

Alured Clarke's attitude towards the men and women who were going to enter his Hospital was, above all, very practical and likely to appeal to subscribers on that ground alone. The Poor, he wrote, 'are very incompetent judges of the true use of money ... money in itself will not provide the instant relief which isalways at hand in those Hospitals'. Moreover, the 'general complaint of our Times' was 'the profligate State of Life'; sickness and incapacity of any kind was regarded by Clarke as the result of un-Christian living, and all his patients were given proper books on religious instruction, and 'laid under such restrictions, as may, by degrees, recover them out of that profligate State of Life'. Clarke was not in favour of any system which gave money to the 'great many families which live in Idleness'. Those who were not really ill would not be treated in his Hospital, and they should not be supplied with money from the ratepayers; they would then be 'obliged to have recourse to some Employment and make themselves useful Members of the Community'.

Clarke's patients were to be the genuinely Poor Sick, and specifically those suffering from Dropsy, Rheumatism, and Paralysis, as well as 'Scorbutic cases' and sufferers from 'Slow and Intermittent Fever'. The 'Lame' were another important group; for the poor country man, walking was often the only form of transport, and anyone with a slight knowledge of even modern village life will have met the old man or woman with a permanent 'bad leg', a term which seems to describe a variety of complaints. Winchester is a hilly place, and the Founder was fortunate enough to get a building in the centre, on flat ground, an easy site for the lame.

By the end of the 17th century, a family called Pescod had acquired the small Winchester estate usually known as 'The Abbey'. Basically, it was the site of St Mary's Abbey, which had passed into private hands at the Dissolution, unlike that Abbey's rented city properties which had all been given to the Corporation in 1554 as some recompense for civic expenditure incurred at the time of the marriage of Philip and Mary.[17] The Pescods were lawyers, some of them were Wykehamists, and their clients included the Rodneys of Somerset, and the Rodney cousins, the Brydges of Avington Park. Robert Pescod, like his son, William, was Steward to the Dean and Chapter, and both were the very influential advisers to the successive families at Avington, the Brydges, and their cousins and successors, the Dukes of Chandos. At first, they seem to have let the main house of 'The Abbey'; one of their tenants was the famous soldier, Hugh Wyndham, whose bachelor habits, fast chariot and gold lace, must have delighted many Wintonians. The Pescod family also owned a medieval house on the western corner of Colebrook Street, but, after Wyndham's death, William decided to rebuild the main house, and to use it himself; for here he could receive the Avington family. He was soon to hold many offices, Steward to the Dean and Chapter, to Winchester College and eventually became Crosse's successor as Recorder of Winchester; he also became Recorder of Portsmouth.

The corner house, an L-shaped building of medieval origin, was empty in 1736, when Pescod agreed to let it to Alured Clarke for the Winchester Infirmary (sic) at a rent of 14 guineas a year.[18] It is too late to attempt to describe the original building, for it was demolished in 1959, but its outward appearance can be envisaged from an early Victorian print, and from a fine bird's-eye view of the eastern end of the Cathedral, drawn by Norman Nisbett, then Architect to the Dean and Chapter, who died in 1919. It stood on the south-western corner of Colebrook Street, at the east end of the Cathedral, and near the parish church, St Maurice, of which only the tower remains. A contemporary plan has survived, made after some early alterations to the interior, printed in the second *Annual Report*.[19]

The lease, dated 28 September 1736, was a grant by Mary Pescod, widow, and her son, William, to Alured Clarke, Doctor John Burton 'Schoolmaster of Winchester College' and Thomas Cheyney, one of the Fellows, and the building is described as 'all that ancient messuage and tenement' formerly in the possession of Mirabella Spence, widow, and John Earle, gentleman. The Pescod lease was enrolled in full in the Governors' Minutes. The building was 102 feet long, north to south, and its eastern boundary was the wall of St Mary's Abbey. It was in very poor condition; the rent, agreed at 14 guineas a year, was reduced by Pescod to four guineas only for the first year. The plan, made in 1737, shows an entrance from Colebrook Street south, by way of an open porch giving on to a large courtyard, where two short flights of stairs led to the first floor. Immediately west of the porch was the Dispensary, then the Hot and Cold Bath Room (right on the corner) and then, in the wing which ran north along Colebrook Street, the 'Elaboratory', followed by a large Board Room and Secretary's office, and an entry and two private wards. To the west of the porched door, along Colebrook Street, was a wash house and brewhouse, and a range of what might be called domestic buildings, a buttery, kitchen, writing room and a very small Physician's Room. The wards were on the first floor, as were the Matron's Room and Store Room and a small Surgery. 'Nurses and servants' eventually slept in the

1. Plan of Cole-
brook Street
Hospital, c.1737.

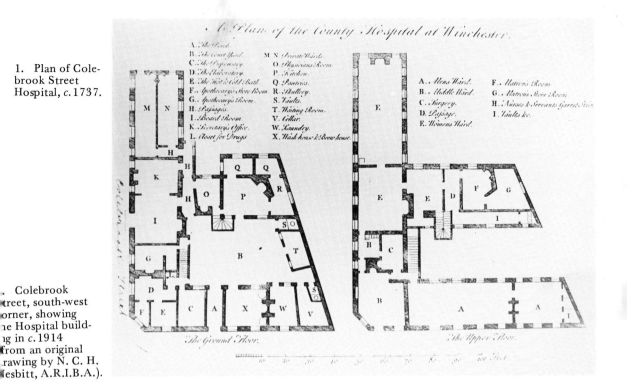

A. Plan of the County Hospital at Winchester.

A. The Beds
B. The Court Yard
C. The Dispensary
D. The Elaboratory
E. The Hot & Cold Bath
F. Apothecary's Store Room
G. Apothecary's Room
H. Passages
I. Board Room
K. Secretary's Office
L. Closet for Drugs
M N. Private Wards
O. Physicians' Room
P. Kitchen
Q. Pantries
R. Scullery
S. Vaults
T. Waiting Room
V. Cellar
W. Laundry
X. Wash house & Brew house

A. Mens Ward
B. Middle Ward
C. Surgery
D. Passage
E. Womens Ward
F. Matrons Room
G. Matrons Store Room
H. Nurses & Servants Garrets
I. Vaults &c.

The Ground Floor.

The Upper Floor.

2. Colebrook
Street, south-west
corner, showing
the Hospital build-
ing in c.1914
(from an original
drawing by N. C. H.
Nesbitt, A.R.I.B.A.).

garrets, but it must be stressed that the plan does not show the very first arrangements for, within a few months of the official opening, additions and alterations had to be made. The wooden lintel over the entrance bore a painted text: 'Despise thou not the chastening of the Almighty', a perfect expression in its way of Clarke's own sentiments. In one of three wards, another painted text promised a more hopeful message to the patients: 'Like as the Father pitieth his children, so is the Lord merciful unto them that fear Him'.[20]

The Cathedral, in some way, was a difficult neighbour. Patients who could walk were required to attend the funerals of patients who had died, for those unfortunates were usually buried in the Cathedral churchyard, simply because they were residents in what had become part of St Maurice's parish.[21] Walking about was not encouraged on the Cathedral's gravel paths, and was soon specifically forbidden. The sad little Hospital parties which had to assemble to attend funerals were probably not always deemed to be desirable additions to the outer Close of a Cathedral whose clergy, very supportive of the Hospital as they were, had spent (or were to spend) large sums of money on improving the area, planting a noble avenue of lime trees (in situ by 1736) and providing lamps, lowering the 'declivities' and also generally improving the neighbourhood for the benefit of the elderly widows in Morley's College – and for the Dean and Chapter. On the eastern side of the building, there was the Abbey Mill and then the gardens of William Pescod's new house which he had completed in a plain and classical manner before he died in 1760. There is an interesting connection here with Pescod's work for the Hospital, for one of Pescod's fellow Governors was Henry Hoare (elected 24 November 1736), the banker and maker of Stourhead and its famous landscape gardens.

Pescod, like Hoare, landscaped his garden with much effect, diverting the stream, building summer houses and masking the view of the mill, an obtrusive industrial building, by erecting a classic temple, and planting trees. Taken as a whole, the area of Colebrook Street was one of large houses in very good gardens, with an ample water supply. It was a desirable part of Winchester in which to live, and only rarely in its Colebrook Street days was the Hospital troubled by crime. In 1752, Stephen Silver appeared at the Winchester Quarter Sessions charged with obtaining 14 pounds of beeswax from a Winchester chemist by fraud, on pretence that he came from the County Hospital. He was sentenced to be publicly whipped.[22] If there were attempted burglaries, and there probably were, they have not been recorded; though St Maurice's parish, as a whole, had come to include many poor families, poverty did not imply dishonesty.

It cannot be said that the conversion of the Colebrook Street building produced a Hospital notable for its convenience. The mere carrying of water must have been a frightful burden, and the wards had to be washed every day. Almost at once, the Hospital had to be enlarged, altered, and a house on the other side of the road purchased to make extra room. The advantages of the original building included, presumably, medieval solidity. Internal alterations were soon in hand and, on 12 April 1737, Clarke was able to report that a new ward for men was just finished, but that an additional building was necessary for the women's ward, to take 12 beds, and with its own private lavatory. Beneath that ward were two small private wards and a 'convenient place for receiving a dead body', known as the 'dead room'. The number of beds for in-patients totalled 60: there were no restrictions on the numbers of out-patients.

One can only guess at the functions of the private wards; perhaps they were for patients who should not have been taken in at all, those with infectious diseases, or who were dying, men and women who could not be turned out. They were certainly not for paying patients.[23] By 11 October 1737, the buildings were finished, including a new waiting room, and only a Herb Room and a Wood Room were needed. The whole place was insured, with the contents, for £500.[24] The Hospital was effectively one year old, and Clarke had been to London to see Sir Robert Walpole and could proudly announce the promise of £200, the Royal Bounty of His Gracious Majesty, King George. Just over a hundred years later, exactly the same sum was given by Victoria.

II The Patients And The Nurses

Opening Day

Clarke obviously believed, rightly, that, once he had collected a fairly substantial sum for his proposed Infirmary, the place should be opened as soon as possible after a suitable building had been found; he was right to press ahead with his scheme, and not endanger the initial enthusiasm of his many supporters. In the two months which preceded 'Opening Day', there was a feeling of general optimism, of willingness to help, in many ways. There was even a hint of democracy; all those who subscribed at least one guinea or more were to have votes. There were clearly many informal unminuted meetings before the first Meeting 'of the Governors of the Public Infirmary at Winchester was held on 23 August 1736 in St John's House. The House formed part of the large complex at the eastern end of the High Street, had been originally used as a Hospital and was still attached to its chapel (in use as a Free School), with a group of almshouses nearby. It had become an important assembly room, and its use as the first meeting place of the Governors was indicative of the status of Clarke's foundation; amongst those present was Bishop Hoadly, himself a Freeman of Winchester, but it was Clarke who became Chairman until he left Winchester in 1741.

At this foundation meeting, the names of all subscribers were read out, as well as 'a Paper by the Governors'. A committee was chosen to draw up Rules for the Hospital before a meeting to be held on 12 October; Robert Waldron was named as Treasurer, Dr Bowles and Dr Bateman appointed Physicians, 'Mr Bacconeau' was to be one of the Surgeons, a lease on Mr Pescod's Infirmary House was to be taken, and Opening Day was fixed for 18 October, St Luke's Day, 'and Doctor Clarke to preach'. This first meeting of Governors was followed two days later on 25 August by the first meeting of 'The Committee of the Infirmary' at the Deanery. There were some 14 members of this Committee, all influential men, including the Dean, the Warden of Winchester, a senior Canon, Joseph Soley, and the local politicians, William Pescod, Robert Waldron, James Crosse, the Recorder of Winchester, Henry Fenton and Alexander Pyott. It was a group well used to paper propaganda, and its first act was to order the printing of a thousand copies of the 'Two Papers relating to the Design of an Infirmary'. The Treasurer and Alexander Pyott were asked to put the Infirmary in order, clean the yards there and put the 'Shop and other rooms in order as soon as may be'. The Shop was for the Apothecary, but as yet there was no official staff, and the lease of the building had not been agreed. On 9 October, the Committee met again, at Alured Clarke's canonical house in The Close, an old building opposite the Deanery and now forming part of Judges' Lodging. This time it was able to appoint a Matron, an apothecary, and a nurse, and to adjourn for the next meeting to take place at 'The Public Hospital' on Thursday 14 October 'at 5 o'clock in the afternoon'.

At the general Court of Governors held in St John's House on 12 October, the Chairman was able to report some important new subscribers, the Dukes of Bedford and Montagu, the Honourable John Spencer, Doctor Lynch, Master of St Cross and Dean of Canterbury, and the three appointments made by the Committee were confirmed. It was a very practical – and urgent – meeting; the hard-working Committee had not done everything expected of it 'because of the multiplexity of Business and Accounts', but a lease of the Infirmary Building was produced, Waldron was thanked for his work as Treasurer and his generosity 'in bringing down the Hospital goods from London gratis'. He announced, as did Doctor Bateman ('and he knew it to be Doctor Bowles' intention to do the same') that he would serve 'without fee or reward'. It was decided that the Infirmary was to be called 'The County Hospital for Sick and Lame at Winchester' and finally, the meeting, already exhausted one might guess, approved the *Orders and Constitution of the Governors of the County Hospital*, dated 18 October 1736, the proposed Opening Day. There were 76 Governors present but, despite the hopeful date on the constitution, it was not until 14 October, two days after this Governors' meeting, that the Committee was told that 'leave to use the Pulpitt at the Cathedral next Monday', St Luke's Day, 18 October, had been granted by the Dean. This Committee meeting was short, and interesting in so far as it met in the Hospital; it obviously considered the arrangements for Opening Day, and invited all subscribers to meet at St John's House 'after Church on Monday next'. It met again on that very Monday, and admitted the first Hospital patient, recommended by Mr James King. The Governors met immediately afterwards and agreed their 'Thanks to Dr Clarke for all he has done, and for his excellent sermon, and he is desired to print the same'. The Hampshire County Hospital at Winchester thus opened on 18 October 1736 and began the first year of its long and honourable history. The occasion was reported briefly, not without ambiguity and some grammatical curiosities, in *The Gentleman's Magazine* for 18 October 1736, under 'Events'. 'The County Hospital at Winchester was opened; when Doctor Alured Clarke preached before a numerous congregation, many of them Gentlemen of Rank who made an handsome collection, beside their annual subscription. It were to be wished such charitable undertakings was to be encouraged all over England'.

Clarke's appeals for money were made on the grounds of Christian charity, but it is also true that they were made in the spirit of the age; he was appealing to men who might be attracted by ideas of practical rationality.Yet it should not be thought for one moment that his interest for the Sick Poor was lacking in affection or true concern. From the very first, the nurses were to be carefully chosen, and they were 'to behave themselves with tenderness towards the patients'. One early nurse who lost her temper and struck a patient was dismissed almost at once, but the first set of *Rules* demanded an equally high standard from the patients. 'In-patients' were not to remove themselves without permission, nor to sleep out 'on paid of Expulsion'. They were to attend Prayers, constantly, not to use bad language, or behave indecently. After one warning, they had to go. Men were not to go into the women's ward, nor the women into the men's ward, without leave; no one was to play cards, dice 'or any other Game' and smoking was forbidden, everywhere. If they were able to work, they were to work, for the sake of the Hospital; there is no mention of payment, but patients were occasionally attended by other patients, and they used to help in the cleaning and washing of the wards, before 7 a.m. in the summer. They could also be required to wash and iron the linen and all 'such other Business as the Matron shall require'. Once a week, every Thursday to begin with, the rules were read aloud in each ward. Anyone dismissed for not keeping the rules, or for any 'irregularity', could never be re-admitted. A high standard was also expected from out-patients, for the taking in of some men and women as out-patients became almost at once a regular feature of the new Hospital, as did their instant dismissal if they failed to obey the rules. They had to be exactly punctual for their appointments, return any medical bottles and unused medicine, and they were not to approach the Hospital, or leave it, by way of the gravel path which ran through the Cathedral Churchyard. They, after all, were the 'Sick Poor', and this particular rule was 'to avoid offence'.

As a Postscript to the *Collection of Papers*, the Governors published a list of 21 patients who left the Hospital between 17 November 1736 and 12 January 1737. These 'discharged and cured' varied from a little boy from Hursley, aged four, with a broken leg and who had had worm-fever, to a man of 62 from the same village, cured of the scurvy. Another child, aged four, from Hyde, had had a broken finger. The very first patient of all, Mary Sellers, of the parish of St Lawrence in Winchester, was a girl aged 17, cured of a very bad ulcer in her leg, which was described in an ambiguous phrase as 'of nine months standing'. The other 'lame' sufferers were Elizabeth Earle of Hyde Street, aged 16 (a sore leg for two years), Catherine Gilbert of Wickham, aged 22 (inflamation of both hands, three years standing), Edward Palmer of King's Worth, aged 38 (a dangerous wound in his leg – 'cured in a fortnight'), and John Smith of St Maurice, Winchester, aged 44, who had been bitten in the leg by a dog. One of his neighbours, George Birch, aged 19, had a fractured collar-bone, and the other complaints treated successfully were 'complaint in her Stomach', intermittent fever, dropsy, fever, and weakness in the lungs, hysterical disorder, rheumatism, giddiness and pain in the head. There was one case of scurvy, one pregnant young woman from South Wonston had left before her time, though cured of a dangerous rheumatic fever, and the two little Rough children, who lived in St Thomas's parish – Mary, aged seven with a scalded head, and William with rheumatism 'cured in a fortnight' – had also been sent home. They were the grandchildren of Cornelius Rough, a well-known local character, an erstwhile keeper of the City's Bridewell.

The list is impressive, and greatly outnumbers what might be called the failures. Two patients had died, a man from palsy, and a woman from ulcered lungs 'occasioned by excessive drinking'. Two had been discharged as incurable, two for non-attendance, and one 'for Irregularity, in not taking his medicine'.

The Apothecary-Secretary gave each new patient admitted to the Hospital a number, and it is this sequential numbering which produced each year the statistics of admissions. It was not an infallible system. St Maurice's church was a medieval parish church which had the nominal responsibility for burying patients who had died in the Hospital, and for whom no other particular arrangement had been made. The statistics for deaths can be partly checked against the words 'from the Hospital' which distinguish the names in its burial registers of the dead from the Colebrook

Street Hospital, and later on for Parchment Street as well. The cause of death and the age of the dead person is not given. It needs to be said that death from old age was unusual. St Cross and St John's were the Hospitals for old people, and the 18th-century registers of St Faith's, the record for St Cross burials, include some very ancient men indeed. At St Maurice, the parish clerk kept the register very carefully and under the regular inspection during the Hospital's early years of the Rector, Thomas Ridding, and then of his successor, Richard Wavell; outbreaks of smallpox were sometimes recorded, as in November 1739 and the early months of 1740.

In the year 1737 (April to April 1738), seven male patients and four women were buried from the Hospital, either in the small cemetery in front of the then medieval church, or (more likely) in the ground to the west which was part of the Cathedral's churchyard, where St Maurice's parish paid a small annual sum for the right of burial. In 1738, there were only three deaths, two men and a 'stranger from the Hospital'. Throughout the 18th century, the burials are recorded of a number of 'Strangers', men and also unnamed women, clear indication the Hospital was admitting casualties from its earliest days. Despite the smallpox, there were only three Hospital burials in 1739, again of two men and a 'stranger' but 1740 was not a good year; there were 12 Hospital burials, three men, four women, four unnamed patients (two men and two women) and 'Henry Hoare, a boy from the Hospital', buried on 9 May. In 1741, the number of burials had risen to 21, including two women on the same day, 4 June. The figures for the next four years are seven burials in 1742, 18 in 1743, nine in 1744, 18 in 1745. What these figures indicate, if anything, in terms of the Hospital's treatment of patients must be regarded as very obscure, for they do not include burials elsewhere, but they do something to explain one aspect of the administration, for all patients were supposed to be provided, on entry, with a form by which their sponsor undertook to pay any burial expenses. For the only method of admission was by recommendation, sponsorship, by a subscriber who had to fill in a form, and there was a sort of means test. The Reverend Mr Ogden, recommended as an In-Patient to the Committee on 22 December 1736, was at first refused admission, because 'he has thirty-five pounds per year', but he was taken in when the Governors were advised that he was 'worth nothing', his annual income had been 'anticipated' and the unfortunate man had 'no friend to answer for him'. He had to agree to repay the costs of his treatment when he could do so, and in the meantime, Mr Dowse agreed to pay the Hospital Ogden's next quarter's 'money' out of the profits of the Vicarage of Wherwell.[1]

In-Patients who did not keep to the Rules were discharged after due warning. How many were literate and able to use the books provided for them remains uncertain, but there was no doubt in Clarke's mind that physical recovery was only of secondary importance to spiritual welfare. One of the early books bought for the Hospital's patients was *The Whole Duty of Man Laid Down in a Plain and Familiar Way, For the Use of All, but Especially the Meanest Reader*; it includes 'A Thanksgiving For Recovery', 'Directions For The Time Of Sickness' and 'A Prayer For A Sick Person', as well as much spiritual advice. First published anonymously in 1657, it is generally thought to be the work of Richard Allestree, Regius Professor of Divinity at Oxford. There is an early edition (1737) in the Cathedral library (Morley XXIV, F.4) which George Cooper, M.D. gave to his wife Mary in 1741.[2] As yet, the Hospital did not have a permanent Chaplain, but the weekly Committee appointed a visiting clergyman, who had to come in every day to read and pray with the patients. The Committee began and ended its own meetings with prayers. Many of the Governors were clerics and the whole atmosphere of the Hospital was permeated by the belief that spiritual health was much more important than that of the body. After all, the Founder himself had suffered from dreadful and repeated haemorrhages on one occasion after he had preached in the Cathedral. He must have been a very determined man to have felt able to preach the Opening Day sermon. There was no chapel in his small Hospital, but communion was celebrated frequently; Lady Lymington gave a silver-gilt communion cup for this purpose, and another benefactor, William Gosse, Junior, provided a fine damask cloth for the table.[3] Daily visits to Colebrook Street by the visiting clergymen was considered to be an essential part of the patients' rehabilitation. When eventually, at the beginning of the 19th century, the Governors appointed regular Hospital Chaplains, who inevitably had other work to do, these men were paid three times the salary offered to the Hospital's physicians and surgeons. A patient in Colebrook Street not only had to obey the rules of the Hospital, he was also required to be a faithful member of the Anglican Church.

Of course, Clarke recognised that spiritual regeneration, vitally important, would have to be accompanied by a regular course of medicine, and in particular, a regular diet. The diet varied; it was monotonous, but intended to be nourishing, and of sufficient importance for its details to be printed in the *Collection of Papers*. At the end of its first year, the Committee noted that one of the reasons for the success of the Hospital was the simplicity and regularity of the diet 'with which the Poor are kept in Hospital ... which contributes much more to their recovery than to their own way of living'. Besides, it was much cheaper than relieving the sick in their own homes.

FULL DIET		LOW DIET	
SUNDAY		**SUNDAY**	
Breakfast	A Pint of Broth or Milk-Pottage	Breakfast	A Pint of Water-Gruel or Milk-Pottage
Dinner	Eight Ounces of boiled Mutton or Veal	Dinner	Two Ounces of Roast Veal with a Pint of Broth
Supper	A Pint of Broth	Supper	A Pint of Water-Gruel or Milk-Pottage
MONDAY		**MONDAY**	
Breakfast	A Pint of Milk-Pottage	Breakfast	A Pint of Water-Gruel or Milk-Pottage
Dinner	A Pint of Rice-Milk	Dinner	A Pint of Rice-Milk
Supper	Two Ounces of Cheese or	Supper	A Pint of Water-Gruel or Milk-Pottage
TUESDAY		**TUESDAY**	
Breakfast	A Pint of Milk-Pottage	Breakfast	A Pint of Water-Gruel or Milk-Pottage
Dinner	Eight Ounces of boiled Mutton	Dinner	Two Ounces of boiled Mutton with a pint of broth
Supper	A Pint of Broth	Supper	A Pint of Water-Gruel or Milk-Pottage

WEDNESDAY

Breakfast	A Pint of Broth or Milk-Pottage
Dinner	Baked Pudding
Supper	A Pint of Milk-Pottage

THURSDAY

The same as on Sunday

FRIDAY

Breakfast	A Pint of Milk-Pottage
Dinner	A Pint of Barley-Broth
Supper	Two Ounces of Cheese or Butter

SATURDAY

The same as on Tuesday

The Patients shall have Bread and Beer sufficient without Waste

N.B. Three Pound of additional Mutton or Veal, is allowed to every Gallon of Broth

WEDNESDAY

Breakfast	A Pint of Water-Gruel or Milk-Pottage
Dinner	Baked Pudding
Supper	A Pint of Water-Gruel or Milk-Pottage, or two Ounces of Cheese or butter

THURSDAY

The same as on Sunday

FRIDAY

Breakfast	A Pint of Water-Gruel or Milk-Pottage
Dinner	A Pint of Barley-Broth
Supper	A Pint of Water-Gruel or Milk-Pottage, or two Ounces of Cheese or Butter

SATURDAY

The same as on Tuesday

Bread Sufficient without Waste. Small beer but a Pint a Day

N.B. Patients on Low Diet are to be served first

MILK DIET

SUNDAY

Breakfast	A Pint of Water-Gruel or Milk-Pottage
Dinner	A Pint of Rice-Milk
Supper	A Pint of Water-Gruel or Milk-Pottage

MONDAY

Breakfast	A Pint of Water-Gruel or Milk-Pottage
Dinner	A Pint of Plumb-Pottage with four Ounces of light Bread Pudding
Supper	A Pint of Water-Gruel or Milk-Pottage

TUESDAY

The same as on Sunday

WEDNESDAY

The same as on Monday

DRY DIET

SUNDAY

Breakfast	Two Ounces of Butter or Cheese
Dinner	Half a Pound of Veal
Supper	Two Ounces of Butter or Cheese

MONDAY

Breakfast	Two Ounces of Butter or Cheese
Dinner	Rice-Pudding
Supper	Two Ounces of Butter or Butter

TUESDAY

Breakfast	Two Ounces of Butter or Cheese
Dinner	Half a Pound of Mutton
Supper	Two Ounces of Butter or Cheese

WEDNESDAY

The same as on Monday

THURSDAY
The same as on Sunday

FRIDAY
The same as on Monday

SATURDAY
The same as on Sunday

Bread: sufficient without Waste. Drink: three Pints a Day, one Part whereof to be Milk, and two Water

THURSDAY
The same as on Sunday

FRIDAY
The same as on Monday

SATURDAY
The same as on Tuesday

Bread or Sea Biscuit without Waste

III The Administration And The Medical Staff

All the resident staff were well fed by the standards of the time, and the Hospital was recognised, too, as being a very clean place. Patients might even have baths, though they had to pay, two shillings for a hot bath, one shilling for a cold bath, a rate fixed in February 1737, when a letter sent by Charles Joyce of St Thomas' Hospital in answer to one of inquiry from the Founder was also discussed by the Governors.[1] It is a very revealing document, a letter of advice based on experience, which the Winchester Hospital certainly tried to follow in two main respects. 'We don't like', wrote Joyce, 'children under seven or crazy-headed people; they could disturb whole wards.' As for venereal disease, 'we don't refuse the Foul Disease, particularly ... because it stops the propagation of the distemper'. In Winchester, patients' families, or those who had recommended them, were supposed to give written undertakings that, in case of death, they would pay for the removal of the body. At St Thomas', 'we don't rely on promissory notes about taking away bodies – we give them to our Surgeons; [they are] of great use to them and their pupils'. There seems to be no evidence that this happened at this stage in Winchester.

By an Act of 1752, the bodies of executed murderers could be handed over to surgeons to be 'anatomized', that is, dissected. In Clarke's Exeter Hospital it became the custom to put the corpses on show, in the Hospital, where they could be viewed for a small fee but only on the day of execution. To be a surgeon in an assize city thus brought its own macabre rewards, and there is nothing to suggest that body snatching was encouraged in Winchester. It was common enough in some Hampshire churchyards; Warblington, for example, if one accepts that the little building there in that churchyard was intended for watchers. Charles Lyford appears to have 'skeletonised' the bodies he was given, and used them for demonstrations after dissection. In 1784, Mary Bailey and her lover, John Quin, were tried at the Lent Assizes for the murder of her husband. She was burnt alive and Quin was hung; the record of the Clerk of the Assizes continues, 'and his body be delivered to Mr Charles Lyford, Surgeon, to be dissected and anatomized'.[2]

Much later on, when the Hospital had been enlarged, the Museum was able to take some extra exhibits, carefully described in the local paper on 17 August 1829: 'The cast of Stacey, the murderer mentioned in our last as being in progress by an experienced modeller, under the directions of the Surgeons of the Hospital, is now completed and placed on a pedestal. By this process, a whole-length statue of the deceased is exhibited, shewing a view of the muscles as recently dissected, whereby an interesting contrast is established between it and the skeleton of Sheppard, which hangs beside it. These, with the other phrenological casts, may still be seen, at a trifling charge, previous to being deposited in the new Museum at the Hospital'.

It needed great strength of mind as well as skill to be a good surgeon, and to be a good teaching surgeon. The wretched process of trying to make some unfortunate patient unconscious was not always completely successful, but it could be achieved by copious draughts of spirits or doses of laudenum. As Mr Russell of Exeter has said, 'A surgeon's career was not for the squeamish'. Standards of medical training were not always as high elsewhere as they were in Winchester, and in 1858, as a result of a Parliamentary Committee on medical education, the Medical Act became law; the Committee had recommended the closing of many provincial medical schools. Henceforth, a statutory body, the General Medical Council, was to be responsible for the training of doctors.

The Staff and the Administration

Alured Clarke was very anxious that his new hospital should be efficiently and carefully administered and the scheme which eventually emerged owed as much to the ideas of Thomas Guy as to those of the Founder. The administrators, a Court of Governors, had much greater powers than the medical men, with overall control over every matter and every body. In October 1739, the Governors numbered 43, but the Court was reduced to 40 in 1740. There were four quarterly Courts, and a General Court on St Luke's Day at which the Annual Report was produced. The Governors were supreme; they made all appointments, and dismissals, and all appointments had to be by an overall majority. The day to day work of the Hospital was done by a Committee of Management, wholly subservient to the Governors and, like them, consisting of subscribers who had promised at least five pounds a year. The Management Committee came to be known as the Weekly Board. It was an administration which continued, basically, as long as the Hospital survived as a voluntary institution. The Weekly Board could engage Nurses 'and other common servants', could receive patients, but not admit or discharge them. Its members were the Hospital's Chairman, Treasurer and Deputy Treasurer, and 12 members elected by the General Court. Enthusiasm and active participation were the essential characteristics of its members, who were expected to provide the two weekly visitors, who had to inspect the entire Hospital every day, and who had to know all the detailed circumstances of the patients whose stay ended with one of the four brief descriptions, 'cured, improved, died or dismissed', the last for irregular conduct.

The Annual Reports, which should include everything of importance in the Hospital's history, are occasionally disappointing; they repeat themselves in some respects year after year, and, as an archive series still in the possession of the Hospital, they are very incomplete, not beginning until 1806. Fortunately, a few early Reports have survived in the family papers of Jervoise of Heriard, in north Hampshire.[3] The first surviving *Report* is No 42, from Lady Day 1740 to Lady Day 1741, and includes a list of subscribers, splendidly headed with 'The King's Most Excellent Majesty', George II. Its main heading is 'A View of the many peculiar advantages of Public Hospitals with the Fourth Annual Report of the State of the County Hospital at Winchester', and it continues with some very factual information; there were 60 beds in the House, but no limit on the number of out-patients for which care can be provided, a fact which was to produce many financial crises. 'Patients are solemnly reminded of their duty to God and their benefactors by no less a person than the Chairman himself.' Exact Registers (i.e.

Minutes) are kept of the Transactions of the Governors. 'On the Books, at Lady Day 1740, 55 in-patients, 71 out-patients.' Perhaps the most interesting item of expenditure, and one which throws light on the difficulties in the household at this early stage, is the cost of Extraordinary Nursing, £15 12s. 0d., but the real importance of this particular document, which resembles a small two-page newspaper, is that its 'frontispiece' is the plan of the Colebrook Street building, and this is probably the only contemporary copy of that plan to have survived.

Only the second page of the Report from Lady Day 1741 to 1742 has survived.[4] In-patients then numbered 51, out-patients 41, but the cost of Extraordinary Nursing had risen to £16 8s. 6d. Wages, gratuities and clothes for the apprentices were £107 12s. 2d., gratuities to Physicians and Surgeons, £100. These appear to be the only surviving annual reports for the Colebrook Street Hospital. Their distribution was wide, the object publicity, and the encouragement of subscribers, and the discouragement of those whose subscriptions fell into arrears.

Though the Governors, without doubt, regarded themselves as infinitely superior to the staff which they had to appoint, Clarke, in particular, was mindful of the need to secure a very high standard of medical care and their choice of the Apothecary-Secretary was particularly fortunate, for he was the most important person in the Hospital, in terms of its practical every-day life. Richard Pratt, appointed on 12 October 1736, stayed with the Hospital for 32 years.[5] He 'lived in', and his salary was £20 a year. In 1736, he was not fully qualified, but he must have eventually passed his final examination for he was allowed to take an apprentice, Thomas Blunt, who became the Apothecary at Clarke's Exeter Hospital in 1747. Another young apprentice was Charles Lyford, the first of the great medical dynasty of Lyfords, who deputised for Pratt in the months before the latter died, and who was later to become Surgeon to the Hospital in 1768. Readers of Jane Austen's letters will recall that rather snobbish comment of hers on Mr C. Lyford, 'a mere county surgeon', who would not have been presented to certain country gentlemen of superior social standing, but it was to a Lyford, in the end, that she entrusted herself in the last weeks of a mortal illness. In 1736, the unqualified Pratt was supervised by a series of monthly visiting apothecaries and by the Governors who kept a strict eye on Pratt's suppliers of drugs.

Not until 1828 was the post of Secretary really separated from that of Hospital Secretary, and then the Secretary could also be the Surgeon. The Governors believed in getting value for money, and the Apothecary was an administrator as well as a member of the medical staff; as a full-time paid officer, he could not be absent from the Hospital for more than two hours at any time without special leave; he was not to 'presume to attend any other business than that of the Hospital', and his arduous duties included the fixing of each patient's diet sheet to every individual bed. All the accounts were to be examined every week, bills paid promptly, and no one was ever to accept or offer any kind of 'fee, reward or gratification' for any service done on account of the Hospital. The regular panel of visitors were to tour the Hospital every day to prevent abuses, and to examine the patients, by conversation, and in the absence of the medical staff.

Clarke had been able to report in 1736 that he had secured the services of two Physicians and two Surgeons who were willing to attend the Hospital without charging any fee; but the fact is that great difficulty was experienced in obtaining doctors and physicians to serve the Hospital in its early years. Not every surgeon would be willing to amputate only when permitted by a Committee, and well-known doctors frequently refused to serve. The first list of subscribers certainly included the local surgeon, Loving Wavell. Wavell came from the Winchester family of great local patriots, a family connected with the city and with Winchester College, and which came to include General Lord Wavell. Loving Wavell died in 1741; he was only 33, unmarried, and almost certainly living at home with his widowed mother and his sister Anne. His early death perhaps suggests why he, who had been offered the post of first Surgeon of the Hospital, had refused it. [6] His father, Daniel, the Rector of St Maurice, had died in 1738, just after the Hospital had been founded; his younger brother, William, died at the very early age of eleven, and he probably could just not afford to take on the job of Surgeon, especially if his health was uncertain, for his branch of the family (originally from the Isle of Wight) was not wealthy.

The first appointed Surgeon, however, was Andrew Bacconeau. By 1713, he had a handsome house 'New Built', lying between the *White Hart* and the *King's Head*, with a paled fence in front of it and a porch, off or in the High Street; that is, somewhere near the shop well known for many years as Hunt's the Chemist, and now the Edinburgh Wool Shop. It had its own small garden near the High Street and near the old Guildhall.[7] He brought up his family, a son Nicholas (d.1778), whose memorial was destroyed when St Maurice's church was demolished in 1957, and three daughters, Anne Maria, who married a naval captain, Roger Frogmore (d.1789), and Lydia (d.1799), and Elizabeth. Lydia is worth mentioning as she shared the fear, current in Winchester when she made her will, of being buried alive. Her coffin was to remain open, but when 'signs of putrification shall apear upon my body, my head shall be cut off and severed there-from'.[8] It is a direction which is not unique, but it must surely reflect her upbringing in a surgeon's household. Surgeons had to operate where best they could, before the days of hospitals and operating theatres.

Clarke's original idea, that the medical staff should serve 'without fee or reward', soon had to be revised, and as early as 1739 the Court agreed to offer the medical staff a proper gratuity.

After Wavell's death, and despite his refusal recorded in the Minutes, the Governors proceeded to elect another young surgeon 'in the room of Mr Wavell deceased'. Richard Baker, who was offered 20 guineas a year, appeared before the Board on 9 February 1741, and was at once admitted as Surgeon, and on 13 April admitted likewise as a Governor. It was a short-lived arrangement; he was replaced on 19 May 1743 by Berrington King, who secured the appointment after a dispute amongst the Governors, some of whom demanded a ballot.[9] The first Doctor, Henry Bowles, that loyal servant of the Hospital until his retirement in 1755, was a Wykehamist from a well-known family from Donhead St Andrew. Born in 1700, he had become a Winchester Scholar at the comparatively late age of 15, went to New College, and was a Winchester Fellow from 1719 until his death in 1765. T.F. Kirby's lists of *Winchester Scholars* describes him simply as 'Physician at Winchester'.[10] He lived, at least for part of his life, in Winchester in 13 Kingsgate Street, a house owned by the Reverend William Bowles, a Fellow of the College, and with whom he was the joint owner of a small Hampshire estate at Lockerly, let by the two Bowles to a yeoman farmer in 1754 for £50 a year.[11]

Matthew Combe (or Coombe), another Winchester doctor with a fine house, was one of the Hospital's medical men mentioned in 1737, whose help was not only honorary but in practical terms, virtually nominal, perhaps non-existent. His situation, 'on the staff' must be described as theoretical in comparison with the service given by Henry Bowles and Roger Pratt. By 1741, he was leaving letters unanswered and failed to attend a Governors' meeting, apparently the end of his connections with the Hospital. He was the son of John Combe of Tisbury, went up to Magdalen Hall, Oxford, took his M.D. and settled in Winchester. His first wife died young, and their daughter, Catherine Finetta, was buried in 1712. He then married an Isle of Wight beauty, Susanna (known as Hannah), the daughter of Sir John Oglander of Nunwell. It was Combe's granddaughter, Anne (née Miller), who married the third Earl of Albermarle, and became the stunningly beautiful girl in Romney's portrait at Kenwood. Hannah's sister, Amy, used to stay with the Combes in Winchester in the large, attractive house with its south-facing garden at the south-west corner of St Thomas' Street. It is a house which has played a very special part in Winchester's medical history. It was from this house that Amy wrote describing the problems of investing in South Sea Stock in early June 1720, for the doctor seems to have been very astute fnancially, and he was very kind to this young sister-in-law, who suffered from epileptic fits. Much later on, he was still advising young Oglanders, including the fourth Baronet's wife, Margaret, whom he suggested should go to Bath, and whose complaints perhaps included post-natal depression. He obviously had a large practice in Winchester, and the fine memorial in the north aisle of the Cathedral, where he was buried in 1748, records him as 'practising his art with a regular happiness in the City of Winchester', and he had lived to the ripe old age of 88, greatly blessed, one suspects, in his second marriage.[12] Hannah Combe died in 1758, and an unmarried daughter, Elizabeth, in 1778. The house in Winchester passed to Villiers Chernocke, who became a Governor of the Hospital in 1751, and it was later bought by Charles Benny, the Victorian entrepreneur, who again had connections with the Hospital, and in 1856 it was sold to the Hospital Surgeon, W.J. Wickham, who died in 1864. His son, H.J. Wickham, sold it to Winchester College, and it was opened as a commoner boarding house.[13] It was used by the Red Cross in the 1914 War and much later on (1973) it became a nurses' home for the staff of the Royal Hampshire County Hospital. It is now (1985) a Probation Office with an adjoining hostel, known respectively as Carlisle and Lee Houses.

In 1741, Doctor Bowles and Mr Bacconeau were offered equal salaries of £100, and henceforth doctors and surgeons were offered what might be called intermittent annuities and the occasional gratuity. The medical burden of these early years fell on three men alone, Pratt, Bowles and Bacconeau. Bowles became a Governor, without any dispute, two months after Berrington King's election, and at this meeting the Governors were feeling generous. Doctor Bowles was offered £40 to buy a piece of plate as a memorial 'of the gratitude of this Court', and the mysterious Mr Bourne, 'the Surgeon', still apparently 'on the staff', was paid 15 guineas 'in consideration of his services to the Hospital and expenses in attending, etc'. Bowles did not accept the offer, and rejected 20 guineas offered (again for plate) in July 1744.

He was standing out for what he in fact got, an annual salary of £30, plus a gratuity of £30 which did not have to be spent on anything in particular; he was now 'the sole physician'. One cannot help feeling that the arrangements for engaging staff were rather haphazard, and that the Governors sometimes decided on a well-known local name – like that of Wavell – and thought it proper to have him on the books, in theory at least. This was certainly the case with Matthew Combe. By 18 July 1744, he had written to make it clear that 'he declined attending patients in ordinary cases'. Bowles was willing to 'undertake the whole care of patients and a settled salary of £30 a year' – he 'seems to have received no assistance from Doctor Combe but in extraordinary cases'. After all, Combe was not getting any younger, and he had always had a great many wealthy patients ever since he first came to Winchester and stayed in Wolvesey as the attendant of Bishop Peter Mews.[14] The number of in-patients at the end of 1743 had been 59, and there were 64 out-patients. For a fashionable doctor like Combe, an additional case load of some thirty bed-ridden patients was probably out of the question; they would have had to have been visited regularly, at least once a week. Bowles and the two surgeons, Baker and then Berrington King, with the aid of the invaluable Pratt and the Matron, in reality did all the work. Poor Doctor Bowles was to ask in 1755 if he might have an assistant 'after nineteen years', as the burden of being the sole physician was getting too much for him, but the request was refused.[15] The brutal fact was that many of the Governors still considered medical men to be of less standing and less importance than the visiting clergy, and in terms of financial remuneration, one Chaplain was eventually worth three physicians.

Mrs Hales' death was reported to the Committee in November 1744 and, as usual, Chancellor Hoadly's advice was sought at once and 'the management of the business' temporarily confided to Pratt. Next month, Hoadly recommended Mrs Owen, 'who had been our Matron at the Infirmary in James' Street for many years'. Three surgeons and three doctors, one of whom was Benjamin Hoadly, signed the testimonial which John Hoadly sent with his letter and Elizabeth Owen started work immediately. She at once began (with permission) to buy supplies for the Hospital which were obviously badly needed; candles, new coverlets, sheets and 'an ordinary canvas or Fustian Frock for the Porter'. Next year, another valued member of the staff had to be replaced. Thomas Blunt, Pratt's apprentice, went off to become the Apothecary at Clarke's Exeter Hospital. His successor was Charles Lyford, an appointment which augured well for the future of the Hospital.

The Lyfords were a family well known in the Basingstoke area, but Charles' father, Giles (whose profession is not known) was living in Winchester when he died in 1783, leaving his son as his executor.[16] In November 1768, the Hospital lost its faithful Apothecary when Richard Pratt died. The Committee decided to recommend Robert Woodford as his successor but, until he could arrive, Charles Lyford was 'to buy what medicines are necessary and now wanting for the Hospital'. The Committee was not quite sure as yet of Lyford, as an Apothecary, and they revived the post of Visiting Apothecary, asking Mr Shipman, one of the Governors, to take on this duty. He was ill, and the drugs had to be sent to his house for inspection before Lyford might 'put them away ... agreeable to the rules of the Hospital'. Pratt's tidy secretarial handwriting disappeared from the minute books and was replaced for a few pages by really awful handwriting, apparently Lyford's, and certainly in the true medical tradition. It would be difficult indeed to over-value the worth of Pratt's years of service to the Hospital. During his whole career not one word of criticism ever seems to have been levied at him and, when an opinion was wanted or some difficult diplomacy was called for, it was Pratt to whom the Governors turned.

The death of Mrs Hales and the increasing burdens placed on Pratt and Bowles by the Committee are reflected in the Committee's administration; half the Committee had to retire each year, after serving two years, and the burden of the work inevitably fell on the permanent members. By February 1749, when Hoadly was Chairman, the number of in-patients had been raised to a maximum of 70 patients, of whom four could be suffering from the venereal diseases; they could only be admitted after 14 days' notice, and only then if there was a spare bed amongst those kept for this kind of patient. Another problem had been the arrival of vagrants, and the Committee resolved that they could not be taken in, 'except in extra-ordinary cases'.

Finally, if there be any doubt as to the dominance of the clerical members of the Weekly Committee and Governing body, it might be added that, in Colebrook Street, the regular inspections of the staff and of the patients were usually described as Visitations, that term long applied to the inquiries by Archbishops, Bishops and Archdeacons within their various jurisdictions. Thus on 14 October 1744, the servants of the House 'were called in and the Rules relating to their conduct read, and they were examined in every article, in which examination the Committee found everything in good order'. The marginal note is 'Visitation of the Servants'. About a year later, the Committee held a Visitation of the out-patients (eight discharged for non-attendance) and two days later (7 October 1745) a similar Visitation of the in-patients followed. There were thus three meetings in early October 1745 (5, 7 and 9 October). Managing the Hospital was not a task for the lazy, or the uncommitted, and the Minute Books of the Governors and of the Weekly Committee do much to counteract any suggestion that the Established Church in Hampshire in the 18th century had little social conscience.

By the time that overcrowding in Colebrook Street was producing all kinds of problems, both Henry Bowles and Richard Pratt had grown old in the service of the Hospital. The Governors' incredible refusal to give Bowles an assistant resulted inevitably in the Doctor's decision to end his work for the Hospital, a sad finish to long years of service. The Committee asked Pratt to visit Bowles 'to know his Resolutions whether he would be pleased to continue his attendance on the Hospital'. His verbal answer was that it required no answer, and on 30 July 1755, the Committee which had refused old Bowles one assistant, decided to appoint two doctors, and resolved 'to apply to Dr Langrish and Dr Hooke'. Langrish was obviously a diplomat, and he returned a 'kind inclination' and came to a meeting on 13 August 1755, and announced he was willing to take on the care of patients 'as far as his Business would permit'.

Brown Langrish had been born in Hampshire, and by 1733 was practising in Petersfield as a surgeon.[17] In that year, he published *A New Essay on Muscular Motion*, a subject which continued to interest him in his examination of the various aspects of muscular contractions. Soon after he began to practise as a physician, having been elected an extra Licentiate, he became a Fellow of the Royal Society in 1734 and the next year published *The Modern Theory and Practice of Physics*. He had learnt much from detailed examinations of blood and excreta. Winchester was probably a more congenial centre than Petersfield, with its association with the death of his first wife; it was attractive with its new Hospital and Hoadly connections, but the new Hospital was certainly fortunate in securing him as Bowles' successor; he was very well known, not just in Hampshire, and combined a forward-looking, inquiring mind, with a kind and gentle bedside manner.

The Committee decided that he should take on the work alternately with Doctor Hooke, but Hooke, though he came to the next meeting, would have none of this, and Langrish was appointed sole Physician. He was obviously a successful appointment. He was thanked by the Governors for his 'regard and humanity to the poor patients' and for 'his obliging and gentleman-like conduct to the Committee', summed up in the brief letter of acceptance he sent to the Committee on his appointment. Dated 15 October 1755, it was minuted in full by a Committee faced with terrible financial problems, not to mention the absence on three weeks leave of the loyal Pratt.[18] 'Gentlemen, I return you many thanks for the obliging Resolutions you were pleased to make yesterday in regards to me; and in return I promise you to take all the care of the Poor and Sick people that is in the power of, Gentlemen, your most obedient and most humble servant, B Langrish.' He became a Governor on 13 January 1757, for not the least of his virtues was that he was willing to lend money for the new Hospital.[19]

His *Essay* was dedicated to Hans Sloane, and a more controversial work, *Physical Experiments on Brutes*, published in 1745, had offered suggestions on how to dissolve bladder-stones without inflicting the agony of cutting. He was both a practical physician, and a researcher with a very inquiring turn of mind, well known in wider medical circles. His series of lectures on muscular motion to the Royal Society in 1747 were followed by another book, *Plain Directions in Regard to the Smallpox*, which showed 'acute clinical observation'. Not surprisingly, Langrish's time at the Hospital was short, and he soon moved on to Basingstoke where he died in 1759, describing himself in his will as 'Doctor of Physic'.[20] He was survived by his wife, Jemima, and their two sons, John and Browne, and left a substantial estate, a freehold house in Winchester (in Parchment Street, in which Jemima eventually lived), a second house there leased from the Corporation, a small country estate in Clanville parish on lease from the Duke of Beaufort, a copyhold in East Meon, and £600- worth of bonds on the Winchester Turnpike to London Tolls. His work in the Winchester Hospital, short-lived as it proved to be, must certainly have added to the distinction of the Foundation, and he may have been one of the voices urging the move to better and larger premises. He had liked Winchester, and was buried in the Cathedral on 28 November 1758; his wife survived him, and was eventually buried in the same grave on 29 October 1781.[21] Langrish's short-lived appointment was followed by an offer on 29 December 1756 to Doctor Welsh 'to be recommended to the next Special Court as Physician to the Hospital' and, in 1760, just after the move to Parchment Street, the Committee thanked Welsh and Doctor Staken 'for their kind and constant attendance'. Welsh had been made a Governor in 1757.

In 1755, Bowles had been getting £30 per annum, the Surgeon, King, a quarterly gratuity of five guineas, Mrs Owen, the Matron, £15 5s. 0d., Pratt £50 a year, and the four nurses (Baker, Browne, Burnett and Winn) their board and lodging and £2 15s. 0d. a quarter. The nurses came and went, but the laundry maid, Elizabeth Alder, stayed with the Hospital for many years, as did the rather unsatisfactory porter, Richard Middleton, reported on to the Committee in January 1756 (by the Matron and Richard Pratt) as negligent and frequently absent from the Hospital.

In the late 1750s, the accounts suggest that some of the patients had hernias, for trusses were bought in July 1753 at a total cost of £3. Langrish obviously believed in preventative medicine, particularly the prevention of scurvy, and continued to order buckthorn juice for the Hospital, as well as 114 gallons of hips; but not all the patients valued his treatment. William Hutchinson (patient no. 4911), admitted on 24 September 1755, was discharged on 5 November after a complaint from the Matron about his 'abusive and disorderly behaviour'; within a few weeks, James Leversuch (patient no.4949) was also discharged for 'continualy going out of the Hospital'.

In 1742, Clarke reported to the Committee that he had accepted the Deanery at Exeter, and resigned the Chair. Henceforth, the Committee had some very different Chairmen, of whom Doctor John Burton, Headmaster of Winchester College, was by far the most successful. Of the other Chairmen, Edward Hooker, a prosperous Wintonian with an attractive house in St Peter Street, was probably too old; he had been Mayor in 1715 and in 1720, but Burton did the job splendidly, and his short tenure began a period when the influence of the Dean and Chapter on the Hospital's work began to give way to that of the Warden and Fellows, and he was succeeded by Warden Coxhead.[22] Doctor Robert Eden, Archdeacon of Surrey, took over next and then, on 4 July 1746, John Hoadly, Chancellor of the Diocese, was elected Chairman. It was to be a very short term of office; in 1749 John Merrill took over for just one year. Hoadly was back again in 1750, and resigned in 1774, when the dropsy which eventually killed him began to have its effect. It was during his second term of office that Richard Pratt died.

Postscript to Colebrook Street

Clarke had always been delicate, and in 1732, after preaching in the Cathedral, had suffered a severe and repeated haemorrhage from the lungs. He had walked through the streets, dined in a cold room and had to be carried home. The attack was so severe that he thought he was dying. He almost decided to apply for a consulship in Algiers, but instead he took two years' leave of absence, visiting Bristol and Bath and then returning to London. He had survived, but only to a limited extent, and the enthusiasm and work which he was able to put into his new Hospital was truly remarkable, for he remained its active Chairman until he announced his appointment as Dean of Exeter on 2 May 1741. Three years previously, Sir William Heathcote had persuaded him to sit for the portrait, by the Reverend James Willis, which still hangs in the Hospital Board Room. It is not a picture which portrays a man in robust health, and he complained to his great friend, Lady Sundon (the former Mrs Clayton, woman of the Bedchamber to Queen Charlotte) that he frequently felt very weary and disinclined to be active.[23] He was probably in the early stages of tuberculosis, but though the haemorrhage was not repeated, he was bled once a month because he – or his doctors – felt that he 'was affected by the moon'. One of these advisers seems to have been Doctor Simon Burton, on the staff of St George's Hospital in London, and brother to the Hospital's future Chairman, that Doctor Burton who was Headmaster of Winchester College. Sufferers from the consumption were not admitted to the Winchester Hospital but were dismissed as 'unfit objects' once the nature of their complaint was discovered.[24] Rest was not part of the treatment, nor was the disease considered to be infectious.

He was away from the Hospital for the two months of February and March 1737, a depressing year which saw his friend Lady Sundon ill and away in Bath, and which ended with the horrifying death of Queen Caroline, his patron, in November 1737. He seems to have been absent again from May to October 1739, and for a total of nine months in 1740, though he was present on 2 November at the Great Chapter when the Close houses were insured for the first time, with the Sun Insurance Company, his own for £550 and his coach house and stable for £50.[25] His signature is large and straggly, but strong. At the June Chapter of 23 June 1741, he was absent again, but his colleagues agreed to contribute two pounds towards the upkeep of the roads near the Hospital. He had probably left Winchester as soon as his appointment as Dean of Exeter was confirmed, but it is not mentioned in the Chapter books. He was almost certainly already very ill, but his clerical ambitions had not faded. His thoughts for his own future included a desire – satisfied – for a stall in Westminster Abbey, and he seems not to have hesitated about accepting the Deanery of Exeter and, though he did not prove an absentee Dean, he continued to keep his Winchester and Westminster stalls, and of course his house in Winchester Close. Weak as he must have been by the time he accepted Exeter, he lost no time in deciding to found a second provincial hospital there.

Mr P.M.G. Russell, the historian of the Exeter Hospitals, has described the foundation and opening of that Hospital, and the laying of its foundation stone on 27 August 1741.[26] That was a tremendous ceremony; there was music, the bells were rung at the Cathedral and at St Mary's and there was 'wine on the ground'. Clarke himself laid the stone; 'Thereby the zealous endeavours of this excellent divine, the Devon and Exeter Hospital justly owes its Foundation ... such a day of gladness has not been known for many years.' The Founder had been determined 'not to give sleep to his eyes nor slumber to his eyelids till he had secured the same blessings for the County of Devon and its Metropolis' as he had done in Winchester. He had seen a site in the part of Exeter called Southernhay for a mere one hundred pounds, money promptly refunded to the Hospital Governors by a generous donor who wanted nothing for his land, but had to ask for a nominal sum lest the Hospital infringe the Statute of Mortmain. Like Winchester, there was a Court of Governors and a Weekly Committee, which met in Mols' Coffee House in the Close until it was possible to use the new buildings designed by John Richards, a prominent Exeter builder.

In October 1741, Clarke nominated John Cholwich to be his Deputy Chairman at Exeter; seven months later, on 31 May 1742, the Founder was dead, aged 46; he had not survived long enough to see his second Hospital, with its very elegant architecture, take in its first patients. The Exeter Hospital opened its doors on 1

January 1743; at this stage, it had 30 beds, and an honorary medical staff of six physicians, five surgeons and one Apothecary, 'Mr Lucraft'. Of the early doctors, it will perhaps be sufficient to note here that Doctor Thomas Glass (d.1786) served the Exeter Hospital for 34 years, and achieved much fame, not least because of an early publication on Pulmonary Tuberculosis.

Clarke had always, apparently, wanted to be buried in Westminster and, since he was still a canon of that church, there was no problem. He was buried there 'without a monument in the north cross (transept) under a large gravestone next to the south angle of the later Duke of Newcastle's monument'. His Winchester canon's house passed to John Hoadly,[27] and his Winchester Hospital continued its progress despite the problems of money and of staff, which had undoubtedly worried the Founder and perhaps added to the anxieties of his last months of life. His obituary, written for *The Gentleman's Magazine* of June 1742, sums up his contribution to the age in which he lived. 'Doctor Alured Clarke, Dean of Exeter, Prebendary of Westminster and Winchester, Deputy Clark of the Closet to His Majesty, etc etc etc. He was an admirable preacher and remarkable for his benevolence, hospitality, and charity, and a very great promotor of the laudable Foundations of the County Hospitals at Winchester and Exeter and other donations.'[28]

Clarke never married; he was certainly not a misogynist; his circle of friends included young Lady Lymington, and her husband, both benefactors of his Hampshire Hospital, and his chief confidante was Charlotte Clayton, woman of the Bedchamber to George II's wife, Queen Caroline, who had become Lady Sundon in 1735 when her husband was made an Irish peer. She had much influence over the Queenand was constantly approached by a variety of correspondents, including Clarke, all seeking the royal favour. Many of these correspondents were genuine friends, and although Horace Walpole, in one of his characteristic cruel phrases, dismissed her as a simpleton, Bishop Hoadly admired her, as did Lord Hervey, whose long and harrowing account of Queen Charlotte's last illness makes the medical terrors of the age only too apparent.[29] She was in Bath when the Queen lay dying in late 1737, she herself apparently ill with a cancer of the throat which eventually killed her on 1 January 1742. Alured Clarke, in fact, understood only too well that even the rich could suffer appalling agonies and die terrible deaths. Money might produce some slight alleviation, but it could offer no certain remedy. His Hampshire Hospital offered more than money to the Sick Poor, an almost unbelievable respite from the harshnesses of contemporary life, the best medical care available and, above all, the consolation of religion and 'tender care'.

IV Moving The Hospital

From the first year of its existence in Colebrook Street, it was obvious to the Governors of the County Hospital that the building opened in 1736 was too small, and that the very success of Alured Clarke's undertaking would make it necessary to move to another site. It must be said that this has been a recurring problem in the Hospital's history, proved almost inevitable with the growth of population, and the conquest of certain types of disease which is usually accompanied by the appearance of others. New kinds of hospital patients have appeared, including pregnant women, and children of tender age. The innovations of technology bring their own problems; the coming of the railway to Winchester in 1840 brought a new kind of patient, men injured or taken ill in the course of the line's construction.

These particular problems did not exist when it was decided to find a new site some 16 years after the Foundation. By 1752, a number of new hospitals had been purpose-built in several English towns. What made the project possible in Winchester was the death in that year of Richard Taunton, a Southampton man, and one of the Hospital's founder subscribers, at two guineas a year. He was an interesting man, who already had friends and patrons amongst his fellow subscribers, for he was a wine-merchant, supplying the Brydges/Chandos family at Avington, and friendly with the Waldrons and Pescods in Winchester. His portrait, still in the Hospital Board Room, shows him for what he was, though not everyone would suspect from that tough-looking countenance that he was a first cousin of Isaac Watts, or that his sister had married a future canon of Salisbury, who was to found the Bampton Lectures at Oxford. He made most of his money as a privateer, that is, an official pirate, but started his successful career just as a maltster when he inherited his father's business, and rapidly progressed up the social ladder by means of electoral corruption and bribery. He was a respectable churchwarden, Sheriff of Southampton and then Mayor in 1734 and 1743. His second wife was of better social standing, and owned an estate near Weyhill, which helped her husband to acquire a coat of arms. By 1745, he had a substantial share in an expedition of three ships, set up by a London syndicate, sent out to attack French and Spanish ships as prizes of war. It was highly successful and made Taunton very wealthy. Though he did not get as much money as he had hoped, he was to maintain that the treasure brought back (to Bristol) was worth a million pounds. In 1751, he fell ill, made his will on his death-bed on 15 February 1752, and left most of his money to found and endow charities in Southampton to maintain the poor and to educate their children. Taunton's School remains today. To the County Hospital in Winchester he left a total of £4,915 in cash and in securities, and his portrait in oil, with its background of the three ships which had helped to secure his fortune.[1] The picture was re-discovered after the First World War in an apple-loft in the Hospital. Taunton's

3. Richard Taunton (1684-1752), Alderman and Mayor of Southampton; benefactor of the hospital (from the portrait in the R.H.C.H.).

only expressed wish as far as the legacy was concerned was that the Hospital would show a special 'regard' for patients from Southampton, particularly for poor sailors.[2]

Once the news of this handsome bequest reached the Governors, they decided to discuss the 'necessity of enlarging the buildings for the reception of more patients', but it was obvious that there was simply no more room for enlargement in Colebrook Street. Taunton's trustees, Peter Dobree, a London merchant and Thomas Harrison, a London attorney, were co-opted as Governors, and the decision taken to buy Clobury House and its garden in Parchment Street, Winchester, on the north side of the High Street and on level ground. It had been built and inhabited by a famous 17th-century soldier, Sir John Clobury, a general in Monk's army just before the restoration of the monarchy.[3] His splendid memorial can be seen, incongruously placed, in the south retro-choir aisle of Winchester Cathedral. After his death, Lady Clobury lived on in the house, but by 1752 it was rather run down, and the three Clobury girls, who had made good matches, were no longer interested in Winchester.

The Clobury title to this very large town house, not surprisingly, proved to be a problem to the potential purchasers. Sir John had had to buy up or lease a whole variety of small properties, houses, cottages and gardens in order to build his mansion. Winchester properties in the centre of the town were still being recorded in the last of the city's Tarrage Books, in the first quarter of the 18th century, in terms of their medieval ownership.[4] The Clobury property is confusing: 16 different smaller properties, at least, can be identified. At the far, north end of the east side of Parchment Street, there were still probably four ponds (not perhaps part of Clobury's estate), and then there began an area of garden land in varied ownership. 'It is the north part of one garden and containeth from the east part from the south to the north 15½ yards and from the east mud wall to the Middle Stone, 27¾ yards and at the middle stone from the north to the south being a Nut tree 21 yards, and from the tree to the stone westwards to Parchment Street 22 yards.' The frontage of the house ran north to south along Parchment Street, an area which is marked in this Tarrage as 'Lady Clobery, now Mr Fletcher', and the site may have consisted originally of some nine different properties, of which one at least at this time still belonged to the city, though that particular garden had been let to Sir John Clobury. There is no need to labour the point, or to be surprised that the Hospital found some difficulty in getting a satisfactory title. Somehow or other, the legal problems were solved, and the *London Evening Post* (No.3995), carried the good news: 'County Hospital at Winchester, June 20, 1753. The purchase of Sir John Clobury's house and ground thereto belonging ordered by the General Court in July last, and the further orders to the said court with respect to securing plans and contracting with workmen having been delayed on account of some difficulties with regard to the title which are since cleared and the purchase made: The Committee before they proceed are willing to have the sanction of as full a general court as possible and therefore earnestly request such gentlemen of the County as are Governors to favour them with their presence of the Hospital on Tuesday the 10 of July being the annual court of Governors at 11.oc in the forenoon and afterwards at dinner at the Sun.' At a cost of five hundred guineas, the seller was William Abree, whose father and namesake was a Winchester clothier and woolstapler.[5] The three most influential men amongst Hospital Governors acted for the purchasers, and as Trustees; the Chairman, Doctor

Benjamin Hoadly, Dean Thomas Cheyney and Doctor John Burton, Headmaster of Winchester College since 1724. James Spearing, a Winchester lawyer, drew up the conveyance and had it enrolled in the Court of Chancery, entirely at his own expense. The Governors paid for the house out of Taunton's legacy, and agreed to spend a further £2,000 which they hoped to get from subscribers.

If Taunton's money made the move possible, it was probably John Hoadly (1711-76), the Bishop's son, who ensured that the Hospital was built. He served two terms as an outstanding Chairman, and his vigorous personality emerges clearly in the Minutes. Like his father, he was very generous, and could afford to be so, though his loans to the Hospital were never interest-free. He was a poet and a dramatist, not entirely successful as either, ordained late in life and the recipient of many episcopal favours. Wealthy livings and the Chancellorship of the diocese of Winchester were bestowed on him by his loving father, but he remained a caring man, though also a great pluralist. He was always mindful of the need to be charitable, a man who, when making his will, remembered what he owed to his servants, to his gardeners, John Hall and Richard Norris and his attorney, Thomas Ridding. His concern for the Hospital lasted all his life, and he left it a handsome legacy of £500, an equal sum for the benefit of Morley College, and £1,000 to the Dean and Chapter to be used for apprenticing one son and one daughter (alternating every year) from families of the poorer clergy. He died in 1776, ordering 'that my body be not nailed up till it is offensive and that it may no be buried till my executrix (his wife) shall be satisfied by the Physician that no life can possibly remain in it', and added precise directions for his grave in the Cathedral.[6]

The Hospital Committee next decided to advertise for 'plans for workmen'; they had not yet made up their minds as to whether to rebuild Clobury House completely, or just reconstruct it, but in July 1753, the Court decided to erect a new building.[7] It remains uncertain as to how much was really new. Sir John Clobury's 'Saxon Doorway' was certainly left and, two centuries later, the auctioneers, who were asked to sell the premises after Romsey Road was finished and who must surely have been instructed carefully by the Governors, described the Parchment Street Hospital in terms of one former mansion house with additions.

The 'new' building was not to cost more than £2,000 and it was to be in part a do-it-yourself job as far as the Court of Governors was concerned. They gave the orders direct for the purchase of 250,000 bricks, some lime and sand, and appointed a Mr Russell as Surveyor; his fee was to be four per cent on all money spent but the Court itself advertised in the Reading, Salisbury and London papers for the building tradesmen required; and in the meantime, a well was sunk, and a quantity of beech wood was bought for piles, and a bricklayer, two carpenters who were father and son, a Portsea stone mason and a plumber were engaged. On 28 April 1755 at noon, the foundation stone was laid,[8] and shortly afterwards, William Blake, a stone mason, provided a marble chimney piece for the new boardroom. Over this there used to hang a painted board with the Founder's arms and the names of the Governors, but this, though still in existence in 1963, appears to have been lost.

Despite the marble chimney piece, all was not well, for the building fund, which had been created by a special appeal, was exhausted; money just had to be borrowed. Chancellor John Hoadly lent £300 (at three per cent), Brown Langrish £250 (at four per cent). The work in progress was the erection of the two wings north and south on beech piling, and for this the Bishop of Winchester lent £600 (at six per cent), which allowed a payment of £550 to the workmen. Despite all these loans, the work had to be stopped, and by Christmas-time 1755 the windows were boarded up, and the site more or less deserted. The Governors needed at least another £1,000 and were prepared to offer £2,000 of Richard Taunton's stock as security. Dean Cheyney, a Trustee and one of the Governors, held out against this and refused to sign the necessary papers.[9] He was a well-known eccentric in financial matters, though very successful, and known also for the number of wills he left behind him.[10] In the end, he agreed, protesting that he had never been against the transfer of Taunton stock and that he had not even been asked to agree to the transaction. The Governors had sought Robert Henley's advice; he wrote, on 8 January 1756, that he could not conjecture why 'A' (i.e., Cheyney) had behaved in this manner.

Building started again in 1756. 'Fir timber' was brought up the River Itchen by Mr Pyott (from Chesil Street), who was paid £30 14s. 6d. for 'riverage and carriage'. Bishop Hoadly had lent a further £2,000 on £3,000 worth of three per cent annuities. The north wing was going ahead, but in February 1757 work stopped again. Poor Pratt was ordered to collect the bills, there were all sorts of rumours, including faulty workmanship and curious financial transactions, allegedly between Mr Russell and the master carpenter. A committee of inquiry decided that all the brickwork in the north wing which carried the stone steps to the front entrance was 'shameful' and that the brick arch would have to be taken down. A new survey had to be made and, at this point, Doctor Burton was asked to write to William Sloane; he refused, but agreed instead to send to Chancellor Hoadly at Bath 'to provide a proper surveyor'. In the meantime, the bills kept coming in from Colebrook Street, though there were some new subscribers, amongst them Mr Richard Hockley of Twyford, and the litle Hospital was being carefully looked after by Richard Wavell, the rector of St Maurice's church. Drugs were bought from Mr Newbolt (£105 4s. 0d.) and Mr Speed (£39 12s. 6d.) and Mr Corbyn, the Chymist's bill came to £28 2s. 0d. Mr Abree had to be paid for malt, Sir Robert Ladbrooke, the distiller, was owed £34. The bakers' bills were left unpaid. It was indeed necessary to sort out the problems of Parchment Street.

Hoadly was able to engage John Wood, junior, son and namesake of a famous architect father, and the future designer of the Bath Assembly Rooms. Wood came to Winchester; he found the Hospital's brickwork safe but 'unpleasing', and proceeded to look at all the accounts and to make detailed recommendations. He was obviously very thorough. Supported by Doctor Hoadly, who described him as 'an eminent architect from Bath', he had come to Winchester to carry out an urgent task and, in a report dated 'Winton, May 17, 1757', explained that he had seen the two carpenters, Peter and John Barton, whose work he tactfully described as 'satisfactory', though 'the purlins of the roof may give way'. Remedial work was essential, strutt or collar pieces and small king posts should dovetail into the centre of each trimming joint. The brickwork was not done in a workmanlike manner 'as to beauty or neatness'. There were no settlements, 'except what is common and unavoidable'. Strengthening inverted arches should be built under the three windows in each of the smaller breaks in the east front and under every window on the ground floor. Wood charged only his travelling expenses, six guineas, paid on 1 June 1757. By that time, the smallpox had broken out, and Colebrook Street was at risk.

So far, the new Hospital had cost £3,700 and another £1,000 was needed. Work started at once, subscriptions were asked for all over Hampshire and, by the summer of 1759, the building was nearly finished, but so was the money. The Treasurer had spent £383 of his own money, and the outstanding debt on the building was £720. The only hopeful prospect were the sums to be derived from known future legacies, and they were 'to be applied to the discharge of the debts as fast as the money is received'. John Hoadly lent a further £800, charging three per cent, and on the security of £1,200 of the Hospital's Bank annuities.

Despite all the difficulties, and despite the ugly brick, there had emerged a handsome-looking building, with a 224-foot frontage on the east side of Parchment Street. Behind (i.e., east), was a garden and a large lawn, though Mr Abree had not sold the great Clobury stable block, nor the ground to the west of it. There were six wards, each with very large windows, and approached by wide corridors six feet wide.

Curiously enough, one important innovation is not mentioned in the Minutes. In 1758, the Reverend Stephen Hales published his *Treatise on Ventilators*. He was the inventor of a method of ventilating ships, and in the Treatise wrote 'The first trial of ventilators in a hospital was made by the County Hospital at Winchester, where they were fixed under the floor, at the further end of the ward from the entrance, so as to be worked with great ease by those in the ward by means of a lever fixed across the ward between the beds. The air is drawn out of the ward through a large tank which reaches near up to the ceiling that it may not incommode the patients with the velocity with which it reaches into the trunk.' It is not certain whether Hale's ventilators were fitted in every ward, or how long they lasted.

It should not be a matter of surprise that the theory grew that disease was carried by effluvium, stink. A medical author in 1771 wrote that Hospitals, intended to cure patients, frequently killed them; but fresh air was valued in the early years in Parchment Street, and patients who were able to walk, but who otherwise might not leave the building, were sometimes given special permission to leave the Hospital daily 'for the benefit o the air'. The new building seems to have admitted its first patients in 1759, at Michaelmas.

The anonymous author of the *History of Winchester*, published in 1773, was probably Richard Wavell, Loving Wavell's brother. He wrote, 'This magnificent edifice was opened for patients at Michaelmas 1759; the front of which is two hundred and twenty four feet long, and is ascended by a noble flight of steps. It contains six wards and is furnished with every other convenient office; besides an extensive green on the east side of the building, wherein the patients are at proper times permitted to receive the benefit of the air'. A neat line drawing of its west front, by William Cave, illustrated the description.

The Patients in the Later Eighteenth Century

Edmund Pyle, who became a canon of Winchester in 1756, was almost as interested in his own health and that of his friends as he was in 'clerical chess', the great game of who gets which preferment in the Anglican Church.[11] Like other of his neighbours in The Close, he suffered from hoarseness, gout and gravel. Gout meant that 'I am consigned over to the joys of bleeding, vomiting, rhubarb, salt and wormwood and Jesuit powder'. Hoarseness consigned him to 'much lying in bed, water gruel, bleeding and physic'. His account of London in April 1743 explains the results of a poor spring. 'London has been a great Hospital wherein there are scarcely persons enough that are well to attend to those that are sick. Colds, attended with a fever, and pain in the heart and back, prevail in every family, but are not mortal.' When the Dean of Salisbury (John Clarke, not a member of Alured's family) died in February 1757, Pyle, describing his death of an ague, added that it was 'caught by living in that vile dank Close in Salisbury, which is a mere sink, and which has destroyed more perhaps than ever it has saved'. Pyle's comments on his clerical contemporaries have some considerable medical interest. Doctor Lynch, Dean of Canterbury, but also Master of St Cross Hospital, suffered two paralytic strokes by 1760. He was 'daily plied with mustard, horseradish, and assafetida'. After he died, Pyle was offered the Mastership. He refused it; he did not want to live 'in a Rat's castle', in a swampy village. Unlike the Sick Poor in the Hospital, he would go to Bath for 10 weeks at a time when the gout became really bad. The fact is, however, that, like Alured Clarke before him and his own contemporary Doctor Hoadly who died of dropsy, and John Mulso, another Winchester canon, money alone could not purchase a cure, and some of the better known 18th-century diseases were sometimes occasioned by or made worse by over indulgence in food and drink. So it is not surprising that details of medical treatment more commonly survive amongst the family papers of the well-to-do, and are not so easily found amongst the records of those patients who were the Poor Sick who came to Clarke's Hospital.

The rise of Methodism, and the development of ready-made, patent medicines, were only two of the features of national history which undoubtedly influenced the patient-clientèle of the Hospital after the move to Parchment Street. John Wesley practised medicine, and his *Primitive Physic* was widely consulted. He once opened two dispensaries in six weeks (not in Winchester), and offered 'infallible' and 'tried' remedies to those who asked for help. The historian of Methodism in Winchester can find no evidence for Wesley's practice of medicine in the city, but Methodist insistence on the value of fresh air and hygiene was very important and a good example. Wesley was aware, too, of the use of lemon juice in the treatment of scurvy and he was convinced of the dangers of tuberculosis. Dr Trail has described his suggested treatment: 'cut a little turf of fresh earth, and, lying down, breathe into the hole for a quarter of an hour', as surely better than the prescription of 'snails boiled in milk' from a well-known member of the Royal College of Physicians in 1740.[12] There is very little evidence about the use of leeches in the County Hospital, or indeed of any particular medicine, all items which must have appeared in the apothecary's books, now lost. One of the best known cases when leeches were applied by a hospital surgeon was reported in *The Lancet* of 1827-8. H.G. Lyford was the surgeon in the case of the unfortunate Thomas Forder, brought in virtually unconscious and hardly able to speak because of a swollen tongue, to which leeches were applied. He died soon after.

The advent of ready-made 'patent' medicines coincided to some extent with the development of local newspapers. *The Salisbury and Wiltshire* founded in 1729, and the

Hampshire Chronicle, first published in Southampton in 1772, and moved to Winchester in 1778, inevitably carried a very large number of advertisements for ready-made medicines,[13] available over the various local counters or through the post. There must always be a number of people who enter a Hospital with gratitude and relief, but a considerable proportion of the human race will do virtually anything in the way of self-treatment and self-medication in the hope of not having to entrust themselves to an institution. Though newspapers were very expensive, and circulations comparatively small, the reading public was large, for papers were borrowed and passed around, and from the 1830s onwards could be read in the libraries of Mechanics' Institutes. Moreover, a large number of books offering advice on home treatment were becoming available to the general public, and they were undoubtedly best-sellers. Thomas Phaer, writing in the *Regyment of Lyfe*, as early as 1546, had advised his readers to 'Flee from such persons as do infect', but the Founder of the County Hospital in Winchester in his sermon on St Luke's Day in 1737, believed that sin was the main cause for disease, and he also, like the Quaker John Bellars in his *Essay on the Improvement of Physic* (1714), stressed the economic value of healthy manual workers; it would not perhaps be unjust to think that Clarke was more interested in cure rather than prevention, except in the one important respect that sinful people were more likely to be ill than those of good character.

There were other, local factors which influenced Parchment Street, and the Hospital's move was more or less accompanied by a period of economic revival in Winchester. The Guildhall had already been virtually rebuilt. There were plans to revive the Itchen Navigation, a new Market House was built in 1776, and from 1766 onwards a newly-formed Paving Commission began to pave, light and clean the Winchester streets.[14] The County Gaol was partly rebuilt, much of it still on its ancient site, and when John Howard came to Winchester to see the prison he also reported favourably on the Hospital. In 1785, a new theatre rose up in Jewry Street, on land which had belonged to the ambitious James Dibsdale (a Chandos man), and innkeeper from Avington who had rebuilt the City's leading inn in 1763, the *George* in Jewry Street; he was a subscriber to the Hospital from 17 onwards. The population was beginning to rise, and the practices of medical men began to increase. Many of them were still making up medicines for their own patients, but the most substantial new house in the High Street was that built by George Earle in 1772, and he was to found a dynasty of apothecary-pharmacists still represented in Winchester today.[15] Yet another local factor was the arrival in Winchester of large numbers of prisoners-of-war, kept in the remnant of Charles II's palace on the western side and considered, not always justly, to be bringing all sorts of diseases with them. The opening of the Naval Hospital at Haslar near Gosport in 1744 had other effects, though it had not prevented Taunton from stipulating that seafarers should have some measure of priority in 'his' county Hospital. There is not any real evidence to suggest that sailors played much part in the Winchester scene or were patients in the County Hospital, though drunken sailors were not unknown and usually ended up in the City Bridewell in the Broadway. Haslar tended to influence through the reputation of its leading Surgeon, James Lind, and Lind was consulted over the outbreaks of fever which emanated from French and Spanish prisoners-of-war in the 1780s, and which undoubtedly scared the Hospital Governors.[16]

It is during this period, too, the early years of the Hospital in Parchment Street, that the plague died away and that smallpox established itself as the great killer; the presence of large numbers of soldiers and the annual camps' militia men undoubtedly helped to spread the venereal diseases,[17] but it was smallpox which was the major threat. Pratt was too valuable a member of staff to go into houses where there was smallpox during the epidemic of 1745. There were out-patients who would have been admitted into the Hospital if infected patients had been allowed, but the Reverend Robert Shipman, a member of the Committee (more expendable than Richard Pratt?) was allowed to visit the sufferers in their own homes. He had to report back, and Pratt mixed up the appropriate medicines which were placed in the porch and collected by a messenger fobidden to enter the main building. Some 10 years later, the Committee had taken a lease of some hop-kilns to convert them into a pesthouse but, by 1757, a small house outside Westgate was leased from a Miss Columbell for the benefit of smallpox patients. It cannot have been very small, for an agreement with the Corporation provided for the admission of any person struck down with the disease within the city boundary, as long as six beds were left vacant for any sufferers from the Hospital itself. Amidst all the worry of the unfinished Parchment Street building, the Governors were aware, and practically aware, of the presence of smallpox.

By far the greater number of patients treated in Parchment Street, as in Colebrook Street before the move, were out-patients, many of whom were troublesome in different ways, unco-operative, unpunctual and, in the terms used so often in the Minutes of the Weekly Committee, 'improper objects'. Five years before the move, the Chairman had reported that, since Opening Day, 7491 cases had been admitted; more than half had been discharged 'cured', but of the rest, 1500 out-patients had been discharged for non attendance, 421 sent away for 'irregularity' or 'at own request', 343 were incurable, 37 'improper objects'; 358 had died in the house, and the remainder, 383, had received 'great benefit' from their treatment. At Christmas 1753-4, there had been 62 patients resident in Colebrook Street, and 122 out-patients. These reports were discussed at the meeting which approved the plans for the new Hospital, plans approved yet again on 14 January 1754. There was a feeling of urgency, not only because of the ever increasing numbers of patients, but because of problems with the Colebrook Street building; William Pescod was proving difficult. The Hospital's Trustees had 'laid out money under a misapprehension', the belief that they had a constant right to renew the lease. Chancellor Hoadly asked for legal advice from a good friend, Robert Henley of The Grange. He took a long time to answer, 'in truth I am mightily idle in the country and when I went to Town last left your papers at The Grainge', but warned them that they must find out from Pescod 'which persons had any interest in the house' and added that their lease was a very bad one, 'it's very inaccurately penned'.[18]

Even after the Hospital had been moved to Parchment Street, the number of patients continued to grow, and soon reached alarming proportions. Non-attendance of out-patients proved again and again to be a major and expensive difficulty. Outbreaks of smallpox were an added complication. At the beginning of 1765, 56 out-patients were discharged for non-attendance, and a vigorous policy began to be applied of discharging any patient who had been on the books for more than six months, and who was not making progress towards a cure or who had not 'quickly benefited'. Patients who had to be discharged for irregular conduct in the Hospital were always reported to their recommenders, especially when the recommenders had also stood security for funeral or removal expenses. Those deemed to be 'improper objects' were quickly discharged, and those who had been on the books too long, and did not show signs of improvement were 'discharged on account of time'. Those who had stayed too long were usually sent off in large numbers; 30 on 14 May 1766, 75 on 30 September 1767. Doctor Hoadly was particularly brisk in enforcing what came to be known as the six months rule, which meant that those who had not made progress after six months, either as out-patients or residents, had to be discharged. Ninety-six such patients were 'taken off' on 3 April 1768. The brutal fact was that the Hospital simply could not afford to keep them. Incurable patients were sent away almost at once; Anne Barnard, admitted on 16 December, was discharged incurable after 24 hours.

Patients who were not the sick poor were also turned out when they were discovered, like David Cooper in 1766, 'improper object on account of his circumstances'; 'lunaticks' were never admitted, though occasionally they were discovered and discharged at once, as was Catherine Sherman in that same year.[19] Hoadly's management of the Hospital was not only brisk; he believed in enforcing the rules: 'Nothing to be sent for from any shop except on order of the Apothecary or Matron'; 'the Cook to preside at the Kitchen Table, no servant to carry anything away, all servants to dine together at the time of meals'. There were to be no illicit snacks, or feeding of poor relations. Over a hundred years was to pass before patients waiting to be admitted could be given a cup of tea or a bowl of broth, or before each resident was given a bun on Easter Day. Venereal patients were always a problem; they were supposed to wait 14 days before they were admitted, though some Governors thought this inhumane.

Hoadly was not only a good Chairman; as a dramatist and a man about town, he knew everyone in London worth knowing, and in July 1767, his friend, David Garrick, sent a benefaction of £21.[19] In the same year, James Harris of Salisbury withdrew his subscription, but new subscribers included the Earl of Northington and Lord Henley, who gave 100 guineas. Pratt, too, collected subscribers when he could, in a number of ways; 'one guinea from an unknown hand by Mr Pratt'; much of the extra money was spent on extra comforts. At the end of July 1767, 20 pairs of sheets, 10 pairs of pillow cases, two kitchen table cloths, two dining cloths for the men's ward and, luxury of luxury, a length of cloth for rollers (towels) were purchased. Blankets and rugs were usually renewed when winter came on, and also night shirts for men and shifts for women. In an attempt to economise, the domestic staff now employed a woman baker, Betty Cole, but this did not last long. Bread might be called the earliest form of convenience food; there were many bakers in the city, bread was not dear, and the Hospital bakery soon came to an end, though barm for baking was occasionally purchased, perhaps for special occasions. Much of the apparatus of medicine could not be bought locally. Galleypots (eight gross at £2 1s. 0d.) and vials continued to be bought from Mr Thompson of London and brought down by the Waldron carriers; but drugs could be bought locally from Philip Newbolt and Richard Speed, and in April 1768 their bills of over thirty pounds were paid as well

4. John Hoadly (1711-1776), dramatist, poet, priest, and Chancellor of the Diocese of Winchester, with Maurice Greene (1696-1755), composer (from the picture by Francis Hayman by courtesy of The National Portrait Gallery).

as £13 5s. 6d. to 'Mr Corbyn, Chymist'. Local suppliers of drugs were official, appointed by the Governors, and at least one druggist, Speed, was cautioned about the quality of his goods. Very large quantities of sugar were always being bought for the Apothecary's shop, presumably to help disguise the taste of some of his horrible medicine; far less sugar was needed in the Hospital's kitchen. Bleeding remained the great remedy, and bleeding bowls were bought a dozen at the time.

In June 1766 it was reported that the 'number of in-patients greatly exceeds' the income available, and there were unpaid bills totalling £182 11s. 0d. The smallpox was soon raging in the city. Chancellor Hoadly's guiding hand was badly needed and he returned to take the Chair after a long absence; and at least the financial crisis was staved off when Hoadly agreed to lend yet another £400 without any further securities. The offer was gratefully noted on 11 June 1766. Smallpox patients continued to be sent to the Westgate House. In 1767, the lease of that Infirmary outside Westgate was transferred to the Corporation. The Governors were not being inhumane, and henceforth the Hospital was always prepared to offer advice and medicine during epidemics, but the Corporation or private individuals had to provide what nursing care could be found.[20] It might be added, however, that it was probably smallpox which broke up the arrangements by which one visiting clergyman and two house visitors were appointed each week. Only visiting clergy seem to have been appointed whilst the epidemic lasted. The number of consumptives taken in was not considerable, though it may have included a few unfortunates discharged as 'incurable'. Mary Barland was discharged on 13 August 1766, after a stay of only a week; Mary Craddock was sent off on 30 September 1767, for both women were consumptives. There are continued items of expenditure which must have made the lives of all the patients more comfortable. In the month that Hoadly made his last loan of £400, 'Mr Curtis' was paid eight shillings to clear away the rubbish, amazingly the first expenditure of its kind noted in the accounts. Two dozen hand basins were bought and benches in the backyard were repaired.

The most common amputation was probably that of legs; wooden legs were bought from a Mrs Smith in 1766 for £3 4s. 0d., but it is not clear how many legs could be purchased for that sum.[21] Hernia patients were provided with trusses, purchased ready-made from Mr Haskell. Patients who were paupers or whose patrons failed to honour their promises had to be buried; a simple funeral cost 16 shillings. Parchment Street had inherited the Colebrook Street furniture and fittings but, of course, new bedsteads had to be bought, though only occasionally. Towels were always rather a luxury; the poor used rags – or hardly washed at all. The towels in Parchment Street were not for individuals, but were 'rollers', certainly not very hygienic. Another problem of quite a different kind appears over payments to Mr James White and Mrs Corbyn for bug traps. Small traps cost nine pence each, larger ones a shilling. Ninety-six traps had to be paid for in October 1767 and, the week before Christmas, the Matron, Mrs James, asked for a 'few shades' for her room. They must have prevented glances from the inquisitive eyes of passers-by; and perhaps made it more difficult to see other unwelcome visitors inside or outside Mrs Corbyn's and Mr White's traps. Curiously enough, mice and rats do not appear to have caused any problems, despite the presence of uncleared rubbish.

Details of individual patients are sadly lacking. Isaac Phillimore, a labourer born in Ludgershall, Wiltshire, where his father had been a woodcutter, springs to life in the settlement papers of the Poor Law overseers in St Maurice's parish, Winchester. Aged 31 when he came to the notice of the authorities in January 1786, he had worked with his father until he was 24 years old, and then moved to Otterborne. After a year working for Mrs Yaldren, he had agreed to work for Farmer Rout, at six guineas a year, after a three months' trial. Then he had two weeks in the Hospital, sent there on the recommendation of Walter Smythe of Bramridge House, the father of the famous Mrs Fitzherbert. When Phillimore came out of Hospital, he went back to work with his farmer, but was discharged by Rout's widow after the death of her husband. Soon after,he married a widow, Martha McNier, of St Maurice's parish, who bore him a daughter, Jane. Presumably they lived on in St Maurice's parish and, hopefully, 'happily ever after', undisturbed by authority. Phillimore's story is known simply because the Poor Law of the time made it very difficult for the poor to live anywhere else but in the parish where they had been born, and which could be required to provide them with financial support.[22]

V Change And A Crisis

After the completion of Parchment Street, the administration of the Hospital seems to have followed a regular routine. The Minutes of the Weekly Committee suggest that the Agenda was always the same; the names of those present was followed by the reading of the Minutes of the last meeting, the appointment of visitors, the names and numbers of patients discharged, and why they were discharged, and the names of the patients admitted 'In' and 'Out' of the House. Subscribers dead were noted and new subscribers added, and sometimes, not always, there was a financial statement and a brief summary of the Hospital's finances on that particular day, 'in Mr Hoare's hands and in Mr Treasurer's hands'. New subscribers to Parchment Street were not always very permanent; Jane Austen's father, the Rector of Steventon, subscribed a guinea on 13 February 1765, but withdrew his subscription in the same year on 4 September.

Some subscribers preferred to pay direct to Hoare, who had become the Hospital's banker; he himself gave five guineas a year, and he produced some useful contacts, including the Earl of Shaftesbury (March 1765, 10 guineas), and the Earl of Dartmouth, another 10-guinea subscriber. William Pescod had died in 1760 and was succeeded on the committee by Francis Swanton, who sometimes acted as chairman, and who allowed over-worked Mr Pratt to go off for three weeks' leave to Worcestershire in 1765.[1] In July of that year, the Duke of Bolton died, and the Hospital therefore lost his annual 10 guineas, a substantial sum when one relises that the Hospital's working weekly balance at that moment was £21 10s. 0d. 'in Mr Hoare's hand', and £9 17s. 2d. with the Treasurer. The staff had to be paid on 2 October; Richard Pratt got his usual £50, Mrs James, the Matron, £15 5s. 0d., Mr King, Bacconeau's successor as Surgeon, one quarter's gratuity (five guineas), and the five nurses £2 10s. 0d. each, five shillings more than the cook, Mary Ford, and 10 shillings more than the laundry maid, still Elisabeth Alder, and all payments in arrears.

It is hardly surprising to find that the long-suffering Treasurer had paid out most of this from his own pocket, and was owed £38 12s. 0d. The Duke of Bolton was dead, so the Duke of Chandos could safely withdraw his subscription. Despite the new building and the regularity of the administration, there was some feeling of general disorganisation, perhaps because Pratt was getting older. There were already too many patients and smallpox was about, and the support of distinguished new subscribers was only occasional consolation; Bernard Brocas of Beaurepaire offered five guineas at the end of May 1766; his was a name from Hampshire's great medieval past, long before the Boltons and Chandos clans tried to rule the county, but one subscription was not enough for running repairs to the Hospital's (lower) stone floors, let alone the ordering of 980 bushels of coal, bought on the recommendation of the Porter, who had been sent to the Wharf to decide when coals were good and cheap; it was one year's supply, and carried up from the Wharf on Mr Pyott's wagon 'if its at leisure'; he lived in Chesil Street, and came from a family distinguished for its members who belonged to the Society of Friends, and distinguished also for the years of service which Alexander and his father, Edward, gave to the Hospital.[2]

In 1772, the Hospital's 'Statutes and Constitutions' were re-issued in a revised form as a small book, published by J. Wilkes in the High Street, Winchester.[3] This important set of rules was not to be altered in any way without the consent of a General Court of at least forty Governors. The rules illustrate changing social attitudes and also the increasing prosperity of Winchester at this time. A great deal was expected of the Hospital servants. Detailed rules for the Messenger and Porter were now included. He was to assist in the laboratory and shop, attend to the keeping of the great or upper door (locked) and wait on the Apothecary and Matron at dinner. He was to brew and to tun; he was to go on all errands 'on the business of the house as the Matron or Apothecary shall direct; to carry all the summones that are sent out ... and obey all the rules of the Chairman, Treasurer, and Apothecary'. In his spare time, when he was 'not otherwise employed' by the Governors or by the Apothecary, 'he shall do all the labouring business of the house according as he shall be directed from time to time by the Matron'.

The Matron, in fact, was occasionally the formidable figure which even a pre-Nightingale Matron could sometimes be; she could employ patients who were deemed well enough to work by their physicians or surgeons, and pay them as she thought fit, though presumably these sums had to be shown in her Incident Book. Thus it was to be a patient who kept the lower door (on the front, but beneath the great flight of steps), and it had, too, to be kept locked. Patients had even to carry all the coals needed in the wards, in the kitchen, 'and to all other places in the Hospital', and presumably had to lay and light the fires, since they were required to sift the cinders. Patients still had to promise to keep the rules and, from 1772 onwards, had to sign a form, the words of which were incorporated in the new Statutes. 'I promise to obey all the House Rules, and if I refuse to comply with the Rules or leave the Hospital without the consent of my Physician, I promise to pay Mrs ... The Matron, for all the Provisions and Medicines I shall have had during my stay in the House, at the rate of 5/- a week. Witness my hand – signed in the presence of ... '

Rule XVI could have been particularly significant in the development of the relationship between the medical staff and the Governors. Before 1772, doctors and surgeons alike had frequently been elected as Governors. Now 'No Person who practices as a Physician, Surgeon, or Apothecary either in the Hospital or out of it be elected or act as a member of the Committee'.[4] 'This Society' was to consist of fifty or more Governors of which thirty or more were to be inhabitants of the city or suburbs of Winchester, and the minimum annual subscription for a Governor was still only £2, or £20 at one time. That latter kind of supporter was rarely described as a subscriber; he was a benefactor. Though there were many generous female supporters of the Hospital, no-one apparently ever considered that a woman might serve on the Committee, let alone become a Governor.

The patients were not the only people to be restricted by Rules. Amongst the new officers, the Auditors were to visit the house every week, to examine the entries made in the record books ... and to see that there were no mistakes. There were Rules for all the other Visitors, House Visitors, the visiting clergymen, and the Visiting Apothecary, when there was one. There was to be a Complaints Book, kept on the table in the board- or committee-room, which every member might use. The strong-box, kept in the board room, had the traditional three keys, held by the Chairman and the two Treasurers. The Box of Writings, kept in the same place, had only one key, for the Chairman or his Deputy; if absent, his two keys were to be kept by the College School Master. The Receivers, whose duties were to collect subscriptions which came from all the many localities where the Hospital had supporters, were outside the mass of regulations; in fact, most of them were retail shopkeepers and newsagents.

When the Governors met on 20 April 1773, they decided to offer Mr Joseph Barker, their senior surgeon, and young Mr Lyford, a salary of £20 a year with 'the thanks of the court to those two gentlemen for their gratuitous service for many years past'; but the attendance of the physicians was unsatisfactory. It was decided to write to Doctor Welsh, with the compliments of the court, asking if his avocation will permit his attendance on the out-patients and his punctual and exact compliance with the rules of physicians, of which he was sent a copy. A stiff answer, in the third person, came back from the Doctor's house in Garr Street,[5] to the effect that the Court could elect a second Physician. He was thanked for his regard for the charity, but as yet there was no suggestion of a second appointment. By the autumn of 1773, Welsh had gone, thanked for his long and great service and a Doctor Smyth (Smith) was approached; and then, at the beginning of the new year, three doctors were elected Physician: Scott, Breedon and John Makkitrick. It seems that Welsh had admitted patients suffering from fits; 'it tends too much to the disturbance of other patients'. The Court was still hoping to attract Smyth, but he was uncertain, perhaps because of the smallpox, for he was asked to attend as soon as it was safe and convenient for him. Makkitrick was already in demand from an increasing number of private patients, and had to be asked in 1776 to visit the Hospital as much as he could, but the real loss of the past 12 months, and one which greatly upset the Committee, was the resignation of Doctor John Hoadly. They did indeed have good cause to hope that 'he will continue his good influences and his good offices', on behalf of the Hospital. He had proved a very able Chairman, and was a generous benefactor in his will.[6]

Parchment Street must have resembled a country lane at the time of the new Hospital, but in the early spring of 1771, the Winchester Paving Commissioners met for the first time. The large body of Commissioners had been set up under recent legislation, but though they included men with connections with the Hospital (Thomas Waldron, the Reverend Richard Wavell and the Reverend Doctor Lee to name only a few), there was no immediate attempt to pave Parchment Street. Surprisingly, very little had been done to the streets of central Winchester since the unpopular attempts of the Parliamentary Corporation after the execution of Charles I, when some of the side streets had been surfaced with grave stones from city churchyards and ruined churches. The new Commission set about its work at once;

it had wide powers, and intended to use them. Overhanging street signs (illegal, since they were theoretically encroaching on the highways) and disused water spouts had to be taken down, at once; the slaughtering of animals in butchers' shops was forbidden. Sheep and cows were not to wander around, and horses were not to be shod in the streets. At its second meeting, the Commission decided to advertise for a Public Scavenger, that is, someone who would contract to clear away rubbish on a regular basis, and 'Mr Grenville' was asked to number the houses, beginning with Mr Penton's great house at the east end of the High Street.[7] The crossing from the High Street into Southgate Street was very narrow, and negotiations were begun to purchase *The Black Swan* on its south-western corner. A search for gravel and sand had already started, and flints were being collected, and stacked in various places, including the south end of Doctor Welsh's meadow in Parchment Street. Soon there was real progress, and the High Street began to be paved in flint, and pavements (footpaths) constructed on both sides from the Westgate to the Jewry Street crossing. In mid-summer, there was a general order that bog houses were not to have their contents emptied into the Brooks, but only into the main river; all green stalls, fish stalls, and other stalls were to be removed to the Square, the entrances to Southgate Street, St Thomas Street and Little Minster Street were to be paved as far as Back Lane (St Clement's Street), the passage way from the Cathedral to the High Street *via* St Maurice's church was also to be paved, and estimates were to be obtained for paving all the streets whose inhabitants had petitioned for paving – and were therefore willing to pay their share of the rates. Parchment Street and Upper Brook Street had not sent in petitions, but estimates were to be obtained for that work, and in fact a petition had arrived by 3 October 1771. Householders did not have to pay a full rate until the work was finished, and Richard Wavell, John Newbolt and Robert Serle, the lawyer, formed a sub-committee to supervise the paving. Surprisingly, it was only a partial paving of Parchment Street at this stage, the entrance to the street and as far as Cross Lane (St George's Street), some 10 yards paved with Guernsey rubble, but with footpaths of good material as in the High Street. Major Poole and Mr Abbot were to assist by taking the levels, and all householders were required to put efficient spouts to their gutters. Twenty-nine Parchment Street ratepayers paid for the work, including Mrs Martha Soley, the widow of Alured Clarke's old supporter, who lived in the street, as did another widow, Jemima Langrish. Wealthy Mrs Langrish owned three houses there, and another owner (of a meadow) connected with the Hospital was Doctor James Welsh. It was a major attempt to improve the Hospital area, but there is no evidence at this stage that the rest of the way down to the Hospital was anything but a mere unpaved lane.The Rates List of 1771 is extremely interesting and shows, *inter alia*, Charles Lyford living in a Columbell House, and Nicolas Bacconeau in his father's house, which by this time belonged to William Kernot; both these High Street houses paid at the rate of one pound per year.

The citizens of Winchester, like the inhabitants of other cities which had county gaols, had always been conscious of the fearful probability that gaol fever might come to their town. It was a much dreaded disease, and in 1767 an outbreak of typhus in the county gaol resulted in the postponement of the Hampshire Assizes for ten weeks. *The State of the Prisons* by the great reformer, John Howard, appeared in

1777, and drew attention to the fact that gaol fever 'was not only widely prevalent, but also accutely infectious and very often fatal'.[8] In 1773, 1774 and 1775, Howard was fully convinced that more prisoners were destroyed by it than were put to death by all the public executions in the Kingdom. At a terrible Assize held in Oxford in 1577, everyone present was dead within forty hours, the Lord Chief Baron, the Sheriff and about three hundred other persons. The smell of a gaol was dreadful, and did much to encourage the belief that all kinds of complaints were carried by horrible odours. In Haslar Hospital, Howard saw a ward full of suffering sailors, all infected by one member of the crew, who had been released from Prison. James Lind, the famous surgeon there, believed that gaol fever was the great enemy of seamen, many of whom were pressed men. When Howard visited the County Prison in Winchester, he was told that until the dungeon there had been improved, 20 prisoners in it had died in one year. Even after the improvements, the place only measured 48 feet by 20, but it had a boarded floor, three large windows, each 12 feet high, and was only five steps below the general ground level.

A short time after Howard visited Winchester, a major outbreak of some sort of fever occurred in the much larger Winchester prison, the King's House on the western hill, used for Spanish and French prisoners-of-war. Doctor Carmichael Smyth (sometimes spelt Smith) was sent down by the Government to inspect that prison, which had its own Hospital. The Committee of Parliament, set up to inquire

5.   The Hospital in Parchment Street.

on the health of prisoners in the King's House, was told that the 'Nurses who attend the sick in the Hospital at Winchester were Prisoners of war themselves'. They also asked if there had been complaints from the inhabitants of Winchester concerning the burials of prisoners. Only one complaint had been received. Doctor Smyth spent a fortnight in the city, and found that the disorder was a fever, 'Extremely contagious, and likely to prove fatal to the attendants and Officers belonging to the Hospital, who were removed into the Town after they were taken ill'; yet he could not find that the Infection had spread to any of the inhabitants, and concluded that it was not 'the real Pestilence' (i.e. Plague) but more in the nature of a gaol distemper. He left behind as a replacement, a naval surgeon, Mr Smith who himself went down with the complaint as did an assistant, Mr Porter; the letters to the Commissioners for Sick and Wounded Seamen, written by Doctor Ferquharson, who had been sent down at the beginning of the attack, have been published. On 4 April 1780, he had been told by London to call in Doctor Makkitrick and report on the nature of the complaint. Makkitrick approved of the treatment 'tobacco burnt round the ward', with Cascarilla, and must have agreed with the verdict that 'the Spanish prisoners are the most Dirty people I know', for he suggested that they should be taken, under military escort, to bathe in the River Itchen ..., 'the most eligible method to get them cleaned'. Three days later, Smith was told to engage 'the temporary assistance of some Practitioner of character in Winchester', and bathing was approved. Makkitrick himself refused to attend the Prison Hospital, saying 'he had many reasons against it', and soon the original medical adviser sent down to Winchester had to write that Mr Porter, his assistant, was dead and that he himself and his Dispenser were not at all well. James Lind came over from Haslar, ordered the whitewashing of the hammock posts, the fumigation of the wards with pots of sulphur, and the sending of prisoners found dirty to the washing cellar for a compulsory bath.

He stayed in Winchester for eight days and examined 189 patients, 47 of whom had a putrid fever ... but no symptom of malignancy. His correspondence with the Commission was also published. He examined the prison water supply (three wells) and found it wholesome, except when the wells were low, and examined the river water, described by him as wholesome, but expensive to carry up to the King's House. Complaints about the bread, supplied by Mr William Meader, of Winchester, were also looked into; the Spaniards liked the bread baked harder than did the French. These were minor matters, compared with the allegations that proper graves of sufficient depth could not be dug (because of the foundations of the old Castle), and suggestions that the prisoners sent out daily for exercise in the Airing Ground to the south of the King's House would merely lie down on the ground, and spend what money they had on intoxicating drink bought from a series of huts, set up quite illegally by enterprising Wintonians. In a comparatively short time, and thanks presumably to James Lind's work and that of Doctor Carmichael Smyth, the outbreak came to an end. In November 1779, there had been nearly 5,000 prisoners in this Winchester gaol, but the outbreak, judged by the numbers of deaths, began to decline in July that same year. It was a very dangerous time for the inhabitants of Winchester and for the County Hospital, and rumours that the complaint had spread to the military garrison under Lord Paget, whose men were acting as guards, and also to the town, were all too rife. The detailed account of the outbreak is extremely interesting for the evidence which it produces as to what could and might be done with the outbreak of any infectious or contagious complaint, and it is surprising that it seems not to have affected the County Hospital.[9]

It is not surprising, however, that Doctor Makkitrick refused to go inside the Prison Hospital. He had his Hospital patients to consider and a very large private practice, and just when the prison fever was beginning to decline, smallpox broke out again in Winchester. Sarah Williams, the young wife of the absentee rector of Compton, wrote to her husband to tell him that she had been advised to go to Smith, the inoculating doctor, to know whether any of her children might be safely inoculated.[10] Doctor Makkitrick, who appears in the Williams' correspondence as 'Dr Mak', was the family doctor, the valued adviser of her husband who was frequently away from home as Chaplain to the Speaker of the House of Commons. In June 1784 'Dr Mak' 'attended by all the Physical tribe in the place, except the strong horseman', fell ill.[11] Poor Mak had to be cut for the stone, rallied temporarily and died on 1 July 1784, between two and three in the morning, and was buried almost immediately.[10a] His private practice had been chiefly in the Soke. He lived in No 68, Kingsgate Street, and there is a memorial to him in St Michael's churchyard. Sarah knew all about his affairs; he had 'got about £520'; had left '£500 to Mr Lee, the Turkey merchant that you saw in his house', and £100 to the son of an apothecary at Sutton called Wickham, and Doctor Butler and Mr Lee were his executors. By the middle of the month, she was able to report further: 'Dr Mak's sale is next week ... [it includes] choice rum in small lots'. She went to view the lots, 'Poor Mak's things', and found that everything was fixed at 'double the value'. She herself had to consult Mr Lyford, the surgeon, in April 1785, because of her many aches of body and mind: 'he considered it due to her children being larger than her frame would stand', but 'no permanent harm was done'.[12]

Makkitrick's death was followed almost at once by the arrival of three potential successors, Doctors Walker, Jones and Scott, 'the same doctor who formerly lived here'.[13] Sarah was staying in College Street, within calling distance of Lady Chernocke's house at the end of St Thomas Street, and that lady was always very knowledgable about the medical world. 'I called yesterday upon Lady Chernocke, who asked me if I had sent to the new Physician yet. She told me so much news and scandal, that I was tempted to come and drink tea with her.' The new Physician was perhaps Doctor John Littlehales, who had eventually succeeded to 'Mak's' practice, and to his work in the Hospital. The Williams' and the Littlehales' families were both members of the close-knit Wykehamical society, which included the Lees and the Blackstones, but Sarah's own life was soon to end. Worn out with child-bearing, she died in childbirth in September 1787.

But all was not perfect at the Hospital when Doctor John Littlehales and Mr Charles Lyford were the chief medical men. John Howard paid a visit on 4 July 1788, when it was far from full. There were only 43 in-patients, and Howard approved of the arrangements for patients able to sit up and who could dine very properly in a room adjoining to their wards. The place as a whole must have looked quite cheerful. The iron bedsteads were painted green, the furniture was blue and white. But it was a high summer's day, and all the windows of the passages and staircases shut, and the semi-basement wards where the venereal patients lived were 'dirty, close and offensive'. There were no opening fanlights over the ward doors such as Howard had seen in the London Hospital, nothing in part 'to prevent the offensiveness of the wards at night'.[14] It was a contrast with Haslar, where James Lind had the windows left permanently open in summer by the simple expedient of nailing them open. His patients wore a Hospital uniform, including a white shirt, and 'all the nurses were women which is very proper, as they are more cleanly and tender, and they more easily pacify the patients who are sea-faring men'. Cleanliness and tenderness had always been required of the nurses at the County Hospital.

John Littlehales was the son of Colonel John Littlehales of Bridgnorth, and his mother, Mary (née Lee),was sister to Lancelot and Harry Lee of Coton. His second wife, Frances Dorothy, the daughter of Lancelot, was thus his first cousin, and Harry Lee (Warden of Winchester College) was his uncle; and Lee's own son and namesake, Chairman of the Hospital for many years, was his cousin, which was not a bad start for a young doctor at a time when the College was very influential in Hospital affairs. There were other useful relations; his first wife had been a Parry and thus a member of a famous medical family.Littlehales was successful, wealthy and kind to the poor, and his fame spread. He was also by far the most highly qualified physician the Hospital had ever had. He had been at Pembroke, had an Oxford degree, become a Doctor of Medicine in 1782, and a Fellow of the Royal College of Physicians in 1787. In 1791, the *Hampshire Chronicle* printed a poem written by one of his grateful patients, a young man who had been given up as incurable.

> *To an Eminent Physician in the County of Hants*
>
> Hail! O those poor man's friend to thee I owe,
> Next, under Heaven, that here I am below.
> A living witness of thy mighty skill
> To save from death, whom dire disease would kill.
> Lo, Health's restorer, precious gift of Heaven!
> In thee, what numerous benefits are given,
> Tis thine to know of herbs and plants and flowers,
> Let not the sick dispair of timely aid,
> Each medicine, from Nature'secrets made.
> He kindly recommends for their relief
> All restoration wuick confirms belief,
> Like Aescu Lapius honoured as divine,
> Example to succeeding ages shine,
> Such fame, O generous active man, be thine.
>   R.B.

It would perhaps be too much to suggest that Littlehales was a herbalist; though the line 'Tis thine to know of herbs and plants and flowers' could well mean just this; it was about at this time, too, that Winchester people were imbibing one of the newer patent medicines, Doctor William Brodum's Botanical Syrup and Restorative Nervous Cordial, which they could buy at the *Hampshire Chronicle*'s office. Doctor Brodum had also written *A Guide to Old Age, or a Cure for the Indiscretions of Youth*, two volumes, price 5s. 0d., and dedicated to George III and intended particularly for 'persons whose delicacy will not permit them to unfold their real situation to their Physicians'.

Littlehales' substantial estate bears witness to his great success with private patients. The *Chronicle* records that 'He followed his profession in this city for many years. Cheerfully lent his assistance to that most useful of institutions, the County Hospital, of which he was at all times the leading Physician and strenuous benefactor. In estimating his character as a Physician he was a point of knowledge perhaps unequalled; as a gentleman, in manners inferior to none. Eminent as a scholar,he united together desirable qualifications, generosity, sincerity and benevolence. Many are the living witnesses of his professional merit, who through his unremitting attentions, under Providence, have been restored from sickness to the blessing of health. The neighbourhood of Winchester will consider him a public loss. Associating with the first classes of society, he was uniformly kind to the deserving in all ranks ... in fact his whole life was one uninterrupted chain of universal charity and interested benevolance [sic].'

His memorial in the Cathedral, where he was buried, is equally laudatory. He left three children, of whom Richard Littlehales, the second son, of Great Minster Street, is commemorated in the east window of St Laurence's church, Winchester, where it was placed there by his sister Maria as part of the great restoration of the church in 1848 and 1849, and Miss Littlehales' name also appears on the Benefactors' Board as the bequeather of seven shares in the Winchester Cemetery Company to the rector of the Parish for the benefit of the parish poor.

Doctor John Littlehales' eldest son, his successor at the Hospital, was Doctor Charles Littlehales, who did not die until February 1868, aged 84 years. His first wife was a daughter of that Harry Lee who was his Chairman at the Hospital. He was survived by two spinster daughters, Frances Louisa, who hung herself on 31 March 1869, and Annie Maria, who cut her throat soon afterwards on 19 May.[15] It is permissible to ask if these two suicides were in any way a result of the marriage of first cousins. Both were women in their thirties. This tragic family lived in Kingsgate Street, and both Charles and Richard were freemen of the city and each appear on the Voters' List of 1835. Both were Tories, supporters of Buller East; in fact, at this time this was the usual political colour of the Hospital medical staff. Charles Mayo, the Lyfords and the Littlehales doctors were not apparently in favour of political reform, but Richard Littlehales was a Whig, and a Reformer.[16]

The *Chronicle* took the opportunity, when it recorded the death of the great John Littlehales, to publish a useful note about 'the Election of Physicians at the County Hospital', on the grounds that there were false impressions about what happened if there was a vacancy. 'This statement [is] to prevent any undue partiality or prejudice on the present occasion [Doctor Littlehales' death]. When a Physician, preparing to practice, arrives in Winchester, it is the custom for him to offer his services to the Hospital.' Doctor Hutchinson offered his services before the death of Doctor Littlehales, and was elected; Doctor Badham arrived; he was also elected, but 'there is no contest between them ... these appointments are gratuitous'. The paper might have added that to some extent 'these appointments were becoming hereditary'.

For much of his life, John Littlehales' chief colleague at the Hospital was Charles Lyford, the Senior Surgeon, and Lyford's son Giles King Lyford, who had been appointed as his successor in 1787. Lyford was not an easy character, and in 1789 the Governors dismissed Doctor (*sic*) John Smith, who had consistently refused to keep Lyford informed about his intentions, as far as operations were concerned, and as he was required to do. One or the other had to go, and it was Smith who went. 'Whereas Mr Lyford and Mr Smith have long been at variance, and these disagreements are likely to be very hurtful to the Hospital, it is very necessary that one of them be dismissed ... agreed that Mr Smith be dismissed'. The decision was taken by a large meeting of Governors, who all signed the record, including Archdeacon Balgy, the Chairman, and John Mulso. The General Court of 12 January 1790 confirmed John Smith's dismissal and appointed William Wickham in his place, 'provided he makes Winchester his constant residence', and 'subscribes to the order of 2 May', which prevented him from operating without Lyford Senior being present. Wickham, who was waiting outside, was called in, and agreed to the conditions. Thus there began the long years when the Wickham family served the Winchester County Hospital. Charles was buried in St Laurence's church in a family vault, on 23 December 1805. There is no record of his death in the Governors' Minutes but he was 68 years old and had done more than anyone to enhance the Hospital's reputation for surgery, and *The Chronicle* provided a splendid obituary.

'On Monday last died, aged 62, Mr Lyford, for more than 40 years an highly eminent surgeon, &c, of this city. The superior judgement and great ability evinced by him in every branch of his profession, deservedly placed him in its highest rank, and introduced him to the most extensive and respectable practice. As a consulting and operating surgeon at the County Hospital his merits were of the most beneficial nature, and they will be gratefully remembered by those who have had the advantage of his assistance at that noble Charity. His attention and consoling manner, if it could not lessen the pain which his skilful hand was often necessarily obliged to inflict, yet it inspired a confidence which gave hope and comfort under the most afflicting circumstances. As a husband and parent his loss is irreparable; and his suavity of manners and general good offices will long leave him dear in the recollection of innumerable friends.' The same issue (23 December 1805) contained an announcement about the future of the firm. 'All persons having a claim on the Estate of Mr Lyford, deceased, or on the firm of Messrs Lyford and Son, are requested to send the particulars to Mr Faithfull, Solicitor; All such as are indebted will have the goodness to pay the amount to the said Mr Faithfull who is duly authorized to settle the accounts. Mr Giles King Lyford avails himself of this opportunity of announcing to his kind Friends, his intention of continuing the Profession; and flatters himself, the many years practice he has had, in conjunction with his deceased Father, will ensure him a continuance of their kind patronage. Winchester. 19 December, 1805.' Six months later, Mr Faithfull was still trying to clear up the estate, but Giles King was not short of money; he soon had a substantial house in Southgate Street, and though the family attended St Lawrence's church (where they had a private vault), Mrs Lyford subscribed to the fund for rebuilding St Thomas' church in Southgate Street.

John Littlehales' patients had come to include Canon Mulso and his family, then living in 10 The Close, with frequent visits to Meonstoke, a living which John Mulso held in plurality with his Cathedral Canonry. Their first Physician in Winchester was

Doctor John Smith, of St Giles' Hill, the famous inoculating doctor. Mulso died in September 1791, after years of letter writing to his greatly loved friend, Gilbert White, letters which are full of his own medical aches and pains, the sufferings of his wife and his family. The family were staying in Sunbury when their daughter was born in 1758, and Mrs Mulso had to endure the agony of breast abscesses. 'Twice her breast has been cut in a most severe way.' Seven years later, when the Mulsos were as Thornhill, and after three lyings-in in just over two years, Mrs Mulso was taking medicine four times a day '... has undergone Emetics and Blisters ...our Faculty says her Cure must be a work of time'. Mulso himself was already beginning to suffer from rheumatism. In 1771, he wrote from his house in The Close, 'there has a sick house ever since I came; for my Cook has had a dangerous illness of great length, and now my wife's maid, her sister, is in a Fever, which has been upon her about Twenty days; their lives have been saved by the Kindness and extraordinary attendance of Doctor Smith, who has been a great Friend to them and us'. A year later, 'we have been all bad here, with Rheumatism and aguish complaints'. Two years later, Mrs Mulso was suffering from a notorious and surprising sort of cough, and Mulso thought his wife's life was in danger; 'we were forced to call in Doctor Smith, to whose prescriptions she is still conforming'. The family had great faith in Doctor Smith, and the four children and five servants were all innoculated by him in November 1773. 'It is an Agreement made by several families in The Close that we shall hazard together ... the Rifeness of it here [smallpox] has urged unto us this measure.' Experience of coughs produced a favourite medicine, which the Mulsos recommended to all their friends, including Gilbert White.

'One pound of Raisins stoned and chop'd and add a Drachm of Olibanum, two ounces of Conserve of Hips, ditto of Roses. Fifty drops of Spirit of Sulphur, and half an ounce of Syrup of White Poppies. Beat all three to an Electuery. Take ye Quantity of a nut meg when the cough is troublesome, especially when going to bed'.

Summer 1778 brought 'Bilious Diarrhoia, gravel etc ... and my wife's maid servant extremely ill'. It is not surprising that, in 1790, Mulso himself was still 'suffering from Gravel, Piles and Ulcers' and, after Doctor Smith had left Winchester, he was seeking the help of Doctor John Littlehales, already establishing his reputation as a brilliant physician at the Hospital, though he also 'had our Physical Tribe here'. There were many doctors in Winchester, and Mulso consulted, too, Mr Hale of Hambledon, and was using a patent medicine, Ward's Paste, though 'all application has been ineffectual'. Dear Gil's 'Old Friend and Affectionate humble servant' died at Winchester on 20 September 1791.[18] There were still so many illnesses which could disable, kill, or just make miserable the lives of even the well-to-do. For the poor, the County Hospital was a continued blessing.

VI Parchment Street Before The Storm

It was Charles Mayo who proved to be one of the Hospital's most famous and successful surgeons. An earlier Mayo had been amongst the Hospital's first subscribers.[1] Charles had been born at Wimborne in Dorset, on 29 December 1788, where his father was the Headmaster of the Grammar School, and he was called Charles after one of his godfathers, the then Rector of Beechingstoke (Wiltshire), a living in the possession of the Dean and Chapter of Winchester Cathedral. He was the fourth son in a family of 10 children and, when he was only 15, he was sent to London to learn the rudiments of medicine. His godfather took a great interest in him, as did a cousin, Doctor John Mayo, who was 'always approachable at breakfast' and who advised him to become a student at St Bartholomew's Hospital. He was a clever young man, working as dresser for one of the most successful surgeons of the time, Sir Charles Blicke, and he was only 23 when he became a member of the Royal College of Surgeons.[2]

Within a few weeks of qualifying, he arrived in Winchester armed with some splendid testimonials in the hope of becoming surgeon to the County Hospital. He had introductions to two of the most influential men in the City, Thomas Rennell, the future Dean, and a formidable member of the Chapter, Canon George Frederick Nott.[3] The interviewing committee was unanimous in its decision, but the local doctors viewed his arrival with suspicion and, when the Governors met to confirm the appointment, he was rejected – by one vote. The whole Committee then resigned, but three months later, Charles Mayo got the appointment, and began his life's work. He was always prepared to risk unpopularity and his concern for all his patients led him, early in 1839, to criticise an attempt by some of his colleagues and some of his Governors to exclude venereal patients from the Hospital. A resolution that this should become policy had been supported by Lyford and Wickham, but the next Court was asked to modify the decision which Mayo felt to be abominable; patients were to be admitted only if they could produce a marriage certificate and a certificate of moral character signed by their parish priest. He exposed the whole affair in *The Lancet*, whose Editor described Sir Thomas Baring, a Baronet (proposer of the resolution) as belonging to the lowest grade of aristocracy. The influence of another Governor, John Keble, was perhaps behind this unfortunate affair which appeared in *The Lancet* (1838-9,2) under the title of 'Charitable Resolution at Winchester Hospital'.

Mayo soon became a well-known figure in Winchester society, where there was a good deal of what he called 'bowing and scraping'. He was asked to Corporation dinners, met the Members of Parliament, and was advised by Canon Nott to give some lectures to ladies, advice which he refused, though the refusal did not impair Nott's regard for him and, through Mrs Rennell's influence, he was elected an adviser to the Winchester Lying-in Society. He soon became particularly known as a competent amputator, and he also sought Abernethy's advice on how to cut for the stone. When the Rector of Beechingstoke arrived in Winchester in autumn 1814, he found his young cousin 'going on very prosperously' and 'much in the good graces of Doctor Rennell'. Soon he was able to buy the large and very attractive house in St Peter's Street which remained his home for the rest of his life.[4] It cost him £1,850, including the furniture, but it was not until 1818 that the Governors offered him an Honorarium of £20 per annum, one-third of what they paid the Chaplain.

'Until 1876', wrote Doctor Druitt, 'Charles Mayo's life was one of the busiest professional work', much of it reported in *Medical and Chirurgical Transactions* or *The Lancet*. The last entry in his case-book, written in 1875, when he was 84, was for a difficult hernia. He always worked a very long day, and expected his students, who valued him greatly, to start their work before breakfast without complaint.[5] His own energy was boundless. He served on the City Council and was Mayor of Winchester in 1839-40, 1844-5, and 1851-2. He was interested in road improvements and had the difficult task of trying, though unavailingly, to reconcile two rival groups of archaeologists and antiquarians who met in Winchester in 1845.[6] The anniversary of his Hospital appointment in 1851 was the occasion of a great public dinner given in St John's House in his honour, but the proposal to replace 'his' Hospital in Parchment Street by a new building in the Romsey road was one of which he could never approve. In September 1869, to his surprise and fury, his appointment as Hospital Surgeon was not confirmed. He alone had survived on the medical staff from the days of Napoleon and Wellington, but he simply could not understand why he should not continue to work, and that meant to operate.

In 1874, he became blind, though he still continued to visit many of his old patients, and used to walk across the High Street every day to attend the Cathedral service. His young wife, Jane, had died of scarlet fever, after only four years of marriage, and was buried in (old) St Thomas' churchyard on the last day of her husband's first year as Mayor of Winchester. She had borne him two sons and two daughters, but the sons went elsewhere to make their homes. The elder son, Charles, joined the Federal Army in America during the Civil War and served as Staff Surgeon Major in the new Hospital in Washington. In 1870, on the outbreak of the Franco-Prussian War, he went to Germany. He obviously felt unable to settle in England for any length of time and, in 1873, joined the Dutch army and served in Sumatra; later still, he went to Fiji and died at sea, about a year after his father's death in Winchester in 1876.

It was Mayo who, perhaps more than any other man, established the reputation of the Hospital as a renowned teaching centre; and the appreciation felt for him in Winchester lived on. Both his daughters remained in Avebury House until they died. Within the Cathedral to which the family was so devoted, the Mayo window in the sixth bay of the north aisle of the nave commemorates Charles and his son, and the nave pulpit, once in the Chapel of New College, was given by members of the family in memory of Jane Mayo, his daughter who died in 1884.

The medical world will not forget Charles Mayo; to the literary world it is the dynasty of the Lyfords which is so well known, because one member of that family, Giles King, attended Jane Austen in the last weeks of her life in Winchester. 'The family of Doctor Lyford has been connected with the Hospital for nearly a century'

IN A
LOVING
AND
CHRISTIAN SPIRIT
HE HEALED THE SICK,

AND COMFORTED THE AFFLICTED.

TO THE MEMORY OF
WILLIAM JOHN WICKHAM, F.R.C.S.
FORTY YEARS SURGEON,
TO THE HANTS COUNTY HOSPITAL.
HE DIED JANY. 19TH 1864, AGED 66.

ERECTED BY MANY FRIENDS,
WHO DEEPLY LAMENT HIS LOSS.

R.C. LUCAS.

ALSO OF HIS GRANDSON
PHILIP ROBERT WICKHAM
PRECENTOR 1906-1919
WHO DIED 31 DEC 1938

6.   Charles Mayo, F.R.C.S. (1788-1876).

7.   William John Wickham, M.D., F.R.C.S.: the marble portrait by Richard Cockle Lucas in Winchester Cathedral.

wrote the editor of the *Quarterly Record* under the entry for 15 December 1863, which announced Mr Henry Giles Lyford's resignation as adviser to the Hospital and to the Prison. Charles Lyford had served the Hospital from 1768 to 1805 as Apothecary and Surgeon, Giles King Lyford from 1790 to 1837, and a grandson, Henry Giles, had worked in Parchment Street from 1816 to 1863 and, when he resigned, was just getting married for the second time. There was thus a measure of quite remarkable continuity. Despite his importance in the last weeks of Jane Austen's life, why she had come to stay in Winchester particularly to consult him, Lyford, as her doctor, remains rather shadowy, though he was able to relieve the pain of what perhaps still may be regarded as an uncertain illness.[7] He emerges more clearly in the reports of the Committee set up to inquire into the state of the County Gaol in Jewry Street. There he probably had an impossible task, perhaps not made easier by the fact that he never examined any prisoner on entry, but only saw them, men or women, when they became ill. For lack of this practice, the Committee reported critically in their report of 1833.[8] Nevertheless, the Lyfords, including 'Mr Lyford the Apothecary' of Alton, had always been regarded as good and helpful advisers by the Austens from Steventon, and were long established in the north of Hampshire as a well-known family. In Winchester, the Lyfords lived in an attractive house in Southgate Street, and G. K. Lyford was Mayor of the City in 1824, 1829 and 1833.[9] Few of the surgeons at the Hospital got a good press after a pupil of Henry Lyford's complained in one of the Hampshire newspapers about his treatment there; there followed a notorious case, well reported in *The Lancet*, with indignant letters from all sides, after Lyford *v* Horsley, and the pupil, Horsley, had been expelled. H.G. Lyford had been the editor of a short-lived predecessor of *The Lancet*; the latter, it is said, was not allowed in the Hospital library.

The edition of the *Hampshire Chronicle*, published on Christmas Day 1837, records 'the death of our most esteemed fellow citizen, for the last half century one of the most distinguished provincial surgeons of this county'. Giles King Lyford had died at his home in Southgate Street, after a period of declining health, but in fact from apoplexy. 'His great professional skill united with the blandest manners will cause him to be long remembered throughout the county'. Lyford was buried in the family vault in St Laurence's church, and 'nearly all the shops partially closed as a mark of respect for one whose loss is universally deplored'.[10]

On the occasion of his last appearances at the Hospital and the Prison, Henry Giles Lyford made lengthy and reminiscing speeches of resignation, and went off the next day to get married at Bishop's Waltham. He was probably not altogether sorry to leave behind the problems of Parchment Street, but he was a good teacher, whose successful pupils included Samuel Wesley's son, John, a Wykehamist, who became in November 1864 the first man from Winchester College to gain a London medical degree. The *Record* noted this particular achievement carefully: 'J. S. Wesley, late pupil of H. G. Lyford, has passed M. B. First Class, of the University of London', and added, 'a very severe examination indeed'.[11]

The early years of the 19th century appear from the Minutes as years of comparative calm in Parchment Street. The Chairmen of the Court of Governors were also Wykehamists. A Fellow of the College, the Reverend Harry Lee, was succeeded as Chairman of the Governors from 1776-8 by the Reverend Charles Blackstone, another Wykehamist, and Blackstone in turn by John Jenkinson.

The son of a soldier, Colonel Charles Jenkinson (d.1750) who had commanded the Blues at Dettingen, John Jenkinson had been educated at Charterhouse but had strong Winchester connections through his mother, Amarantha Cornwall, and was born in the city in 1734. His elder brother, Charles, became the first Earl of Liverpool. He was thus a member of what might be called a family of courtier-politicians, a page to George II from 1748-52, Gentleman-Usher to the Queen in 1761, and in 1773 served the Government in Ireland as Second Secretary to the Lord-Lieutenant. His contemporaries thought highly of him; 'a most prudent and sensible man who has attended the meetings of the session most assiduously (with) an accurate, good understanding.' His political career was made possible by the fact that his great-grandmother had been a Bankes, the family who controlled the constituency of Corfe Castle, and where Jenkinson was returned as M.P. without contests in 1768 and 1774. He wrote to his elder brother in that same latter year hoping that Charles would get him some sort of job in England, 'on this side of the water', or 'a small Irish pension'. He was rewarded with a salary of £400 a year for acting as joint-secretary to the Lord-Lieutenant in England but, by 1779, he obviously knew that Henry Bankes Junior, just coming of age, would need the Corfe Castle seat; he gave it up, and though the two facts are not apparently related in any way, succeeded Blackstone as Chairman of the Hospital Governors.[12] As Chairman, he was a fairly assiduous attender, a regular signer of the Minutes. He lived in Winchester, in Kingsgate Street, where he died on 1 May 1805; a very brief obituary notice in the *Hampshire Chronicle* simply records him as Lord Liverpool's brother. His regular attendance forms part of the Lee-Sissmore period of the Hospital's history, and he was succeeded by long years of renewed Wykehamist administration.

During Jenkinson's tenure of office, the Hospital endured the notorious outbreak of fever amongst the prisoners of war in the King's House; Doctor Makkitrick died and was succeeded by John Littlehales; smallpox was virtually conquered by the inoculators led by Doctor John Smith; the Hospital's former apothecary, Robert Woodforde, set up a luxurious nursing home at Winnall; Winchester's famous artist, William Cave, painted a controversial portrait of the unfortunate George III in a straight-jacket; and the Hospital Governors appointed the first Hospital Chaplain. On 17 May 1782, the Committee asked Harry Lee[13] 'to treat with the Reverend Mr Westcombe with a view to his becoming the Hospital's Chaplain'. The negotiations were successful, and Nicolas Westcombe was elected on 9 July 1782 at an annual salary of 12 guineas. He had no chapel, but his honorarium was soon increased to five guineas per quarter, and his other employments must have given him a modest sufficiency.[14] The Cathedral register simply records 'the Reverend Nicolas Westcombe died 14 August 1813', but in fact he had been brutally murdered in a lonely pathway from Hyde Street to the Winchester-Andover road. At first, it seemed as if his son, Thomas, would succeed to the Chaplaincy. His name was put forward, but 11 days later, the Governors chose the Reverend W. Tugwell Williams. The younger Westcombe had married the daughter of the leading Liberal reformer, Samuel Deverell, and did not suit the Tory rulers of the Hospital. Williams was already Chaplain at St Cross, where the Master, Francis North, was a great pluralist and an influential Tory.[15]

The every-day administration of the Hospital was almost entirely in the hands of two men, Harry Lee and the Treasurer, Henry Sissmore. Lee's father and namesake had been a controversial Warden of the College. His had been a disputed election, and Doctor Burton's opinion had been that 'Lee's sovereignty will be our coup-de-grace', but the second Lee, whose name appears so frequently in what might well be called the Lee-Sissmore Minutes, proved a not unable administrator, loyally supported by the Treasurer, a Fellow of the College, who did not die until 1881 aged (at least) ninety-four.

The Minutes of the Quarterly Courts of Governors were sometimes kept in the same books as those of the Weekly Committee, which had ceased to appoint House Visitors, and which was often attended by only a few clerics, sometimes just two, sometimes only one, and once or twice by nobody at all, except the Apothecary-Secretary, who wrote out the Minutes showing that there was no-one present, and nevertheless got them signed and approved at the next meeting. A few examples will illustrate this unsatisfactory situation. When a new Minute Book was begun on 13 July 1803, the Weekly Committee of that date was attended by only three members, all of them clerics. Two in-patients were discharged, two admitted, and six out-patients taken on to the books. A few subscriptions were received; a new kind of subscriber was appearing, for the parishes which still bore so much of the burden of maintaining the 'Sick Poor' were now many of them subscribers, therefore entitled to recommend patients for admission. At this particular meeting, King's Worthy paid its annual two guineas; The Winchester United Parishes, as usual in arrears, paid 10 guineas for two years. An unknown Miss Croft paid a guinea, and Charles Shaw Le Fevre, whose family were to provide much valuable support in the future, paid up for three years, at two guineas a year. The Minutes of this short meeting were signed by Henry Sissmore, who had by this time become the Hospital Treasurer, and Harry Lee, the Chairman. Again, on 18 August, they were the only members present when a thousand bushels of coal were ordered, but Sissmore as Treasurer was of course in control of the Hospital's expenditure; the working weekly balances usually varied between £25 and £50, according to the subscriptions received. Again on 7 September, only Sissmore and Lee were present and, on 28 September, Sissmore alone had to consider an important letter from Doctor Percival, offering his services as Physician to the Hospital. Sissmore, at this time in his active middle age, ordered the Secretary to write to Percival with the thanks of the Committee, and to say that the offer would be considered at its next meeting. That did not happen, but the next Governors' Court on 11 October did approve of Doctor Percival, taking the wise step of writing to Doctor John Littlehales to see whether he would agree to work with the new man; if the Minutes produce a feeling of calm, it is probably because the medical staff at this time were men of exceptional ability. John Littlehales was working on an honorary basis, but the rest of the establishment, the paid staff, had long since settled down, aided by five nurses, a cook, and a laundress; the Matron was Mrs Shenton, a member of the well-known family of mill-owners (£5 10s. 2d. a quarter), Mr E. Whittle as Apothecary Secretary was getting £12 10s. 0d. a quarter. The two surgeons, Giles King Lyford, who had succeeded his father, Charles, and W.N.

Wickham, each got a quarterly gratuity of £5, and the Reverend Nicolas Westcombe got the same sum. He was still Chaplain, presumably under the friendly eye of the Warden and Senior Fellow, for he was also a Chaplain at Winchester College. In general, the atmosphere might be described as reasonably comfortable, even cosy, though from the patients' point of view there were already signs of occasional overcrowding, and the Apothecary's work was not satisfactory. Wickham was making up his own medicines and Whittle was paying him for them, but on Boxing Day 1810 the Apothecary was warned that 'if complaints against him' continued, 'steps will be taken for the more regular discharge of the duties of that department'. Presumably this threat implied dismissal, but nothing further happened in the next four months.

At the beginning of 1810 when Doctor John Littlehales died, there were almost too many physicians wanting to work in Parchment Street. On 17 January, Doctor Charles Badham was elected Physician; he had only offered his services the week before, and the day after his appointment, Doctor Andrew Hutchinson was also recommended by the Committee to the January Court of Governors. A further formidable application was already on the way: a Special Court of Governors, held on 3 February, received a report on Andrew Crawford, and resolved that he should be made a Governor, i.e. not as Physician to the Hospital, though the next Quarterly Court (10 April) appointed Hutchinson, Badham and Crawford as Governors. By this time, the Apothecary had ceased to present his Incident Book, and in August, the Committee (in reality only Sissmore) at last began to 'discuss' complaints against Mr Whittle, alleged to be absent from the Hospital without leave and to neglect his duties in other unspecified ways. It is clear that the complaints were not all on one side, and in September the Committee asked for Whittle's laboratory to be repaired. Not long after, and when he had been given a short leave of absence, the Apothecary resigned on 29 May 1811. There were difficulties in replacing him. Advertisements in two provincial newspapers produced a suitable candidate, Thomas Peachey, but he withdrew his acceptance after being interviewed by the Committee. Further advertisements at length produced a new Apothecary, with the most important qualification of being an unmarried man. Whittle stayed on during this difficult time, and, when he finally left on or about 3 July, he was given a gratuity of £21 and thanked for his services.

By that time, some of the Governors were becoming anxious at the increasing number of patients admitted to the Hospital. Sissmore was still Treasurer, but a new and formidable financier had begun to make his presence felt, Thomas Deane, the Winchester banker and a partner in the firm of Waller of Minster House, Winchester, who had succeeded Hoare's as the Hospital bankers.[12] Some Governors wanted to enlarge the Hospital and some thought it would be best to employ an additional Surgeon, but the Governors' resolution to the effect (of 9 July) is crossed out in the Minutes, after what must have been a stormy meeting. When the Committee met on 10 July, only Deane was present and again only he appeared on 17 July. There must have been a great deal of discussion going on in the background. On 24 July, only Gilbert Heathcote and one other member, John Richards, appeared but, the week after, there were more members to hear of Peachey's withdrawal. An August Court of Governors decided to 'revise the Present Regulations of the Hospital' and, the day after, the Committee recommended the appointment of Doctor Charles Littlehales,

John's son, and a Wykehamist, as Physician to the Hospital; a few days later, Charles Fowler was appointed as Apothecary at a Court of Governors called specially for that purpose.

Throughout most of these years, Henry Sissmore was by far the most constant attender at Committees, sometimes with Lee, or occasionally with Frederick Iremonger. By 15 May 1811, when the problems of the Apothecary were rapidly reaching the stage of Whittle's resignation, he and Iremonger were really running the place. Occasionally, not one single member appeared, but 'Minutes' were taken and signed at the next meeting by Sissmore and Iremonger. It was apparently some time before the 'new' men elected at the Governors' meeting of 10 July 1810 could prove effective. There were then 63 in-patients and 193 out-patients on the books. Lee and Sissmore were elected Chairman and Treasurer respectively, but Gilbert Heathcote and Thomas Deane were elected House Visitors, and Deane's partner, Nicholas Waller, was appointed Assistant Treasurer. The governing body included seven other clerics and two other laymen, John Richards and John Ridding. In other words, the administration of the Hospital was still dependent on the care and kindness of Anglican clergy and, in particular, on the sustained efforts of a group of Wykehamists.

In contrast to the Apothecaries, the medical staff (the men who were committed to its service, not the so-called consultants who came and went) seem to have been on good terms with the Lee-Sissmore administration for, after all, John Littlehales was the Chairman's cousin and son-in-law. There were other, useful links with the Corporation and the College. Charles Lyford and his son, Giles King Lyford, were Freemen and Mayors of the City. W.N. Wickham, appointed Surgeon in 1823, belonged to a family which had served Winchester College for many generations. When Charles Mayo arrived in 1811, he continued the connection between the Hospital and the Corporation, and between the Hospital and the Dean and Chapter; as the 19th century advanced, the new Winchester and Hampshire institutions found themselves inevitably involved with the Hospital. It is possible to criticise its administration at almost any stage of its history, but nevertheless, the Court of Governors did succeed in giving the new Diocesan Training College a real interest in the Hospital; one of its Principals, the Reverend Charles Collier, proved an admirable Hospital Chaplain; and the new Hampshire Police Force provided a very formidable member of the Court of Governors in the person of General Forrest, the County's Chief Constable.[16]

The Court still proved less adaptable in other respects; it was years before women – other than the Matron – had any real influence, or any official position on the various Committees, and this despite Florence Nightingale, let alone Queen Victoria. It was years too before the basis of representation on the Court was widened to include industrialists, certainly not 'working men', a curious contrast with much of the 18th century, when the Hospital owed so much to so many varied occupations, including stonemasons, canal barge owners, carriers (including one bankrupt Mayor), and inn-keepers. By the last quarter of the 19th century, the distrust of the middle-classes, those people whom Sir William Heathcote genuinely believed would ruin England once they were given the vote, had largely disappeared, but these were the men who were prominent on the new Sanitary Authorities, and they were particularly to be found on the staff of the new local authorities including, eventually, the Hampshire County Council. The Hospital Governors did not always find it easy to accept sugggestions – orders in some cases – which originated with these new men in the new forms of local government. After all, most of the Governors had behind them years of traditional service through the County Magistracy. At the time when the Hospital celebrated its one hundredth anniversary, political reform had split the country and most of the Governors, and practically all the medical staff were men of the old school, unrepentent Tories opposed to the extension of the franchise, who could believe only too easily that the worst excesses of the French Revolution might spread to England. So perhaps it is not altogether surprising that there was not much change in Parchment Street, until a situation developed there which made drastic change inevitable.

There is a suggestion of professional rivalry in the Committee's continued references to their surgeons. At the end of 1818, Giles King Lyford and Wickham wrote to the Court asking for their sons to be appointed Assistant Surgeons. The Committee agreed to tell Mr Mayo and the Physicians about this matter, and to consider it again. A week later, the proposal was turned down – 'it may lead to future inconvenience' – and both Surgeons asked for a reconsideration. There was no moving the Governors, and on 6 January 1819, W.N. Wickham and G.K. Lyford both resigned, and their sons, Henry Lyford and W.J. Wickham were appointed in their places, though they were not to perform any 'great operations' without the approval or presence of one of their fathers.[17] Charles Mayo was now the Senior Surgeon, and the Committee marked the occasion by offering him a small annual salary. Other changes quickly followed. The medical men reported on the nurses and the Matron was 'examined' with the result that Mrs Shenton resigned in May 1821 and was replaced by Mrs Sarah Thomas.[18] Two years later, there was a new Apothecary, Nicholas Adams. It was probably always unwise to consult all the medical staff about proposed new appointments, better to confront them with a *fait-accompli*. Thus, in 1824, Doctor Litlehales and Doctor Crawford were written to with the news of the appointment of Doctor Kane, and Doctor Philips was told he was unsuccessful. A year later, Philips got the job, and was also made a Governor. Men wanted to come and work in Winchester, for, despite the problems of too many patients and not enough money, the Hospital's reputation was very high indeed, and not least as a teaching Hospital, and this despite the fact that, in 1821, H.G. Lyford and W.J. Wickham had not been allowed to read lectures to their pupils in the Hospital building. Operations for the stone were particularly successful and the *Annual Report* ending in July 1817 contained some very unusual information about three successful operations. George Munday from Overton, aged 30, had had a stone weighing one ounce removed, and two little boys from Portsea had also been successfully cut.

The Hospital's finances were always a major concern and the *Annual Report*, sent out to all subscribers and to some other hospitals, was in fact the chief effort by the Governors to encourage existing subscribers and to get new supporters. Apart from changing statistics, the format altered little from year to year, and one suspects that James Robbins, the well-known Winchester printer and book-seller, kept much of the type standing. There were constantly repeated standard forms for the use of new subscribers and warnings about the wrong kinds of patients; for many years, there was one illustration, in the form of the Parchment Street frontage, and of course, the long lists of subscribers, some marked 'M', which meant their subscription fell due at Michaelmas, the other monies being due on Lady Day. Those marked with an asterisk formed the Weekly Committee. The proportion of clerical subscribers was always high, but country gentlemen were loyal supporters and produced many of the patients from amongst their employees.

In the *Report* for the year of Trafalgar, 1805-6, there were some 29 women subscribers, headed by the Duchess of Chandos, who gave five guineas a year, and including Mrs Bradfield of Winchester (one guinea), soon to be widowed, and then become Mrs David, the wife of Mathew David and Jane Austen's landlady in College Street. Jane's brother, the wealthy Edward of Godmersham Park in Kent, was a five guinea subscriber. The small Hampshire village of Titchfield produced no fewer than five lady subscribers; there were five subscriber members of the Heathcote family, and four Earles from Winchester, headed by Mr Alderman Earle, by far the most flourishing of the Winchester apothecaries. Winchester was well represented, too, on the 'Weekly Committee', hardly surprising since the burden of daily visiting fell on its members; of the three laymen, one was the Deputy Treasurer, Nicholas Waller, the banker, John Ridding was the Chapter Clerk, and the third, James Pyle, was of independent means. The other Winchester members were clerics, a parish priest, four Canons and three Fellows of Winchester College.[19]

The 'ordinary' members of the Committee were elected but, in theory, anyone who gave more than twenty pounds was also a member, and there were 16 such subscribers, headed by Bishop Brownlow North who had given one hundred guineas. The Bishop's son, Francis, soon to be in trouble as Master of an unreformed Hospital, St Cross, was another clerical subscriber. Not one woman supporter had given more than the Duchess of Chandos, but the problem of whether or not the Committee could include ladies did not arise, nor does the Matron's name appear in the *Report*. Membership was effectively confined to the upper strata of society, and to the professional classes, clerics and lawyers. More than one hundred years was to pass before the Committee would consider including amongst its members a representative of the working, industrial class, but the tradition was already established amongst some Hampshire county families of long and continued support for the Hospital. Even so, out of a total income of £1029 1s. 0d., virtually a quarter was in arrears, £227 17s. 0d. and, just before Trafalgar and *pace* Richard Taunton, there was only one seafaring subscriber, Captain Yates of the cutter *Rose* of Southampton, though there was considerable support from individual civil subscribers in Southampton, Portsmouth and Gosport.

The problem of arrears was always a difficult one. The year before, in the Annual Report for 1804-5, the Governors had thought it necessary to urge subscribers to pay early, and they also began to publish an arrears list, filled in, where necessary, against the names of the defaulting annual subscribers. One clerical culprit was six years behind with his promised subscription of two guineas. If only a small run of surviving Annual Reports is taken, the figures speak for themselves; the fact of publicly black-listing the names of defaulters in this way had drastically decreased the arrears.

Year	Income Promised			Arrears		
	£	s	d	£	s	d
1804-5	983	18	0	215	5	0
1805-6	1029	1	0	227	17	0
1807-8	1246	0	0	281	8	0
1808-9	1212	11	0	97	13	0
1810-11	1447	15	0	15	15	0

The Hospital's Founder had intended that its work should relieve ratepayers and lighten the burden of the many local Poor Houses and (later) Poor Law Unions. There were soon an increasing number of corporate subscribers, including incumbents with churchwardens subscribing for their parishes. To these can be added the numerous Friendly Societies, some centred round inns and ale houses, like the *Rodney's Head* in Winchester in 1810-11, which should surely have had some ex-navy patrons and which subscribed one guinea. The Heart-in Hand Society and the Preston Candover Friendly Society were each paying two guineas in 1851-2, though the Cordwainers' Society of Winchester paid a single guinea. Later on, amongst Winchester firms, Browne and Caplens, the High Street drapers, and Jacob and Johnson, publishers and owners of the *Hampshire Chronicle*, also subscribed two guineas annually; they employed comparatively large staffs.

On the other hand, as the century progressed, and although new subscribers were being found in Winchester and the surrounding countryside, new Hospitals had begun to appear in other parts of Hampshire, and were beginning to call on more particular and local loyalties. It is perhaps surprising to find the Peninsula and Orient Steam Navigation Company, which used Southampton as its great port, supporting the County Hospital with an annual subscription of five guineas in 1852.[20] It probably supported the Southampton Hospital as well. Southampton was growing fast and so was Bournemouth, another town with its own Hospital.[21]

8. Robert Specott Barter (1790-1861) (from the portrait in Winchester College).

By 1851-2, the *Annual Report* was in a more robust form, though the same words, even entire paragraphs, were still being repeated year after year, and the Report issued for the year ending 30 June 1852 gave no indication of the problems affecting the place. The heading set out the names of the Chairman (The Warden of Winchester College, Robert Barter), the Treasurer (William Whitear Bulpitt, a successor in the bank begun by Nicholas Waller and continued by Thomas Deane), and the Chaplain, the Reverend J.H. Janvrin, all in large print. Below, in slightly smaller type, were the staff, three physicians, all of them qualified doctors, Edward Phillips, G.E.W. Wood, and Thomas Hitchcock, and the three surgeons – all three of whom formed part of medical dynasties, Charles Mayo, H.G. Lyford, and W.J. Wickham; on the final line of the heading appear the Apothecary and Secretary, John L. Jardine, and the Matron, Mrs Jane Anne Haynes. Money, as usual, was still the chief problem. Contributors were reminded that they could not recommend patients unless they had already been subscribers for a year, and there were again numerous subscriptions in arrears. There were particular problems with venereal patients, who could not be admitted unless there was room, and there was only space for six men and six women patients. 'The Charity had been much abused by persons of abandoned characters and common prostitutes', and this complaint was to be repeated year after year. Rules to prevent other problems were constantly repeated in the *Annual Reports*. A subscription of one guinea a year allowed the taking in of one patient; five guineas upwards permitted two. In-patients were required to provide security from their sponsors to pay funeral expenses, or removal in the case of smallpox. Children under seven years of age could not be treated at all, and pregnant women, disordered persons, persons subject to fits, or suffering from smallpox, itch or other infectious diseases, were not admitted. There was a sort of general arrangement by which emergency cases could be dealt with, but patients who took themselves off, or who were discharged for irregular conduct, could never come back again. Special care was taken to avoid the arrival of dying patients; 'it is injurious to the reputation of the Hospital that they should die in it'.

Halfway through the century, by 1852, the Hospital's records showed that, since the foundation, the in-patients had totalled 55,431 persons, the out-patients 41,640; every patient was still being given a number by the Apothecary-Surgeon-Secretary. But it is the national Census Returns of 1841 and 1851 which are so valuable for their brief descriptions of the inhabitants of Parchment Street.

VII Overcrowding Again: Not Enough Room And Not Enough Money

The *Annual Report* for the year ending 30 June 1824 included a much larger list of medical advisers than was usually the case. There were three Physicians, Charles Littlehales, Andrew Crawford, and 'Doctor Kane'; two 'Extraordinary and Consulting Surgeons', Mr G.K. Lyford and Mr W.N. Wickham; three Surgeons, Charles Mayo, G.H. Lyford (*sic*), and W.J. Wickham; the Apothecary was Nicholas Adams, and there were 60 in-patients, and 277 out-patients.[1] Francis North, the controversial Master of St Cross, had given a donation of £100, the Hampshire Club in London provided £25, and other interesting supporters included John Nash, the architect of East Cowes Castle. The Iron Duke (100 guineas), Alexander Baring (50 guineas), and the Earl of Malmesbury (£55); Sir Thomas Heathcote (£155), and William Clarke (£177 10s. 0d.) had provided these handsome sums over a period of time, and all the local members of the Littlehales family were subscribing on a regular basis, as was Charles Mayo himself.

In 1827, when it had already been decided that the accommodation in the Hospital was inadequate, the medical gentlemen were given permission to set up a circulating medical Library in the Physicians' Room. Books were not to be given out on Wednesdays or Saturdays, and only to members of the staff. By this time, Richard Littlehales, a banker, was the Chairman of the Committee, ably assisted by a very important supporter, another banker, Sir Thomas Baring.[2] The problems of the Hospital building, and the rising number of patients, produced a famous 'Appeal to the County', dated 13 October of that year and signed by Sir Thomas Baring. He was a comparatively new man in Hampshire, and he must have looked at the Hospital with a fresh eye. The Appeal began by pointing out that the Hospital was too small for the numbers applying for admission, and that it was particularly crowded in autumn and winter. Many patients were discharged before their treatment was completed, though lodgings had been found for some in the neighbourhood. In one week, 11 would-be patients had been turned away. 'They are impelled to be in crowded wards, inhaling the effluvia of discharging wounds.' Convalescents were obliged to stay in the same wards as seriously ill patients. There was not a chapel, 'nor a building of any kind in which divine services could be performed'. In fact, services were held in a room used by the women patients, and which could only hold half the number of patients wishing to attend. The room was filled with sufferers affected by diseases, disorders and sores, 'productive of an offensive effluvia'. The officiating chaplain had fainted on more than one occasion. The only classification of patients was one of sex; medical and physical cases were nursed together, indiscriminately.

This disastrous account of the state of the Hospital was sent out all over Hampshire. In terms of publicity, it seems today to be dreadful, but it was not counter-productive; indeed, it produced a sum large enough for the Governors to decide to go ahead with their object of providing additional wards and a chapel. By 5 April 1828, the contract had been offered to Mr Martin Filer, a Winchester builder, a descendant of that Martin Filer who had been a paper-maker in Hampshire in 1663, and who had given the Dean and Chapter his valuable collection of the works of Martin Luther. A sum of £3,000 had been set aside for the new building, and for alterations to the old, and a Building Committee set up. A nearby property had to be bought, 'Mr Young's Premises', not expected to cost more than £1,000. The Building Committee included some formidable characters; not only the Chairman, Lee, but Sir Thomas Baring himself, Richard Littlehales, William Portal, and Samuel Wall (from Worthy Park), all experienced businessmen, and the young baronet from Hursley, Sir William Heathcote. Filer was ordered to complete the work by 1 October 1829; but even in the new buildings, and despite the Governors' vote of thanks to the Building Committee, there were still problems with the ventilation, and in January 1830 the medical gentlemen were asked to give their attention to the problem. Meanwhile, Nicholas Adams, the Apothecary, had resigned in 1828, and had been replaced in April of that year by Robert Corbin, a name of long standing in the Hospital's history. When Robbins and Wheeler published their *New Winchester Guide* in 1829, they were careful to describe the Hospital in glowing terms; it had been 'recently enlarged by the addition of a handsome wing', could take in 120 patients, and 'numbers of indigent persons also receive the best assistence and medicine as out-patients ... the character of the Institution ranks high ... [because of] the active and unremitting vigilance of its charitable managers, it may challenge comparison with the most popular Hospitals of the Kingdom'.

Hardly had the Hospital's new wing been opened when rumours began to reach Winchester of a disease more terrible than the gaol fever and smallpox. The prospect of an outbreak of cholera made Harry Lee very anxious, and in 1831 his College gave the Hospital £30 'for supplying the poor inhabitants of the city and suburbs of Winchester with proper food, warmth and clothing to relieve them of the danger of an attack of the malignant cholera'. In fact, the cholera did not arrive, and a disgraceful affair in summer 1829 had not improved the Hospital's status.

Early in August 1829, the two John Staceys, father and son, appeared at the Hampshire Assizes charged with two murders at Portsmouth. The younger man was sentenced to be hung, and the execution was carried out at 8 a.m. on 10 August, after a merciful prison chaplain had removed the prisoner's father to another part of the building in order that he might not witness his son's death. It was, of course, a public execution and there were crowds of people present in Jewry Street, and it was followed by some disgraceful scenes in the Hospital. In the course of the day, the executioner was seen wandering around Winchester in an ever-increasing state of intoxication, and in the evening, very drunk indeed, he fell down the steps of a public house and, bleeding profusely, was taken to the Hospital, apparently seriously hurt. He had with him Stacey's shoes, the cords which had pinioned his arms, the cap which he had worn – and the noose. He was put into a bed in the mens' ward, with Stacey's cap pulled low over his face, and was 'repeatedly assailed by the patients' with scoffs and jeers. All the ghoulish souvenirs were either stolen from him or sold by him, including the rope, which changed hands again in the early morning, when its purchasers sold it at a profit, piece by piece. The whole dreadful scene is reminiscent of Hogarth or Henry Fielding, but it is a valuable reminder that the patients in the County Hospital were far from being perfect, whatever their physical condition might have been.

As for the wretched Stacey, his body was taken to the Hospital at once, but the public were allowed to view the corpse. Before Charles Mayo – or perhaps Giles King Lyford – began the anatomising, a cast was taken of the head, separately, and also of the whole body, in a position intended to show the man's muscular strength. He was not tall, but much had been made of the fact that he was remarkably powerful. The process meant incasing the whole body in cement, composed of plaster of Paris and leaving it to harden for several days.

The years of comparative peace and slow progress in Parchment Street, although they were years of almost continuous war against the French, culminated in 1836 with a magnificent celebration of the Hospital's first one hundred years. The celebrations proved to be even more magnificent than the programme suggested. The last music festival to be held in Winchester on behalf of the Hospital, some 19 years previously, in 1817, had been a great success, not least financially. In 1836, the Archbishop of Canterbury, Howley, began his visit to Hampshire by staying with Sir William Heathcote at Hursley; Wolvesey at this time was not used by the Diocesan Bishops. On the Monday of the Hospital's anniversary week, Doctor Howley arrived at the Warden's Lodging, and was then received with all the traditions of the ceremony *Ad Portas* reserved for distinguished visitors. He, too, was a Wykehamist,[3] able to reply in good Latin, the bells of the Cathdral and the College rang out, and dinner followed at the Archdeacon of Winchester's house in The Close. In the meantime, the Mayor had given a public Breakfast at *the George Inn*, and then the Corporation went in procession to await the arrival of the Archbishop at the Cathedral. After a short choral service, the sermon followed, preached eloquently on the text, 'The blind receive their sight, and the lame walk, the lepers are cleansed and the deaf hear, the dead are raised up, and the poor have the Gospel preached unto them' (Matthew XI, v.5). He had some wise words to say in a long sermon. 'The Hospital confers its benefits on everyone, without distinction of rank or party ... it enters not into discriminations of characters or causes of suffering ... this Institution has the recommendation of constancy and perpetuity ... it was entitled to the warm regard of all Christians.' Over £700 was collected for the Hospital as a result of this splendid eloquence.

All the arrangements for the dinner which followed were made by a Committee, under the patronage of the Bishop of Winchester and some distinguished vice-presidents, including the High Sheriff of Hampshire, the Duke of Buckingham and Chandos, the Marquis of Winchester, Lord Rodney, the Earl of Malmesbury, Lord Palmerston, J. Buller East (a Winchester MP) and the Reverend F.B. Baring, as varied a collection of the nobility and gentry of Hampshire as could be imagined. Needless to say, only Gentlemen Subscribers could buy tickets (no ladies attended) which cost a guinea each, 'no entries at the door' and tickets were to be purchased at the County Newspaper Office. The *Hampshire Chronicle* in fact ran a kind of central office for the occasion, and left a book open with the names of Wintonians willing to let lodgings during the Festival which went on for two days. Many more speeches followed on this evening, a late dinner at 7 o'clock, attended by about 230 noblemen and gentlemen, presided over by the Earl of Caernarvon (Heathcote's friend) who had the Archbishop on his right hand, and, also at the High Table, the Duke of St Albans, the Earl of Cavan, Lord Ashburton, the High Sheriff (Sir Charles Hulse), the Mayor of Winchester (John Young) and Lord Palmerston. The healths of King William and the Queen were drunk and also that of the Princess Victoria, and the Archbishop replied at length when he was also toasted.

There were 19 other speakers to follow, finishing up with short replies on behalf of the Hospital from Doctor Phillips, the senior physician, Doctor Crawford and Richard Littlehales, the Chairman of the Management Committee. The only noticeable absentee was the Bishop of Winchester, who was ill, but the Archbishop was in excellent form. He stayed the night at the Warden's Lodgings where, next day, he received addresses from the Dean and Chapter, and the neighbouring clergy, to which he again replied at some length, in a speech which contained one of the few references made to Alured Clarke during the entire Festival, as well as a notable tribute to 'a Fellow of this College, endeared to me by early acquaintance, by a friendship of long standing', the Chairman of long standing, the Reverend Harry Lee. Lee had indeed taken the Hospital through some difficult years, but he had not the problems which were to face his greatly loved successor, Warden Barter.[4]

At two o'clock on the same afternoon of 18 October, there was a concert (of sacred music only) in the County Hall and the next day, a 'miscellany' concert of all kinds of music in St John's Rooms. Doctor Chard presided at the pianoforte and many famous musicians appeared on those two occasions. Finally, there was a Fancy Dress Ball in the evening of 19 October, again at St John's, and the list of noble ladies bringing partners was headed by the Marchioness of Winchester, and the Marchioness of Clanricarde. The Stewards were all well-known Hampshire gentlemen, including Charles Shaw Lefevre. Mr Weiffert attended in person to direct his First Quadrille Band, tea, coffee and other refreshments being included in the cost of a ticket, ladies at ten shillings and sixpence, gentlemen at one guinea. Fancy dress was not compulsory, dancing began at 10 p.m., and in order to exclude any undesirables, 'no masques or dominoes admitted'.[5] Soon England would have a young queen who loved dancing, and who, as the Princess Victoria, had already passed through Winchester accompanied by her mother; they had changed horses at *The George*, right in the centre of a loyal city soon to become infamous as one of the most unhealthy towns in the kingdom.

In 1836, there were undoubtedly some supporters who attended everything, and the celebrations illustrate the stamina which became such a necessary characteristic of men and women taking part in public activities in later, Victorian, Winchester. Huge processions, great public dinners – and breakfasts – lengthy public meetings, huge and joyful demonstrations like those which marked the arrival of Kossuth in Winchester, were always happening and it is difficult to believe that this vast expenditure of private energy occurred in a city which was slowly acquiring a dreadful reputation as an unhealthy place. For Winchester, like many another town, was rapidly out-growing its old walled area; at first, the wealthiest citizens were reluctant to move from the town centre, and it was only in the last quarter of the 19th century that successful shopkeepers built new houses on the slopes of the eastern and western downs, and that it became unfashionable to live 'over the shop'. Most of the population had to remain in the increasingly crowded and undrained town centre, and in the eastern Soke, where at one stage the average expectation of life for a man was only 35 years. Children were wading out into the polluted river to escape floating sewage in order to fill their buckets with drinking water. The new diseases were beginning to appear. Doctor Jenner had published his work on vaccination in 1798, and smallpox as the great killer was dying away, but typhus and typhoid were becoming more common and, by 1832, the cholera had come to England.[6] In the Parchment Street Hospital, the medical staff still held to the belief that disease was spread through the air and could in some way be prevented by fumigation and by fresh air. The various remedies included the burning of pitch, though one local undertaker had written down a current prescription in his account book in early 1830.[7]

'Cure for *Cholera Morbus*, or Bowel complaint.

One ounce cinnamon water,
One grain ipecacuanha,
35 drops tincture of opium,
1 Drachm spirits lavender,
2 Drachm tincture of rhubarb.
To be taken at once, and the complaint will be instantly relieved.'

It was dysentry rather than true cholera. The belief that cholera was carried by smell was widespread, and it was a long time before the medical world accepted that what was killing people in most towns was what they were drinking. It is said that in London, five hundred people were killed by one pump, but it was not until after the creation of Registry Offices in 1835, which provided statistics and causes of death, that water was accepted as a killer. The death rate was so much higher in places on rivers and estuaries; the Thames was revealed as not much better than an open sewer and, in Winchester, the Itchen and the Brooks were frequently as disgusting and as dangerous. One of the difficulties was that Winchester soon had a Water Company, which could produce piped, tap water for houses, and which flushed the street gutters for the Paving Commissioners. Some householders were now buying water closets, but the overall problem was simple; where was the dirty water to go? Winchester had a water supply, but it had no main drainage, no sewerage. The eventual foundation of this Winchester Water Works Company by a local entrepreneur, Charles Wittman Benny, supplying piped water from the western hill, added to the complications.[8] Water could be thrown into the streets, emptied into the Brooks and the main river; if you were a householder with a well, it could be thrown down the well which was no longer needed, and in the case of the Hospital, it would be emptied into that great bubbling cauldron, the Hospital cess-pit. The Hospital had its own well, one of the first things constructed when the Governors bought Clobury House. The first man to draw attention to all these problems was Mr A. Newman, who was in effect the town's Sanitary Inspector. His platform was a popular one, the Winchester Mechanics' Institute, and a lecture there in 1844 attracted wide attention, for the speaker was advocating a proper sewerage scheme for Winchester. The difficulty was that the majority of the city's Councillors were shopkeepers, small tradesmen devoted to keeping down the rates, and nothing was done.

An Act of 1848 set up the Central Board of Health, but there was no compulsion on local authorities, that is boroughs and cities, to form local boards, except after a petition from 10 per cent of the ratepayers, though there was a power of enforcement in places with a high death rate. In 1848, the town of Southampton was in the grip of cholera, and the area around the Docks was worst hit. It was much in use by the steam ships of the Peninsula and Orient line, and Captain Engledue, a former captain of a P. and O. vessel, was the Company's Port Superintendent. He ordered the Port Medical Officer, Doctor Moore, to carry out a private examination into the causes of the epidemic, and Southampton emerged as a dreadful place, or at least parts of it; 'Abodes of misery, ... and vice had found a permanent home'. It was probably Engledue's influence which encouraged the P. and O. to subscribe to the Hospital. There was a second outbreak in 1866; Doctor Cooper, Southampton's first (and heroic) Medical Officer of Health died; and eventually James Lemon, who had worked under Sir Joseph Bazalgette in London, was appointed as Borough Engineer, and the problems of Southampton's drainage began to be solved, but not until thousands of people had died.[9] The story of Southampton is worth this brief mention here if only because it shows, in its way, the faith which Victorians put in engineers; what happened in Southampton was closely observed in Winchester.

Soon there were letters in *The Times*, and widespread outbreaks of cholera, though not in Winchester. Newman gave a second lecture in 1857; nothing had been done, and the Corporation was divided into Muckabites and Anti-Muckabites.[10] 'Even the High Street', said Newman, 'was filthy', and in some of the close courts of tightly packed houses, 'the ground is little better than one mass of corruption'. The evil, he went on, is proved, and one of the worst offenders was the County Hospital in Parchment Street, where the cess-pit was leaking into the Upper Brook, and there was additional pollution from pig-styes. The remedy could only be an efficient drainage system, with a main sewer from the north end of the town, passing under the river via College Meadows to the little lane called Bull Drove, where the effluent could be pumped up to Morestead and Chilcombe: 'both need fertilizers'. Nothing was done to provide sewerage for the town until the Church, the College and the medical profession took up the cause, with the important exceptions – and they are very important exceptions – that the County Gaol in Jewry Street was closed, sold off in lots and a new building opened in Romsey Road ('to be occupied 13 October 1849'), and the County Hospital likewise moved to a brand new building almost opposite the new Prison. Those inhabitants who wished to move away from the town centre did so, and Winchester's important suburbs on the eastern and western hills began to grow. Those who believed that disease was air-borne, caused by effluvium, in particular that cholera was carried by smell, had their belief strengthened until Bazalgette cleaned up the Thames, and Southampton likewise began to benefit from clean water and main drainage.

One of the communities which could not move was Winchester College and the story of the Moberlys shows what could happen even in a relatively affluent family. The Headmaster of Winchester College, Doctor Moberly, the head of that family, kept a journal in which he described not only much of his public life but also the lives of his greatly loved family of 15 children. He had arrived as Headmaster in Winchester in 1835, and lived in College Street; in 1839, for health reasons, he moved the household out of Commoners to Kingsgate Street for two years, but 'terrible illness in the School' broke out in 1843; there was 'Scarlet fever', College was dispersed, all the Moberly children and two of the servants were very ill indeed. The eldest son's paralytic stroke in 1846 was a different matter and did not prevent him from having a successful career. The Warden's young footman, Oiku Aga Faraghk, died in the Hospital in March 1853, and in the first quarter of that year the deaths there were all of young people.[11] In 1858-9, there was 'an epidemic of sore throats among us'; the son, Arthur, became desperately ill and probably remained delicate for the rest of his short life. Eton and Winchester were both sent home, the Warden's butler died, the Moberly's butler and one of their house maids died, all the children were ill, and just before Christmas 1859 the weather became wretchedly hot and humid, and clouds of midges and gnats could be seen flying around in Winchester. Against this sort of background, the Headmaster took the decision to open new boarding houses for Commoner boys, and henceforth the problems of Winchester drainage and the health of the School were not forgotten by the College authorities.

One of those Houses was Doctor Matthew Combes in St Thomas' Street, a part of Winchester which the Headmaster considered very healthy. Even after the new School boarding houses were opened, there were still problems, and Selwyn Moberly (by this time his father had become Bishop of Salisbury) died in 'Sergeants' in 1871, and of 'scarlet fever'. J. S. Furley, the future historian of Winchester and a Scholar from 1867 to 1873, wrote in his reminiscences that 'F. Morshead went on the Town council soon after his appointment as Master and was Mayor in 1872-73. We always believed that Ridding [Moberly's successor as Headmaster] pursuaded him to stand in order to get through a drainage scheme for the city, for Winchester had a bad reputation for health in the sixties'. It certainly had, but on 31 July 1866, Archdeacon Philip Jacob's special committee to consider the sewerage problem met at the Mechanics' Institute. Jacob by this time was soon to be Hospital Chairman; on 2 August, a memorial was presented to the local Board of Health (in effect the Corporation) signed by all the leading doctors, including Charles Mayo. No immediate action followed, but on 3 May 1873, a letter from George Ridding was read at a meeting of the Winchester Literary and Scientific Society; at last, a Sewerage Scheme was going ahead; a pumping station was opened in Bull Drove, soon renamed Garnier Road in honour of the Dean of Winchester. The memorial stone on that building records its main dates 1874 and 1894, and it surely must be the only building of its kind to be called after a Dean of the established Church of England.

In the meantime, and when this major battle was being fought out, the minor skirmish which Florence Nightingale's biographer called the 'Battle of Winchester', was being decided in Parchment Street.

VIII The Battle of Winchester

The National Census of 1841 included the Hospital. On Sunday 6 June of that year, there were 111 members of the resident household, whose head was the young Apothecary, Arthur Paul, aged twenty-five. The Matron, Mrs Maria Somer, was 56, and was assisted by eight nurses, of whom the eldest was 61, the youngest 20, but the return is slightly ambiguous and almost illegible in several places; one of the nurses may in fact have been a patient at the time. Both the Porter and the Under-Porter were both aged 20, and the female servants were also young. Two boys, Matthew Finch ('medical pupil' crossed out), and the Dispenser, Albert Bower, were both 15 years old, the age at which Charles Mayo had begun his medical career in London. Most of the male patients were general agricultural labourers or working countrymen with defined skills, several shepherds and a thresher. There was a group of railway labourers, many of them young men, an elderly blacksmith (aged 68), a mercantile traveller, a joiner, a seaman, and some sailors. There was a comparatively large number of children; those of 14 years or under evidently had no occupation, but there were boys of 15 who were working as railway labourers, agricultural labourers, a young sailor, and a paper maker. A boy and three girls were all aged only seven; the Founder's belief that young children should not be admitted was clearly not being sustained.

Ten years later, another Census was taken on Sunday, 30 March 1851. By this time, the head of the household was an older man, the House-Surgeon, William Martin, M.R.C.P., aged 47, and the Matron was Mrs Jane Haynes, aged forty-six. There were two Chemists' Assistants, George Comely, and Henry le Croix, aged 22 and 25 respectively. There was a Porter, but not an Under-Porter, six day nurses of whom the eldest was aged 66, and five night nurses. The patients form a separate section in this return, and the total number of men and women was eighty-one. That is, the number had declined, but the amount of nursing help had increased, and the number of children had gone down to six. There was a farm labourer, aged 13, another boy whose age is given as seven (Henry Harrison, born at Easton), a girl from Weeke (Emma Aldridge) who was only six, and another girl born at Sparsholt, who was fifteen. The household, in all, totalled 101 residents, but of course the doctors and surgeons had their own private houses.

The Hospital had always avoided the treatment of patients who were mentally ill, but it was a long time before any real provision was made in Hampshire for those 'improper objects'. Wealthy patients could be sent to private doctors to live in their care in small private asylums. George Pescod, William Pescod's only son and a brilliant Wykehamist who eventually lost his reason, was moved from Winchester to such a private house in Chelsea, at just about the time that William Tuke was founding the Retreat at York, the first Humane Asylum in the Country. In Hampshire, after the Powletts left Lainston, that Hampshire house became a Private

Lunatic Asylum. It appears as such in the Census of 1841, when it was under the direction of Doctor John Twynham and his wife, Mary. His young staff consisted of two male 'keepers' (sic) and five female nurses, responsible for 43 men and 53 women, most of them of humble origin and living in wards created by the partitioning of Lainston's large rooms. The place was empty by 1851. It must have taken in Winchester patients, for it is very near Winchester; many of them were supported by private benefactors in their parishes, though all classes of society were nursed there. After Lainston was closed, some later Hampshire 19th-century patients were sent to the Old Manor, in Salisbury, where the Winchester City Council had representatives on its governing body. Hampshire Quarter Sessions had begun to consider the problem in 1850.

It is against the general background of population growth and potential disease that the fate of the Hospital in Parchment Street was determined. A matter of additional importance was the sudden opening of a second Hospital in Parchment Street at the end of March 1858. The Army, not surprisingly at this stage of the nation's history, was in difficulty. A new Hospital in the Barracks was soon overcrowded, and the barrack authorities took on a large empty house in Parchment Street, just opposite Mr John Parmiter's premises; he was the Winchester Postmaster and lived and worked at the south end of the street, next to the southern end of the County Hospital.[1] How long the army stayed here is not certain, but the arrival of a military Hospital must have been just one more disaster. The County Hospital was doing its own work, and in 1853, to take one particular year, the number of patients on the books varied from 392 in January to 306 in August. Of these, the numbers actually 'in house' changed each month. The so-called 'six months' rule still occasionally resulted in a mass discharge, based on the then realistic assumption that six months' treatment ought to produce results of a definite nature. The day-to-day running of the Hospital was in the hands of its Infirmary Committee, under the chairmanship of that much beloved man, Robert Speckott Barter, the Warden of Winchester College. He did not always agree with George Moberly's suggestions for reform, but he was a personal friend of the family and must have realised the dangers to health in the city.[2] He had the loyal support of his Hospital's architect, John Colson, senior; Colson, born in Shedfield, had gained his early experience in the office of Owen Brown Carter, a distinguished and local exponent of the classical style, and had worked in London and in Norwich before returning to this city where the patronage and friendship of Bishop Sumner produced for this quiet and retiring man his appointment as architect to the Dean and Chapter, a post which he held until his death in 1895.

A glance at his Diocesan Training College, in the Gothic style, but plain and almost severe in its stonework, reveals his best kind of building, but Colson's real contribution to Winchester was the great remedial programme he initiated at the Cathedral, and for which Thomas Jackson got most of the credit. By 1861, he was beginning to be well known in Winchester, but his honorarium as architect to the Hospital, five pounds a year, was not enough, even by the standards of those days, to allow him to devote much time to the building and its drainage problems. The Governors thought it desirable to have the opinion of a civil engineer, and Robert Rawlinson of Westminster was engaged. He actually spent a whole day at the

Hospital, which he visited on 16 January 1861, in company with Colson and Mr William Wheatear Bulpitt, the Treasurer, a Winchester banker, soon to be financial adviser to the Tichborne Claimant. Rawlinson's report, its limited scope indicated by its heading *The Sanitary Conditions of the Hants County Hospital*, was presented to Warden Barter within five days, and it was damning.

The site 'is undrained', and the sub-soil was wet; everything poured into one cess-pool, 20 x 15 x 9 ft, with a capacity of 11,250 gallons, but the surface drainage from land and buildings alone equalled that capacity, and the result was continual saturation. 'How much of the solids of sewage remains combined with the sub-soil cannot easily be ascertained', but it can be imagined. The total number of beds, on three floors, was 112, and certain extensions suggested by John Colson were not supported by Rawlinson; 'to enlarge the Hospital on the present site would not remove any objections focussed on existing sanitary defects', 'but would cause the waste of a large sum of money'. The estimated cost for 112 beds, with 1559 cubic feet of space to each bed, was £6,000. Rawlinson thought that the right ratio was 2,000 cubic feet per bed, and he estimated the cost of a new building at £100 per bed. 'Tainted by putrid sewage to an extent which cannot be computed ... no comprehensive scheme for the City ...'. He could only recommend the complete removal of the Hospital, a new site, a new building. He reinforced his arguments with a quotation from *Leviticus*, Chapter 14: 'the precautions set forth by Moses ...[in cases of leprosy] are still necessary ... He shall break down the houses ... the stones of it and the timber thereof', and in case this comparison seemed remote, even to his clerical chairman, he finished with the words, 'The city of Winchester ought to be sewered ... it is only a question of time ... as to when a devastating epidemic shall prevail'.

There was already widespread unease, and many rumours, and a feeling that it was not good to have a hospital with such a drainage problem in the midst of such a crowded city. Hospitals were in the news. The Mechanics' Institute in Winchester had provided a platform for Newman, and a focal point for local opinion, but the Crimea War, ended in 1856, had done much more; Florence Nightingale was well known in Hampshire and her father was a Hospital Governor. It should also be remembered that there were those who considered that architects were extravagant, frivolous men, not concerned with the practicalities of life, and that engineers were much more practically suited to advise on buildings in an increasingly industrial age. That opinion was always to hover over John Colson, and to haunt William Butterfield.

Perhaps it was a mercy that the old Warden was already ill; if Barter was able to read the report, Rawlinson's words must have clouded the last days of the dying man; when the Infirmary Committee met on 27 February 1861, the Archdeacon of Winchester, Philip Jacob, a new Chairman, referred in moving terms to Barter's death, and his love of the Hospital: 'His cordial and engaging manner endeared him to all classes within its walls'.[3] Early in March 1861, the Committee agreed to circulate Rawlinson's report, but on 20 March, 'after further consideration', its publication and printing was suspended. At about the same time, too (13 March), the nearby 'old Assembly Rooms' were bought for £74 (paid for nearly a year later) from

Charles Wittman Benny, Winchester's great entrepreneur, a purchase which might have foreshadowed improvements in Parchment Street.

By this time, the case for and against a new hospital was being argued furiously, but in the background, sometimes with discretion, and sometimes without. Miss Nightingale's biographer, Cecil Woodham-Smith, has described this argument in one brief sentence: 'A pitched battle was fought at Winchester'. In 1859, that most famous book, *Notes on Hospitals*, had appeared from Florence Nightingale's pen; it ran into three editions, and ensured that its author was asked continuously for advice about all new hospital buildings. Not only was she asked for advice; her advice was inevitably given in return for information. By February 1861, she was in possession of the statistics of an outbreak of erisyphilas which occurred in the Hospital between June 1860 and March 1861. In May 1861, Miss Nightingale felt able to urge the Committee to 'new construction' but she was rebuffed. If the erisyphilas figures were revealed 'it would give a very unfair impression as to the ordinary state of the Hospital'. However, though the official Minutes do not reveal this, the medical staff (Mayo in particular), did not want to remove from Parchment Street, and discussions continued until 4 September 1861, when a notice was sent out to all members of the Infirmary Committee, requiring their attendance at a special meeting to appoint a sub-committee 'to consider adapting the present building or the erection of a new Hospital, or [and this part of the minute is in a pencilled addition], postpone consideration of the question'. The sub-committee met on 18 September 1861 and recommended the adoption of Rawlinson's report; that is, a new building.

A building sub-committee was soon set up and at its first meeting (20 January 1862) it appointed Sir William Heathcote as its Chairman. In February 1862, the medical staff were 'ordered' to consider extracts from Miss Nightingale's *Notes on Hospitals*, extracts concerning 'the absorption by walls, floors etc, of dangerous, absorbed, organic matter'. Perhaps it should be mentioned here that, at this time and during the whole of the period of the rebuilding of the Hospital, Miss Nightingale was virtually confined to her bed or to a sofa, and that she had no direct contact with the Committee. Mr E. Nightingale, her long-suffering father, was occasionally present at full meetings of the Infirmary Committee. The advice which his daughter gave was offered only by correspondence; her letters have long been known, but some of those written by Sir William Heathcote appeared on the market in 1972, and the Hospital was fortunately able to acquire them. Heathcote's Committee was a powerful one, Lord Eversley and Lord Ashburton, the Archdeacon of Winchester, Henry Compton from Lyndhurst, Melville Portal, John Bonham Carter and William Barrow Simmons, but its efforts were unlikely to prosper without Miss Nightingale's advice and, as soon as he was Chairman, Heathcote wrote to ask her opinion of the proposed new site, an area on the south side of the road to Romsey, which the Committee hoped to acquire, and in fact did acquire, from two owners for £2,225.

There was much local anxiety about the new site, for it was outside the municipal boundary, which might upset the Corporation (it did), it was difficult of access, even to the able-bodied, and it was very near the County Gaol. The site had to be paid for, and money raised for the new building and an architect had to be appointed. The sub-committee met in a variety of places, frequently at *The George* at 1 o'clock on a Monday, but it was at Lord Ashburton's house in Piccadilly, on 13 February 1862, that William Butterfield was chosen as architect after some general discussion of other names not specified in the Minutes. On 3 October 1862, the Court of Governors sanctioned the purchase of the Romsey Road site, but there were legal difficulties about the title to one of the pieces of land, and the purchase was not completed until April 1863. By this time, the appeal for funds had been much encouraged by a gift of £200 from Queen Victoria, and a promise of £100 per year for the future. Osborne was considered to be in the Hospital's catchment area.

On 14 October 1863, a meeting was held at Hursley Park, Sir William Heathcote's house, to consider the architect's plans, and the Chairman reported that Butterfield had 'thrown himself into this work with a zeal and interest far beyond the mere performance of a professional engagement'. He had even foregone his summer holiday and, with Heathcote, had gone on a tour of new hospitals, and consulted Doctor Sutherland and Captain Galton of the War Office, 'several' (note, not all) of the Medical Officers at the Winchester Hospital ... and Miss Nightingale, 'though in her case only by means of correspondence; she was unfortunately too ill to be seen ... but perfectly able to scrutinize the plans which were sent to her'.

The Hospital doctors, from their experience, were asking for a Museum and a Library to be incorporated in the new building, a larger number of small wards (five instead of three), a central bathroom for the use of convalescent patients, and a balcony along the south front of each ward. Doctors Heale and Christe recommended Day Rooms for convalescents, as well as balconies; Doctor Lyford and Mr Langdon opposed them. A few weeks before this Hursley meeting, on 23 September 1863, Charles Mayo, the Hospital's senior surgeon, had replied to the toast of the professions, at the usual dinner in honour of the retiring Mayor. He was outspoken in his attack on the proposals to build a new Hospital, criticised the Bishop and the Archdeacon for their letters in the *Hampshire Chronicle* asking for funds, and maintained that six of the eight 'medical attendants' concurred with him in opposing the removal. His speech, incidentally, was seconded by Thomas Watton, a Winchester lawyer, who was about to go bankrupt.

Miss Nightingale's comments were very carefully considered by the party at Hursley. Her main objection, read aloud, concerned the proposal to admit men and women suffering from venereal disease, although they were to be housed separately. 'The whole principal of these wards is objectionable' and 'Where are we to find such a Head Nurse as I describe to overlook a ward of six patients?' Moreover, men and women suffering from this disease ought to be in separate buildings. She was also opposed to Day Rooms – if you were well enough to use a Day Room, you were well enough to go home ... balconies (the English climate made them unsuitable) and small wards – 'necessary evils', producing neglected, unsupervised patients – each [ward] really requires a first-rate Head Nurse'. Yet her report, on the whole, was favourable to Butterfield; 'I think you may justly congratulate yourselves on having planned a model hospital'. When the meeting ended, her advice had been accepted; the venereal patients were to be in a 'distant' building, there were to be no Day Rooms, only three wards, and balconies only at the east end of the building. The advice of the staff had been accepted in some measure. There was to be a central bathroom, a Museum, a Library, and a microscopic room. Inevitably, the space per bed, in terms of cubic feet, was 1560, much below Rawlinson's recommendation of 2,000 cubic feet.

The Hursley meeting was followed on 11 October 1863 by what the local press called 'a long and desultory discussion' at the Quarterly Meeting of the Governors. The plans were not finally accepted until 18 November 1864. Then tenders were asked for, and a new crisis arose. The lowest figure, that of the London builders, Jackson and Shaw, was for £21,993, a sum far in excess of what had been expected. Further appeals for money had to be made. It looked as if the whole project would have to be postponed, and the illness of the Chairman was an additional complication. Under Statute 20 of the Hospital's constitution, he was allowed to serve by Deputy; in effect, this meant that, for about five years until 22 July 1868, Sir William served by means of his chosen Deputy, the Reverend Edward Stuart of Sparsholt. In one way or another, the money began to come in. An anonymous donor gave £500 towards the cost of the Chapel, which was to be a memorial to Warden Barter. Much later on, Heathcote revealed that this gift had come from Butterfield; generous support too came from the Baring family.

In the meantime, of course, the everyday life of the Hospital was going on its usual way. The War had directed attention to matters of hospital food and, in 1857, the patients' diets were revised.

Daily Allowance	EXTRA DIET	ORDINARY DIET	
	8 oz. uncooked Meat	6 oz. uncooked Meat ⎫	5 days
	Broth	with Broth	a
	16 oz. Bread	and ½ lb. Potatoes ⎬	week
	½ lb. Potatoes	12 oz. Light Pudding ⎭	2 days
			a week
		12 oz. Bread	
	¼ pt. of Milk	¼ pt. of Milk	
	1½ oz. of Tea ⎫	1½ oz. of Tea ⎫	
	¼ oz. of Sugar ⎬ per	1¼ lb. of Sugar ⎬ per	
	¼ lb. of Butter ⎭ week	¼ lb. of Butter ⎭ week	

	SIMPLE DIET	MILK DIET
	12 oz. Bread	12 oz. Bread
	1 pt. of good Broth	2 oz. of Rice
	¼ pt. of Milk	1¼ pts of Milk
	1½ oz. of Tea ⎫	
	¼ lb. of Sugar ⎬ per	
	¼ lb. of Butter ⎭ week	

In October 1858, the quantity of bread for men was increased to 16oz per day. The Hospital's reputation as a teaching Hospital was still being maintained, and the Statutes of 1857 relating to the Library and the Museum were widened in 1864 to allow their use by other practitioners in Winchester and its neighbourhood. Medical pupils were allowed to read in the Library, but had to pay a guinea for its support when they 'enter to the practice of the Hospital'. Any wilful damage would be punished by 'exclusion from all future use'. The 1857 Regulations for Pupils were quite clear:

'9. That Pupils be admitted to the Hospital under the following Regulations:

I. The Physicians and Surgeons of the Hospital shall be allowed to introduce, under the sanction of the Committee, a certain number of Pupils, who shall be maintained without any charge or expense to the Hospital, and shall be liable to be removed either by the Physicians or Surgeons by whom they may have been introduced, or by the Committee, at any Board specially convened for that purpose.

II. That every Pupil so admitted into the Hospital shall be under the immediate direction of the Physician or Surgeon by whom he has been introduced, and shall attend him in his visits to the different Patients, assisting in any manner he may be required to do; but he shall not be entitled to witness the practice of the other Physicians and Surgeons without their permission. He shall have the privilege of attending every Clinical Lecture, and of being present at all the operations and post-mortem examinations performed in the Hospital, but he shall not prescribe for any Patient or perform even the minor operations of surgery, or dress wounds or ulcers, unless by order of the Medical Officers.

III. Pupils of properly qualified Medical Practitioners not belonging to the Staff of the Hospital may, with the consent of the Committee, become out-pupils, and see the practice of the Hospital under the direction of the House Surgeon, on the payment of Ten Guineas for one year or Twenty Guineas for an unlimited attendance; the whole of such fees to be given to the Institution.

IV. The times of attendance for the Pupils of each class shall be at the hours appointed for going round the Wards, and they shall remain at the Hospital only during the time that is employed by the Medical Officers in prescribing for and dressing their Patients, except when their services are required to assist in the dispensing of medicines.

V. When any Pupil or Apprentice shall leave the Institution, such a certificate of merit as his general conduct shall appear to deserve may be delivered to him by the Chairman, engrossed on parchment by the Secretary; and such certificate shall be recorded in the register of Pupils.

VI. In the absence of the Physicians and Surgeons, the Pupils shall be under the direction of the House Surgeon; and should they be found in any instance to act in opposition to the established discipline of the House, the Committee shall have power to suspend for a limited time, or wholly to prohibit, their future attendance.'

A Special Committee met at the Hospital on 13 January 1864 to consider Lyford's successor.[4] His place at the Prison had already been filled by Doctor F. J. Butler, and Lyford was now appointed as Honorary Consultant at the Hospital, but Butler had not applied for the post as his successor there. Of the three candidates, Doctor England, who had succeeded to Lyford's private practice, decided to withdraw. On a vote of nine votes to seven, T. C. Langdon was appointed, victorious over R. W. Smith who had a good Winchester practice. Langdon had a number of advantages; he had been the Hospital's House Surgeon, and he lived close to Parchment Street, in a delightful house at the north end of Jewry Street, which he had bought in 1851 from old Thomas Westcombe. Incidentally, at the Annual General Meeting in July 1864, the Governors approved some new arrangements for the medical staff. Henceforth, the House Surgeon could only take in one pupil at a time into the house.

Thomas Charles Langdon, Lyford's successor, was the first young House-Surgeon not to serve also as Hospital Secretary. He had qualified as M.R.C.S. at St

Bartholomew's, in 1858, and in 1863 became F.R.C.S. From 1873 till 1905, he was on the Winchester Board of Health as Medical Officer, and was also the Public Vaccinator. His last official appointment was as Superintendent of the Victoria Hospital for infectious diseases. Langdon was only one of the characters who appeared in some doggerel verses collected in c.1866 by one of the patients, a woman who had part of her foot amputated:

Of all the doctors in the west
Dr Hitchcock is the best
His name is known to one and all
For the Good he does to the Hospital.

Dr England is also kind
And with his skill is not behind.
He is to all both kind and good
And orders his patients plenty of food.

Mr Mayo is very clever
To cure his patients do endeavour
With his lance he tries to ease their pain
And hopes they will be better when he comes again.

Dr Butler walks up the stairs
With his kind majestic air
He looks so kind and smiles so free
His patients cannot but happy be.

Mr Langdon meek and mild
He says now how are you today my child
Are you better, are you worse
Can't you speak where is the nurse.

Mr Rundle is very charming
Visits his patients night and morning
Listens to all they have to say
And with a smile he walks away.

Mr May is very tall
He comes in and sees us all
And with his skill I think you will find
He helps our wounds to dress and bind.

Mr Foster I do declare
Mixes our medicines with care
He makes us pills which do us good
And helps us to digest our food.

It was indeed a time of change. At the very beginning of 1864, just after Lyford's resignation, the great W. J. Wickham died, aged sixty-six.[5] William John Wickham had been Consultant with the Hospital for some 40 years; his memorial[6] in the Cathedral provides his best epitaph, 'in a loving and Christian spirit he heeded the sick and comforted the afflicted' and the *Record* for 19 January 1864 helps to complete the story, though it has rather an odd entry. 'Died in St Thomas Street, Winchester,

William John Wickham Esq, F.R.C.S. aged 66. His loss will be universally lamented as a native and old inhabitant of this city ... he succeeded his father in a large general practice and was for many years successively Surgeon and Consulting Surgeon to the County Hospital, and would have been followed to the grave by the staff of the Institution had they been aware of the time of his internment'.[7] It is a sad omission, but the staff were very occupied in various battles about the Hospital's future, and Sir William Heathcote had not yet recovered his full strength.

It was soon possible to go out to tender again, and on 28 December 1864, at *The George Inn*, a tender from Rogers and Brooks of Gosport for £22,582 17s. 0d. was accepted and approved on 18 January 1865, inevitably well above the figure turned down previously. Once started, and despite the bad winters of 1866 and 1867, the contractors made good progress. Sir William Heathcote was able to report, at a meeting of the building sub-committee held on 23 May 1868, 'that the building is nearly complete'; soon came the good news, announced in the *Hampshire Chronicle* of 13 June 1868, that the Queen had agreed that the new Hospital should be 'Royal' and on 30 June 1868 the Chapel – the Barter Memorial Chapel – was opened with a service of Holy Communion and a sermon preached by the Headmaster of Winchester College, Doctor Moberly.

When the Committee of Management met for the first time in the new Hospital on 5 August 1868, it admitted 16 in-patients and 14 out-patients. In the words of the 130th Annual Report, published on 9 October 1868, the Hospital had, at last, 'removed to new premises'. The Annual Report on the state of the County Hospital ended with the words 'Removed to New Premises, and aided as may be hoped, by new and improved appliances, the Committee trust that it will please God to make the Royal Hampshire County Hospital a blessed means of extending to the sick and afflicted the benefits of medical staff and science, and while the physical necessities of those, who in a long succession of years resort to its Wards are relieved, that their sprirtual wants will ever be remembered and supplied.'

....

It was important to explain to the public how the £34,312 18s. 8d. collected for the new building had been spent. The site had cost £2,225 0s. 0d., the building £24,713 1s. 1d., the Chapel £1,430 18s. 6d. There had been a Clerk of Works who received £463 11s. 8d.; administration and the fees of a quantity surveyor cost £411 18s. 8d, and Butterfield's fees amounted to £1,499 19s. 6d. His biographer has suggested that his annual income was about two thousand pounds, and though he had given £500 to the Chapel fund, the Hospital commission cannot have been unimportant to him financially. The building had taken a long time to complete, and there were years ahead when it must have provided more worry than fees and, for the last careful remedial work he did at the Hospital, he refused to accept any money at all.

The truth probably was that there were still people in Winchester who remembered the disastrous result of employing 'a London architect' to restore the High Cross; the balance of Gilbert Scott's fees for that work were never paid, and to some people the definition of an architect was a person appointed to take the blame. Butterfield was working in Winchester for a Committee of county gentlemen, all

9 & 10. The Royal Hampshire County Hospital (architect William Butterfield), south and north views.

used to having their own way, and Sir William Heathcote, who could certainly be described for much of the time not only as a friend as well as a patron, was frequently ill; moreover, at a very critical time in the history of the Hospital, he had suffered the disaster of the death of John Keble, and was absent from meetings. Melville Portal's relationship with Butterfield is more difficult to estimate. In the last critical months of the architect's relationship with the Hospital, he certainly supported Butterfield, but significantly he does not appear to have consulted him about his own great project, the restoration of the Great Hall of Winchester Castle. The support of Lord Eversley was clearly significant. Butterfield had done work for him in Heckfield church, built some almshouses in the village there and, above all, had been entrusted with the design of Lady Eversley's memorial, one of the architect's best and most delicate pieces of work.

There were still years before main drainage arrived in the centre of Winchester, and there was certainly none in the new Romsey Road building. There is a tradition and some evidence that Butterfield usually destroyed his plans, and certainly his original drawings seem to have disappeared. He had already been subjected to endless but probably necessary economies, and his plans had been passed to an engineer to make sure that they were not too architectural, too decorative, too extravagant. At first, everyone seems to have been pleased with everything, except perhaps Charles Mayo. In September 1869, his appointment was not renewed, and he could not really understand why; at nearly eighty, he was deemed by some people not fit enough to continue as a surgeon. It is not too much to say that the new Hospital was in itself in part his memorial, and the pulpit in the nave of the Cathedral is another reminder of the importance of his family in Winchester. Even Mayo must have felt pleased at the first impressions of the new building. All was openness and light, space and fresh, bracing air around, and a developing garden. The most immediate difficulty was access, the long walk up the Romsey Road from the town centre, and from the new Railway Station, and there was no public transport.

It was necessary to sell off the buildings in Parchment Street as soon as possible, and it was thought best to sell by auction. T. S. Morris, of St Peter Street, a well-known local auctioneer, was asked to arrange the sale, and he advertised it in a number of successive issues of the local newspaper. The 'large and important property' was to be sold at 3 p.m. on the afternoon of Thursday, 15 October 1868, and there was a crowded room. The auctioneer's printed particulars have not survived, only an overall plan of the site, and Morris' descriptions in his advertisements. Interestingly enough, he described it as 'The centre building originally a large family mansion', with wings added later, and a chapel wing with a superior stone staircase. Perhaps more of Clobury's house had survived than has been suspected.

The *Chronicle*'s report of the sale in its issue of 17 October 1868 announced that the whole 'Hospital estate' had fetched 3000 guineas, and had been bought by a local firm of builders, the Govers, on behalf of a London firm with whom they had family connections. The Govers were well-known Winchester carpenters and builders. They had done much work for William Garbett, the Cathedral Architect (d.1835), including the making of the present episcopal throne in the Cathedral, and they had also built the three attractive terrace houses opposite the Hospital in Parchment Street (nos 13, 14, 15), traditionally said to have been inhabited by the members of the Hospital's medical staff.[8] The whole site was soon redeveloped as two rows of town houses, in Parchment Street and in Middle Brook Street. The original Foundation Stone had been removed, and was built into the new Hospital in Romsey Road, where it can be seen on the east side of the main entrance. Ironically, the original Hospital in Colebrook Street survived some mid-19th century demolition there, and was divided up into cottages.[9] The local remembrance of what it had been in Winchester's history remained, and the writer recalls the late Mr S. Ward-Evan's antiquarian notice on the building, *in situ* until 1959; then it was demolished by the Corporation. No such antiquarian description survived in Parchment Street, but the very tall, almost out-of-scale chimneys at the south end of No. Upper Brook Street may represent some slight survival and a Roman coin remains, which had been found at the laying of the foundation stone.

IX Romsey Road – and Its Problems

The Romsey Road Hospital needs to be seen as part of the major 19th-century development of Winchester's western downland. When Thomas Stopher, its future architect, was a young boy and his father began to design the new County Gaol in 1847, there had only been one building along the road from Winchester to Romsey. The coming of the railway in 1840 did not hinder this western development, and new fashionable areas grew up, Clifton Hill, and Clifton Terrace, and to the south, 'St James', a survival, in terms of the name, from the Cathedral's monastic past, deriving from a long-demolished parish church.

The site of the Hospital was an open space, sloping towards the south, with a northern frontage along the road from Winchester.[1] There were few other approach roads; on the eastern side, where the municipal boundary stone of 1835 can still be seen, an ancient lane marking the southern line of the enclosure of the royal castle had formerly twisted its way to the entrance of the new prison of 1847, and also to the churchyard of St James, the burial place of Winchester's Roman Catholics. It had been called Barnes' Lane, after a local family of brewers but, before the new Hospital was completed, it had come to serve part of the fashionable new area, and was henceforth called St James' Lane, with fine houses springing up on its northern side, even though their immediate southern outlook was Mr Charles Wittman Benny's new cemetery. To the west of the cemetery was Mr Colson's new Diocesan Training College, on the other side of another narrow lane, lying below the Hospital. There was, of course, no public transport available to serve any of these new buildings, but the generosity of a local brewer, Mr Richard Moss, a future Member of Parliament and a great Conservative, produced a free and regular omnibus service for the Hospital; it started from the Broadway and toured the town, and was viewed with genuine suspicion by Mr Moss' political opponents, who had doubts about the motives which lay behind his many gifts to Winchester.

Mr. Rawlinson's original suggestion, to be fair to him, had never really been examined, but his calculation that a new Hospital might cost £6,000 was a hopeless under-estimate. Before a brick of Mr Butterfield's building had been laid, yet another engineer had been asked to look at the plans. Butterfield survived, with unaltered plans, and his insistence on quality as well as practicality in the new building proved a valuable asset; he took great care with the drainage and ventilation, but even he could not have contemplated the vast improvements in that respect which were to develop in his lifetime; of course, there was still no main sewer in Winchester and, in any case, the Hospital was outside the main city boundary.

The building accounts show that £13,091 4s. 8d. had been received in subscriptions; church collections amounted to £1,730 4s. 10d.; the rent from part of the site before building commenced amounted to 18s. 0d. and the Exchequer Bills produced £626 1s. 6d., making a total of £15,465 11s. 0d. in receipts. The not inconsiderable sum of £1,430 18s. 6d. had been received separately for the building of the Barter Memorial Chapel; this included a deficiency item of £65 15s. 1d., paid for out of his own pocket by Sir William Heathcote, and Butterfield's donation of £500. The sale of Parchment Street produced £3,150 0s. 0d., but with some interest and the proceeds of the sale of some of its furniture, the total was £3,221 8s. 0d.

In all, £34,312 18s. 8d. had been gathered in for the new building and its Chapel. It was in the Chapel that William Butterfield was most able to display the characteristics which made him one of the most successful architects of his time. Though Butterfield's plans have not survived, his building is still to be seen, despite the many later additions, and the various functions of its original component parts are not in doubt. It was not a pavilion house, like Netley, but relatively compact, running east to west for 255 feet, with a central block and two wings. It has been called 'a slab'. In the central building was a vast and impressive staircase, three small wards for special cases, and the limited administration offices. Here, too, were the only operating theatre, apartments for the House Surgeon and the Matron, 'nurses and servants' day and sleeping rooms', a Board Room, and the kitchen 'and offices'. The wings on either side contained five large wards, two on the ground floor for men (one medical and one surgical) and two above, on the first floor, similarly described, for women. On the second floor on the eastern wing was the Barter Memorial Chapel, with a fine east window, and the corresponding western floor was a second surgical ward for men. These large wards all terminated in turrets, where there were bathrooms, lavatories, and storage closets, and there were 'convalescent balconies', of which Florence Nightingale had not approved. They are shown in one very early drawing of the building. The larger wards could each take 18 patients; they were 20 feet by 24 feet wide, with enormous windows almost to the ground, supplying a constant flow of fresh air, and they were warmed by coal fires. Their walls were coated liberally with Kean's cement, easily wiped down, and the floors were splendid, of polished oak and walnut.

Beneath the ground floor were 'two spacious waiting rooms', an unspecified number of consulting rooms, the Dispensary, and 'the Library, etc.' All around was open ground, the promise of an excellent garden and even of a plentiful supply of home-grown vegetables and fruit. In 1885, Warren's *New Illustrated Guide to Winchester*, like its predecessors describing Parchment Street, referred to the new Romsey Road Hospital in glowing terms. The number of beds was fewer (108) than those available in Parchment Street in 1829; it was 'in need of more funds'. The Hospital Chapel was apparently open to the public, since it is described as well worth a visit, and the two windows by Clayton and Bell in memory of Sir William Heathcote and Archdeacon Jacob were particularly to be noticed; it added that the chapel had been recently redecorated by Westlake, Barand and Company.

In 1876, Sir William Heathcote felt some concern about the heating and ventilation systems, and in the next year, 1877, the water supply was sometimes irregular. Cases of sore throats and bouts of unexplained 'fever' began to appear amongst the patients. By this time, main drainage had at last been allowed to come to Winchester, thanks almost entirely to the influences of Dean Garnier and of the Headmaster of the College. It soon became a panacea, a remedy for all complaints, but the Hospital was just outside the City boundary and, as yet, there was neither

11. Sir William Heathcote, Bart. (1801-1881)
(from the portrait by George Richmond).

a Hampshire County Council, nor a Rural District Council in terms of elected local government. The City Council could not or would not act, and the matter does not appear in its Health Committee Minutes. Further down the hill was the Winchester Union Workhouse, whose medical officer was Doctor Earle, a great advocate of drainage and the professional man to whom at least some of the Hospital Governors preferred to go for advice when they heard the many complaints of Hospital staff about bad drainage, horrible smells and even an allegedly tainted water supply.[2]

The problems of the Parchment Street Hospital had almost all derived from the absence of main drainage. By 1879, Doctor Earle was genuinely concerned at the condition of Butterfield's complex drainage systems, and he put his concern in writing. The physical presence of three very large communities, all just outside the City boundary, was bound to be a matter of common concern; if patients could be affected by bad drains, infection might well spread to prisoners in the nearby County Gaol, or to the inmates of the Union. Much of Winchester was already sewered, and an efficient arrangement made, *via* the Pumping Station in Garnier Road, to dispose of the sewage, suitably filtered, on the neighbouring downs at Morstead and Chilcombe. Doctor Earle was concerned at the horrible smells which had become a feature of Hospital life, and also at what he considered to be the possibility that the water supply was contaminated. In fairness to Butterfield, it needs to be said at once that his plans for drainage had been most careful, and the work of building that system was carried out with great exactness and care, and much in advance of the time. In his new building, sewage was generally kept separate from the waste water from sinks and baths, both were separated from the flow of rain water from the roofs, and there was a complicated but very well-built system of traps and ventilation. It was a good system, but it relied on careful maintenance, and regular cleaning. In the years after the new building had been opened, the system was not given the respect it deserved. Irregular, unauthorised alterations had been made, and haphazard maintenance, and an unwillingness to involve a London architect in small problems had produced the inevitable result. There were too many plumbers prepared to proceed 'by guess', as a contemporary said, and in fact the electric wiring was also subject to the same risky repair work, and large areas of the Hospital were occasionally plunged into darkness.

Butterfield, whose devotion to the Hospital cannot really be questioned, found himself constantly criticised, and most of this criticism was uninformed and from members of the Hospital staff or Governors. It ought to be said that there was no adequate provision for maintenance staff, and that the great majority of the male patients were unused to the refinements of main drainage and water-closets. Relations between the Architect and the General Committee had come to boiling point long before August 1879, when the General Committee met and decided to set up a special sub-committee, whose main duty was 'to confer with Mr Butterfield' and 'earnestly request him to resume his relations with the Hospital'.

The four members of the Committee included two of Butterfield's friends, Sir William Heathcote and Melville Portal, and their appeal was answered promptly. He came down at once and, in three days, inspected the whole system and made detailed and careful recommendations as to how it was to be maintained, and how the ventilation could be improved. He was not pleased with what he found; the careful, framed plan of the system, presumably displayed in the Secretary's Office, had been too often ignored, and he was struck with the 'carelessness with which the drains had been attended to and dealt with'.

The House Surgeon had complained about the drain opposite the south-west turret of the surgical wards. This was the scullery drain, blocked completely by years of grease accumulated from washing-up water. Two of the drains from water-closets had been deliberately closed with tow; only a few months previously 'a person under discharge from Miss Freeman' had maliciously stopped up another sewage down pipe. Not surprisingly, the Sub-Committee made a point of stressing that 'no structural arrangement, however complete, can contend against carelessness, nor neglect, nor misuse', and they recommended that the Porter should flush and clean the drains regularly, as part of his normal work – 'he should be a person of some practical intelligence'. Doctor Richards, one of the Hospital staff, had complained particularly about the smells in the Post-Mortem Room, and from the cess-pit in the garden. The cess-pit was to be thoroughly cleaned out, the charcoal in it replaced, and ventilation in the Post-Mortem Room improved. These were some of the chief recommendations and the Architect had prepared detailed specifications, and obtained estimates. The entire cost for all the work recommended was £196 9s. 0d.

As for Butterfield himself, 'the foregoing Report shews in every part of it that, so far as the present emergency is concerned, Mr Butterfield has, without hesitation, accepted the invitation of your Sub-Committee, and has devoted to the service of the Hospital an amount of labour and time, of which the value can hardly be appreciated, except by those who realize the very great eminence of Mr Butterfield in his profession, and his constant occupation.

'They have felt some diffidence in attempting to carry out this instruction, fearing lest their estimate of the footing on which alone such relations can be tolerable to an Architect of Mr Butterfield's position, may not agree with that of the General Committee.

'Your Sub-Committee could not shut their eyes to the appearance of late, in communications with Mr Butterfield, of want of confidence in him and his professional skill, and of passing over, apparently without consideration, certain elaborate letters on the subject of the Hospital, which Mr Buterfield had written.

'But Mr Butterfield, putting aside all personal considerations, has generously consented to super-intend the proposed alterations, and to renew his relations with the Hospital until the end of next year, when he reserves to himself the privilege of re-considering the matter. Your Sub-Committee congratulate the friends of the Hospital on having, even for this limited period, secured the continuance of his valuable advice and assistance.' The Report was signed by Melville Portal, as Chairman, from Laverstoke on 21 October 1879.

The most important decision taken by the Sub-Committee was their agreement not to recommend the alteration of Butterfield's drains in order to connect the entire arrangement with a main sewer. His suggestions were duly carried out and complete by 22 May 1880, and in June the Sub-Committee received a further report. Despite repeated efforts, the drains were still not being properly maintained and cases of sore throat and of erysphilas had occurred. The Sub-Committee had taken expert advice on the causes of 'hospital illness' and had been told that bad drainage was far from being the only cause for the differing kinds of outbreak, for that great authority, Sir James Paget, was consulted. The case of the St Thomas' Hospital surgeon was quoted. Despite St Thomas' splendid drains, Mr Simon, a surgeon there, had found that his operations had been most successful when carried out in the temporary buildings of the Surrey Zoological Gardens. Nevertheless, the Sub-Committee could do nothing to increase the General Committee's confidence in Butterfield and they found themselves 'affected to some extent' by the 'somewhat irritating communications' which the Architect was always receiving. It was all getting too tiresome for Butterfield, and he sent Melville Portal a splendid letter of resignation.

4 Adam Street
Adelphi
22 May 1880

My Dear Sir,

    In presenting my Report to the Committee of Winchester Hospital, will you be good enough to inform them that, notwithstanding my offer in my former Report to continue as their adviser until the close of 1880, I have, during the last few months of my connection with the Hospital, been forced to reconsider the question.

    I have great satisfaction in remembering the terms of professional confidence and personal kindness on which I worked for many years with the Authorities of the Hospital; conditions, the want of which (except so far as your Sub-Committee are concerned) are now so marked, that having concluded the works which I undertook with you to carry out, I must beg leave to withdraw at once from all connection with the Hospital.

    In my former relations with the Committee, it was always a pleasure to me to give professional advice whenever Sir William Heathcote consulted me, and to give it gratuitously, except in cases where plans were not only prepared but carried into execution.

    In the present position of affairs, no money charge that I can make would compensate me, and I decline to make a charge or to accept remuneration for the services which I have just rendered.

I am, my Dear Sir,
Yours very faithfully
W BUTTERFIELD

In the words of his biographer, Butterfield 'liked to work with patrons whose confidence in him was unquestioned'.[3] He was eventually succeeded by a Winchester architect, Thomas Stopher, whose father and namesake had designed the County Gaol in 1847, and who was already well known for his local patriotism and love of local history. Stopher's private practice became considerable, and he designed some very interesting buildings, but he lacked Butterfield's national status, and the architectural story of the Hospital after Butterfield resigned is largely one of endless economies and small alterations. In 1881, the Governors decided that they really must try to provide separate accommodation for infectious or infected patients, and they also provided each ward with its own bathroom and lavatory.[4] Not until 1897 was the City Council's offer to deal with all the sewage accepted, and by this time the problem of where to put the increasing number of nurses had become acute.

Throughout these years of problems in the new building, the Weekly Committee were dealing, as usual, with important concerns mixed with trivial matters. On one occasion in 1883, the only item on the Agenda was the purchase of a new rope for the lift.At one meeting, two Generals, a Colonel, a senior cleric, and a well-known solicitor were called together in order to inspect the Hospital's strong box. It is a great pity that the Visitors' Books, which would have told so much about the life of the household, have all disappeared. These years of renewed crisis with the Hospital's drainage system were also years of very bad winters, and cold and wet summers, and of decline in Hampshire's long-standing agricultural prosperity. Vast harvests of grain could now be imported from overseas, particularly from Canada, and this, with the growth of refrigeration and of various canning processes, meant the import of foreign meat. A period of depression began, from which the country took years to recover. Agricultural patients were often to be found amongst the Hospital's patients. By 1881, a Census Year, the in-patients were all working people, many of them labourers, still the 'sick poor', and men greatly outnumbered women. In the Census of that year, 45 male patients are recorded, but only 19 females; out of the men, 19 were farm-workers, including a wood-cutter, a carter, an old shepherd and a young shepherd boy (aged 14), both the latter from Sir William Heathcote's estate. The Hursley influence can be seen, too, in the fireman from Ampfield and in the Porter, a Hursley man whose two children had been born in the village. All the men were manual workers with the exception of a solicitor's young clerk from Chawton, aged only 16, and an elderly musician, James King, born in St Albans.

The women patients were nearly all in domestic service, variously described as housemaids, housekeepers, 'generals', or nursemaids; there was a needlewoman from Longparish, and a female hawker. There were children, all described as scholars, more boys than girls, but the list included a carpenter's apprentice from Lasham, aged 15, and the Porter's daughter of the same age, but not employed. Amongst the employed boys, Frederick Bowen, born in Winchester, aged 15, is described as 'choir boy coff' (i.e. his complaint). There were six boys between five and 12, all presumably being nursed with the men, of whom the two eldest were 66 but there were only four girls, aged seven and nine, and two aged ten. Very few girls were being sent to be nursed away from home; the nine-year-old came from Winchester, the youngest child just from Harestock, nearby.

The odd omission is the name of Miss Freeman as Matron, and Lady Superintendent, but this must be an error, as two Miss Freemans appear on the list, both Lady Superintendents and both described as visitors in terms of their relationship to the young head of the household, Jonathan Hutching, M.R.C.S., the House Surgeon, aged only twenty-one. There were five ward sisters, all in their thirties, of whom two came from Ireland, three nurses, of whom two are described as 'private' nurses, and nine probationers, of whom the eldest was 54 and the youngest nineteen. The ratio of nursing staff to patients was 17 to 64. In addition to the Housekeeper (Mrs Mitchell from Yorkshire) the domestic staff consisted of a parlour maid, one domestic servant, a housemaid, a ward maid, and a young scullery maid, aged only sixteen. Presumably the cook did not live in, or was absent on the night of the Census, and the nurses were probably still serving up the breakfasts as they had been in 1736. The total household numbered ninety-one.

It was during Miss Freeman's time as Matron that Sir William Heathcote resigned as Chairman of the Court of Governors in 1877. Four years later, he was dead, aged 80, and is commemorated by a tablet on the south wall of Hursley church tower; it indeed recites in part only, 'The life work of this much loved and respected Baronet' for it says not one word of his work at the Hospital, the work which he had begun as a young man in his twenties.

It was under Miss Freeman that the diets for in-patients were considerably modernised.[5]

The Chairman of Governors who succeeded Heathcote was that much loved man, Archdeacon Philip Jacob, in whose memory the great central crucifix of the Cathedral's reredos was erected. Mrs Suckling was appointed Matron at the end of 1881, when there was a new Secretary, a retired army major who soon seems to have fallen out with Doctor Earle. The Matron and Major Terry, new brooms, began almost at once to make small changes; Mrs Suckling's salary was fixed at £90 a year, new furniture was bought for her room, and a month's notice given to her subordinate, the Hospital's Housekeeper, whom she replaced with someone of her own choice. Most of the groceries were being bought from Harrod's (of Winchester), and continued to come from that firm for many years. As yet, there were only three permanent Sub-Committees; Finance, Visiting, and Dispensing; the Reverend J. Slessor was Chairman of Finance, but he had a formidable colleague there in the person of Charles Warner, a Winchester solicitor; the Warners, father and son, were to become invaluable members of the entirely voluntary administration; it was the younger Warner who guided the Hospital through the First World War and the difficult years that followed. As well as the Sub-Committee, the Weekly Board continued to meet regularly and, in March 1882, a close debate resulted in a decision to allow Physicians and Surgeons to be members of the Board, an important step carried by nine votes to eight. By the end of April, there were other changes; the old Chaplain (Firmstone) resigned; in the advertisements for his successor, the average number of in-patients was given as 70, and the salary ofered was £120 a year, an interesting comparison with Mrs Suckling's £90. In all the splendour of Romsey Road, there was thus said to be 10 patients more, on average, than there had been in little Colebrook Street.

It was still a small Hospital, which could be very shaken by changes in personnel. In April 1882, Doctor W. England resigned as Physician to become the Surgeon after old Doctor Butler's death.[6] England was succeeded by Doctor Beresford Earle, and the young House Surgeon, F.J. Pound, resigned to go abroad. His successor was not found easily, despite advertisements in *The Times*, the *British Medical Journal* and the *Lancet*, which offered board and residence and £100 a year, and a temporary man (Aslett) was appointed at two guineas a week, until Herbert McDougall arrived in July 1882.[7] There were other changes; in January 1882, the Weekly Board heard complaints about the nurses' food; four months later, it was decided that each nurse would be allowed an extra one pound of bacon a week, or, at the option of the Lady Superintendent, three eggs and three quarters of a pound of bacon. Accommodation for female servants whose family did not live locally was another source of anxiety. John Colson, the Hospital's old pre-Butterfield architect, was still active, but his description in the Minutes as 'Colson, an architect' is decidedly odd; the Secretary was probably suspicious of architects, but it was Colson who produced plans for rooms in the roof for the domestic staff, and who pointed out that the roof was in need of repair. It is not really surprising that Romsey Road had not been the object of an annual architectural report; perhaps there was a feeling among some of the senior administrators that, having achieved a new building, the day-to-day problems of a Hospital would somehow or other disappear. What the Minutes call 'Complaints about the Household', especially complaints about insufficiency of food, were supposed to go to the Lady Superintendent of Nurses, to the Secretary, or to one of the Visitors; matters could not or were not usually raised at Committees unless notice had been given beforehand, and inevitably it took a long time for small grievances to be remedied.[8]

Yet there were major changes; Ward 2, the 'Infectious Ward' for women, was taken over as a Children's Ward, and Fever Cottage opened with a service on 3 May 1882, but a proposal to set aside a much smaller ward for paying patients, sent up by the Weekly Committee to the Board of Governors in December 1882, did not find favour, and was eventually turned down, though 'with much regret', in April 1883, after consultation with the medical staff. The occasional taking in of individuals in cases of emergency was almost always allowed and it was neither deemed improper nor unusual for grateful patients to give donations. The Board of Governors and the Weekly Committee were still dominated by ecclesiastics but, at the end of May 1883, Archdeacon Jacob announced his intention to resign. By that time, Charles Warner (the Hospital's Treasurer) had died, and the problem of who was to succeed as Chairman was a serious matter. In some ways, the obvious choice was General Forrest, Hampshire's strong-minded Chief Constable, though he was not renowned for his tact, and it was perhaps fortunate that he decided that his other duties prevented him from taking on the work.

Forrest could have been an excellent choice in one respect for, once again, the Hospital's drains were in disrepute, and in September 1883 a letter arrived from Mr Frank Faithfull, solicitor to the Rural Sanitary Authority. It asked that the Governors take immediate steps 'to render the drainage effective ... nothing could answer so well as connecting it with the City system'. The Basingstoke firm of Milson and Glover reported on the complaints to the Governors in September; the ventilation pipe to the main drains on the south-east side was blocked at the base, and foul air was coming out of the Post-Mortem Room because the manhole cover nearby was not properly bedded. Otherwise, the system was 'free, clean and in good working order', though the 'apparatus' of some of the water closets was dirty; the lavatories, of japanned metal, were a real problem, and it was suggested that they should be replaced by ones made of earthenware. Incidentally, the firm had made that particular recommendation in the past but, in this new situation, it was agreed that one Ward (No.1, Mens) should be fitted out with 'The National Closet'. This was all that happened, and Frank Faithfull wrote again, asking what had been done; on 19 October 1883 the Rural Sanitary Authority was informed that the drainage system had been inspected by Milson and Glover, who had in part improved the drains for Butterfield in 1880, and that 'the drainage of the Hospital is now quite effective'. The Sanitary Authority simply refused to believe this statement, and Faithfull wrote again; it was not possible to accept the reassurance, made 'on the authority of a day-labourer and an Army Major', and the advice given to the Governors 10 years ago had not yet been properly implemented. The deep cesspool was full of offensive sewage, the whole should be connnected with the City system and, in the meantime, the cesspool should be emptied at short intervals. The Chairman himself wrote the answer for Major Terry to send: 'No illness of any kind of late years could be attributed to the Drainage'.

By 30 January 1885, the Committee heard that the cesspool had been emptied and, more encouraging, that the Empress Eugenie had sent a letter promising to subscribe £20 a year. Next month, the walls and roof of the chapel were reported to be damp, and Butterfield himself was approached for help; he simply suggested the problem should be referred to Mr Norris, the builder, of Sunnyside, Ascot, who had done the original work. Norris came down, and the Committee, always suspicious of instant decisions, referred his suggestions back to Butterfield, who agreed with the experienced Mr Norris. In the end, Norris was asked to deal with the chapel (he was not allowed to attend to the main staircase) but only after further delays caused by the Chaplain's request to postpone the work until after Easter. This seems to be the very last occasion on which Butterfield, as usual unpaid, did anything for the Hospital.

X Some Victorian Matrons And Their Nurses

The first Matron in the Romsey Road Hospital was Miss Freeman, whom the Governors sent in 1867 to the Florence Nightingale School for Nurses in the temporary building of St Thomas' Hospital at Stoke Newington. All her staff subsequently underwent the same nursing training, but the new superiority of the Lady Superintendent of Nurses upset some of the medical staff, and the result in 1869 was a Memorandum intended to establish good understanding between the Medical Department and the Nursing Department. 'All matters regarding the management of the sick are placed absolutely under the control of the medical men.' Miss Freeman was responsible only for the selection, discipline, and dismissal of the nurses. This indeed she achieved, as the first Nightingale Matron of the Hospital, where she remained for 15 years, and to her must go much of the credit for establishing a scheme for the training of probationers, though by a small majority, in 1885, probationers were declared not to be part of the permanent staff.[1] Mrs Suckling, who succeeded her, had been Matron and Lady Superintendent of Nurses at Highgate Infirmary. She was appointed on 21 December 1881, at the same meeting which selected Major Terry as Hospital Secretary, and she was a lady who knew her own mind. New furniture was bought for her room, and the Housekeeper was given a month's notice, so that the Matron could engage a woman of her own choice. It was probably Mrs Suckling who suggested that a bun should be given to each patient on Easter Sunday; bread, milk and meat were bought locally. In April 1882, the Lady Superintendent of Nurses was allowed to use the Board Room for lectures to her nursing staff, and next month Mrs Suckling got an increase in their rations; each nurse was to be allowed one pound of bacon per week, and at the option of the Lady Superintendent, three eggs and three quarters of a pound of bacon 'if eggs easily obtainable'. Night nurses were given an extra pound of butcher's meat per week; there were four of them. It took her several months to get that strange sounding item, 'an oven for infectious purposes', but the Committee were quick to agree to other suggestions; all sheets were to be of linen, not cotton, and she could make what use she thought best of nurses' rooms when they were absent on leave. Some of the nurses living in the Hospital were, in fact, private nurses, sent out to nurse in patients' houses, usually at the medical staff's recommendation, and their use of rooms in the building was a matter of some concern. Mrs Suckling went off for three weeks' Christmas leave in November 1882, leaving the Hospital lift to be put into complete working order, at an estimated cost of £4 to £4 10s. 0d. Next year, she had a new Chairman, R. Jones Bateman, of Otterborne Grange, in succession to the old Archdeacon. Her chief concern was still her nursing staff, and she asked if the Honorary Medical Officers might give a course of lectures to the Probationers, a matter referred by the Governors to the Weekly Committee. It seems to have been difficult to get an immediate decision about anything and, in April 1883, she sent in a long letter of report on her work, and was asked to discuss it with the Governors. A few weeks later, the Governors' attention was distracted by the re-appearance of the problems of the Hospital drainage, but the relationship between the Governors and the Lady Superintendent did not seem to have produced any difficulties.

She emerges from the Minutes as a caring person, conscious of a world outside the Hospital; after March 1884, patients coming in from the country and kept waiting to be admitted, were offered a cup of tea or a basin of broth with a slice of bread; and her lectures to nurses were well known – sufficiently known for the Governors to agree that they could be attended by some non-members of the Hospital Staff. There were still occasional difficulties with patients. In May 1884, Alice Stockwell was discharged for disorderly behaviour, but was readmitted at Doctor England's request. Surprisingly, too, the Hospital was not able to deal with emergency cases on the point of death. Fanny Pidgley, brought in in a semi-drowned state, died within two hours. It was bad publicity, but the Hospital, unlike the Union Infirmary or the Police Receiving House, did not keep 'Proper Restoratives'. What exactly was meant by 'Proper Restoratives' is not clear, but alcohol must surely have been included and, by 1887, its consumption in the wards was increasing in a way which caused the Governors much anxiety.[2] Alcohol was dispensed, like other medicines. In 1914, the medical staff were to maintain that it was impossible to separate the prescriptions of alcohol and drugs, since both were connected with the treatment of patients. The increasing use of alcohol in Mrs Suckling's time was raised again in 1889, 1893 and 1894, when an investigation into its use in the wards led to Mrs Suckling offering her resignation.

By the beginning of 1894, it was clear that the relationship between the Committee of Management and the Matron had become a kind of armed truce, sometimes threatening to break into open warfare. Mrs Suckling was a highly professional woman, and there is nothing to indicate that she was not devoted to the promotion of nursing as a very skilled profession. The Chairman of the Committee, Colonel Wyndham William Portal, was also a determined character, and Matron found herself continually at odds with him and several members of the Committee. In February 1894, she asked for her own letter box, not at all an unreasonable or extravagant request; but it was refused. Some of her nurses' rooms were damp; nothing was done. Much more serious was the complaint brought to the Committee in March that the assistant nurses who were supposed to have been engaged to help the ward sisters (and there were still only five wards), had not been 'supplied', that is, engaged by Mrs Suckling. Doctor Beresford Earle bought up this matter, based on the allegation that the Matron's Weekly Reports had deliberately misled the Committee. The Committee had agreed in November 1890 to engage these five extra nurses. Evidence was called for from Sister Walkington of Heathcote Ward, Sister Strange from Victoria, Assistant Nurse Bartlett, the House Surgeon, Mr Clarke and Mrs Suckling herself. It appeared that Matron's Reports were correct and described the working state of the Hospital when they were written. 'Doctor Earle's statement was not well founded', and he was asked to withdraw it, for five Assistant Nurses were being employed, but Mrs Suckling was asked to appoint such nurses in future in the same way as she appointed sisters, by reporting the matter to the Committee, and they were not to be sent out on private nursing work, which is what had been happening – 'the Patients of the Hospital were the first call'. There was no suggestion that the patients had been neglected.

Soon afterwards, Matron sent the Committee a letter 'relating to nursing matters'. It was not discussed (its exact contents are not known) and it was sent to the Dispensary Committee, though the subject matter appears to have been the accommodation – or lack of it – for nurses. The remedy, as usual was not action, but yet another Sub-Committee. At this point, the House Surgeon gave in his notice. In May 1894, the Reverend James Baker complained about the admissions and the patients; vagrants were being nursed (contrary to the Rules); worse still, nurses were actually having to look after evil-livers and infidels, but the Chairman replied to this letter himself, and the complaint stopped there, though yet another Sub-Committee was set up to deal with admissions. In June 1894, there was a typhoid scare; the staff's verbal assurances were not enough, and every medical adviser was written to, demanding to know whether or not typhoid was infectious. A unanimous series of replies assured the lay members that typhoid was not an infectious disease. For the next two weeks, the Matron does not seem to have sent a Weekly Report, but the Committee had plenty about which to think.

General Forrest, that tough Chief Constable of Hampshire, had received an anonymous letter making certain allegations; what these allegations were about was not revealed, and it was by no means certain that the letter complained about the Matron. If it did, Forrest probably should have treated the letter with the contempt it deserved, and it is surprising that the Committee decided to investigate it by referring it to the Finance Committee. There was no Matron's report offered at this meeting, nor in the following two weeks, and in the meantime the new House Surgeon was complaining about the drainage, and someone, it is not clear who, was objecting to the fact that sisters were being moved from ward to ward. There will be differing opinions about the wisdom of this, in terms of nursing experience, but Matron was told that it should not happen. Some members of the Committee were clearly looking into nursing matters and, whoever they were, discovered that no Register of Nurses and Probationers had been kept since 1891. Also, illness amongst the nursing staff was not always reported to the House Surgeon or to the Matron. At this stage, Miss Powell, the Housekeeper, resigned. It was midsummer, there was probably not a refrigerator in the place, and there were complaints about bad soup. It was Mrs Suckling who was told to pay particular attention to the quality of the provisions. The week after (1 August 1894), it is hardly surprising that she sent in her report book without any current entry. Bad soup could have had dreadful results, but her nurses and the probationers were just about to undergo a general examination by Mr Langdon, and he reported favourably on all the staff.

Soon there was a new Housekeeper, Miss Moor, from Addenbrooke's in Cambridge. Two senior sisters resigned, Sister E. Saunders from the Accident Ward, and Sister E. Cross in Bartlett. Matron went off on a week's holiday, and Miss Moor took over in her absence. When Mrs Suckling came back, the Committee had begun to discuss the consumption of alcohol, alleged to be excessive, and then asked for an explanation from her.[3] They had also to consider the laying of a proposed connection to the main sewer of King Alfred's College, but no one knew if Training College Lane belonged to the Dean and Chapter. It did, and Warner was asked to inquire and report on the matter. The matter continued to be discussed for several weeks but, in the meantime, some one seems to have realised, at last, that Mrs Suckling had too much to do and, on 19 October 1894, some of her duties were placed on the new Housekeeper. It was not much of a relief for, at the very next meeting, the Housekeeper was told that she had to send all her requisitions in to the Matron for Mrs Suckling's approval. On 21 November, the Finance Committee was asked to arrange for a complete inventory of all the Hospital's effects.[4] A professional accountant had recently been called in and, on 5 December, the Chairman told his Committee that he had told Mrs Suckling that she could see the accountant's report, but that she had replied that 'she had no wish to do so'. Christmas passed, and then on 15 January 1895 and 'having regard to all the circumstances of the case', the Committee was told, 'with much regret', that Mrs Suckling ought to be asked to resign. Three days later, Mrs Suckling wrote the briefest communication. 'I hereby resign my office of Matron. E. Suckling.' It was accepted, at once, by the same meeting which heard that a further investigation of the accounts had shown that the Hospital owed Mrs Suckling £50 for monies to which she was entitled but had not claimed.

So ends the story of the second of the two Matrons, the only two Matrons, with whom the Hospital voluntary administrators fell out in more than a century and a half. It has been examined here in some detail, without conclusions, and without some of the vital documents which might provide an answer to some of the questions. What is clear, however, is that there was, at least, some conflict of personalities, and that Mrs Suckling, an experienced woman in the matter of institutional nursing care, had too much to do, and probably much too much interference in her performance of her own duties. Fortunately, the Suckling Papers have survived as a small bundle amongst the Hospital Archives.[5] They are labelled, 'Original Papers concerning the Enquiry into the management of the Hospital by Messrs Edmonds Son and Clover, November and December 1894. Re: Mrs Suckling, the Matron'. The most important document is probably J. Henry Slessor's *Defence of the Matron*, printed privately, 9 December 1894.[6] Slessor had been a member of the Weekly Board for 20 years, and Chairman of the Sub-Committee of Finance, and Treasurer of the Hospital for 10 years, and his account reveals what the Minutes do not, that the anonymous letter accusing Mrs Suckling had almost certainly been written by a servant of the Hospital discharged by her for misconduct, and known to bear ill-will to the Matron: 'When the letter was put into my hand, I said it ought to be put into the fire'. The Chairman had never told Mrs Suckling that her accounts were being investigated, and that the investigation would cover a period of three years. 'It does not follow that because an accountant is familiar with figures he is an expert on Hospital Management. It reads like the report of men resolved beforehand on bringing about her dismissal in any case.' Slessor described in detail the procedures which Mrs Suckling had followed in her care for the Hospital's money, and her scrupulous honesty in always paying over to him any monies sent her by grateful patients. It was he who wrote to Thomas Kirby, the College Bursar, pointing out that in fact the Hospital owed Mrs Suckling certain monies, and Kirby in turn wrote to Warner, suggesting 'that the matter could be settled without re-opening the account'.

It was obviously a controversial and unfortunate business, and one which did neither the Hospital nor the Matron any good. Perhaps it needs to be seen as the kind of unfortunate matter which might arise from the new status of nurses and matrons. Mrs Suckling must have read Miss Nightingale's *Notes on Nursing: what it is and what it is not*; and Miss Nightingale had believed that the work of nurses depended on the standard set by the Matron, and 'no good ever came of anyone interfering between the head of a nursing establishment and her nurses'. Nurses were not to be passive, devoted and obedient; 'Consider how many women there are who have nothing to devote'. It was very unlikely that the Hospital's long history would never include at least one incident of conflict between a trained matron and a governing Committee of laymen.

The resignation of Mrs Suckling was certainly not the end of Colonel Portal's problems. The drains were still a cause for anxiety, a Special Committee was set up in 1896, and, at last, in January 1897, the Governors accepted its recommendation (and that of Doctor Corfield, M.D.) that the Hospital main drains should 'join up to that of the City of Winchester'. The work appears to have been entrusted to a firm of architects, Salters and Adams, and the Secretary, Major Edward J. Bigg-Wither, yet another retired officer. He resigned through ill-health in May 1898, and was succeeded by a well known local personality, Thomas Kirby. The Drainage Committee of 1896 was contemporary with another Special Committee set up on 15 April to consider the method of appointing physicians and surgeons in other well known hospitals. Its terms of reference, even today, seem slightly tactless, though to be fair to the Governors not all the appointments made in the past had proved brilliantly successful, and there had been much reliance on personal recommendation, the old boy network. The Governors wanted to increase the number of Consultants from four to six, but the staff 'did not want a stranger to the place and neighbourhood'. At the end of October 1897, when there were 208 in-patents and 302 out-patients, the matter was coming to a climax, and on 9 March 1898 all the medical staff resigned, en-bloc, at the news that a certain Cyril Wace had been elected as Surgeon by 29 votes out of thirty-nine. Wace was a brilliant Londoner, and the opposition was led from Northgate House by T.C. Langdon, the Senior Consultant, he who had once been described as meek and mild. The letter, signed also by R. Margerson, W.M. Harman, and C. Fuller England, was accompanied by an assurance from Langdon that he and his colleagues would continue working till new arrangements could be made. In the event, the crisis, though sharp, was short-lived, and on 28 April all the resignations were withdrawn, Wace was accepted as a colleague, and it was his skill as a surgeon which did so much to help the Hospital through the Great War.

At the end of 1899, the Chairman resigned after a term of nearly seven years. He was succeeded by Colonel Heathcote. The next year there was a new Matron, Miss A.H. Gwyn, of the County Hospital in York, and in 1902, a Wickham was back on the staff with the appointment of the Reverend P.R. Wickham as Chaplain. When Langdon himself resigned at the end of 1903, his successor was Herbert James Godwin,[7] and early in the next year the Governors agreed for the first time to take in certain military patients. When the Matron's post was advertised at the end of 1904, there were 51 applicants. Emily Carpenter Turner's appointment completed

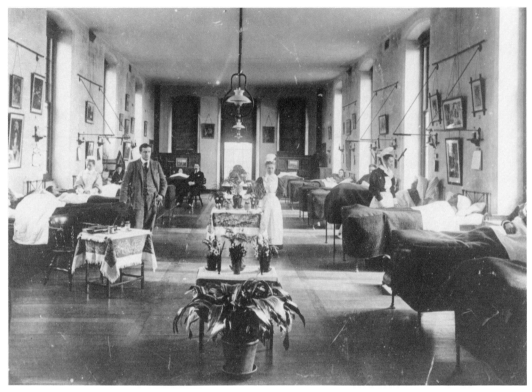

12. A ward in the Hospital, *c.*1895.

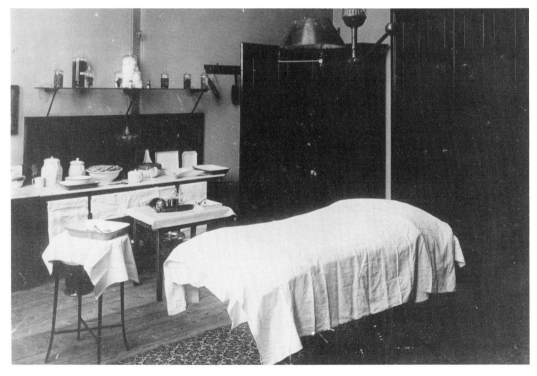

13. The operating theatre, *c.*1896.

the band of colleagues who took the Hospital into what was to prove the dangerous new century.

The change of all changes, which seemed to mark the end of an era, was the death of Queen Victoria, the Hospital's Royal Patron, and the Governors' resolution of respectful sympathy to the King and the royal family was duly recorded in the Governors' Minutes of 13 February 1901.

The nurses of the County Hospital had long been held in high esteem in Hampshire, ever since the days of the Founder, but it was Sir William Heathcote's admiration for Florence Nightingale, and his insistence that the nurses who were to work in Romsey Road should all have a Nightingale training, which did so much to enhance the reputation of the Hospital in the second half of the 19th century. In November 1855, when the Hospital was still in Parchment Street, a public meeting in London, chaired by the Commander-in-Chief of the British Army, the Duke of Cambridge, had inaugurated the Nightingale Fund for the training of nurses; Miss Nightingale was still in Scutari but, when the Crimean War came to an end and she was back in England, the important decision was taken to set up a nursing school in St Thomas' Hospital. It was here that Miss Freeman had been sent to the temporary building at Stoke Newington, and by 1868 all the nursing staff had been sent in turn for this training. One of the main objects was for these trained nurses, generally known as sisters, to train others in their own hospitals, and 'probationer' nurses began to make their appearance, as did 'assistant' nurses. At this time in Winchester, there were several regular day nurses, two regular night nurses, and one assistant; extra nurses were taken on if absolutely necessary, and nurses with spare time stayed in the Hospital and were sent out to attend to private cases. The trained nurses owed much to the formidable Mrs Wardroper, Superintendent for 27 years at the Nightingale Training School. Her trainees lived in, worked on the wards of St Thomas', and were paid from the Nightingale Fund, and started as 'probationers' or 'paying probationers'. It has been said that one of the most revolutionary aspects of the scheme was the positive mandate, that the entire control of a nursing staff must be taken out of the hands of men and belonged in those of a woman.[8]

Improvements in nursing, the emergence of a class of trained professional nurses, followed some of the most important medical discoveries of all times, in particular, the use of anaesthetics; chloroform was made reputable even in childbirth by the example of Queen Victoria.[9] Lister's work on antibiotics revolutionised surgery, the vacillus of typhoid was discovered in 1880, that of tuberculosis in 1882, and of diphtheria in 1884. It took time for these new ideas to win general approval, and for the experiences and expedients of war-time surgery to affect the routine of civilian surgeons. After the dreadful siege of Paris in the Franco-Prussian War, a new English Hospital was set up in the French capital, and trained nurses from Winchester were asked for in 1874.

During Miss Freeman's time, the usual number of trained nurses at the Hospital was eight; they had board and lodging, and by 1879 were getting a salary of £29 5s. 0d. a year. Miss Freeman received £80 per year. The prestige of individual hospitals depended very much on the standard set by the Matron and applied to her nurses. Winchester nurses were highly regarded, but Miss Nightingale, fearful of standardisation, was opposed to any form of state recognition, or registration;

although the Medical Act of 1858 allowed women to register as medical practitioners, it was a long time before Parliament permitted nurses to be registered. Indeed, although Nightingale nurses were experienced in ward work, not everyone thought that nurses needed theoretical training, or that they should attend lectures. There were even nurses (not in Winchester) who had to be taught to read and write. The lectures on surgery given in the Hospital by Langdon in 1882, and on medicine in 1884 by Doctor Beresford Earle, were of considerable importance. They enhanced the reputation of the nursing staff, and encouraged the demand for private nurses, R.H.C.H. trained.

In 1886, a new building was provided as a dormitory block for private nurses and much of the credit for this part of the Hospital's work must go to Mrs Suckling. In 1888, prizes were given to the three best private nurses, and another step forward was taken when the Hospital joined the newly-formed British Pension Fund for Nurses, whose President was the Princess of Wales. By this time, the Hospital had built up a sizable fund from its profit on private nursing, and half the Pension Insurance Premium was paid for from this fund. The in-Hospital training of nurses had come to stay, under Mrs Suckling's successors, Miss Mary Mocatta (1895-1901) and Miss Gwynn (1901-5). Courses of lectures were a regular part of the household's routine, and the Annual Nurses' Prize-giving a joyful celebration, held at first outside the Hospital, at Malshanger, the home of the Committee Chairman. The part played by the Hospital in the Hampshire community as a whole had become important to all strata of society, and the demand for private nursing and for the services of private nurses continued to increase. By 1911, the Hospital's income from private nursing had reached £1,575.

By that time, the profession as a whole had helped to create the Central Committee for the State Registration of Trained Nurses, and the College of Nursing was now in favour of a nationally-recognised registration. The war of 1914-18 really determined the matter and, in 1919, the Nurses Registration Act created the S.R.N., the State Registered Nurse. By that time, Emily Carpenter Turner was Matron of the Hospital, a post she had held since she arrived from Leicester in 1905. Hardly had the new Matron arrived, than a flood of criticism was aimed at the Hospital and its alleged extravagances. It was left to the *Hampshire Observer* to answer the critics, in a thoughtful leader which began with the words 'If we were asked to select a series of subjects for articles under the heading "Unknown Winchester", the Royal Hampshire County Hospital would be amongst the first.' The Hospital was 'that great and noble institution which is such an ornament to the landscape of Winchester's West Hill', and the writer went on to refute the allegations made against its administrators. Last year, 1907, the deficit was £907 6s. 1d.; in 1906 it had been £1,128; in 1905, £1,600. In 1905, the average cost for in-patients per day had been 3s. 7d.; in 1906 it was 4s. 0d.; in 1907, 3s. 9d. The small ward used for children had recently been re-papered, for the first time since 1867. No money was being wasted on alcoholic liquors. The expenditure on strong drink was 8s. 4d. per bed per year, and each bed, on the average, was being occupied three times a year. Malt liquors were not given to patients on any occasion, and in 1867 they alone had cost £139. There was no extravagant use of medicine or surgical dressings; the case was quoted of a woman patient recently admitted with terrible burns; her bandages alone had cost £25. Another woman patient was being given medicine three times a day, at a cost of six shillings a dose. These sums were trifles, compared with their effect, the saving of life. Moreover, the Hospital produced many of its own vegetables and, finally, 'fresh air is the only commodity the use of which may be called extravagant'.

XI The Hospital And The First World War: The Thirties

The outbreak of war in August 1914 did not find the Hospital in a happy financial situation and, moreover, the Management Committee were at once aware of the problems and practicalities of the situation. When it met on 5 August, the usual routine reports were considered, and a long report from a Sub-Committee on the whole question of the prescription of alcohol '... in the treatment of in-patients'. It accepted, gratefully, from its Honorary Dental Surgeon, Mr L.M. Balding, his offer of flowering shrubs to be planted along the new iron fence on the Romsey Road frontage. The war made its first appearance in the Minutes of this meeting when members decided not to hold the Annual Ball in January 1915, and when, 'in view of the present state of the financial world', the Treasurer was asked to consult the Bank Manager about possible rates of interest on the current overdraft. It was unwelcome news that the contractors supplying groceries had already written to say they could not fulfil their contracts 'in view of the unsettled state of the nation'. Miss Carpenter Turner had cut short her annual holiday 'voluntarily', and she was now told to order an ample supply of hospital dressings, and to recall all nurses whose leave had already extended to one week's holiday. The New Block building was indefinitely postponed.

The Minutes, though as impersonal as ever, breathed a spirit of uncertainty, combined with a feeling of anticipation and strong sense of urgent duty. The Dispenser, Mr Joyce, offered to give up his annual leave, the Honorary Consulting Surgeon, Mr Cyril Wace 'had placed his services at the services of the Committee in case of emergency', and Mrs Gould, Commandant of the Voluntary Aid Detachment of the Red Cross Society No.34, had written to ask if she might spend some time on the wards to gain nursing experience. That request was granted, and the V.A.D.s became a familiar part of the war-time scene in Winchester, and of the Hospital in particular.

A War Emergency Committee was set up, its Members being the Chairman, the Treasurer, W.D.F. Sergeant, and Captain Mitchell, R.N., and the Members of the Honorary Medical and Surgical Staff; but even in this Hospital, in a garrison city, there can have been few men or women as yet able to realise what was to lie ahead for the nation.

As the early months went on, the old administrative routine continued. Committees were, usually, very well attended. It was decided not to alter the working arrangements; the efforts of successive Mayors of Winchester were very helpful, and one member of the Committee produced a new contributory plan which wiped out the deficiencies.[1] It was another kind of problem, the nursing staff, which placed a considerable burden on the Matron. One Sister went off to Paris to nurse there, two nurses were warned that they would soon be needed to serve with the Territorials. These three experienced women could only be replaced by two Probationers and one

Red Cross nurse. The Matron was having to deal, too, with a large number of enthusiastic V.A.D.s who had to be told that they must make their own sleeping arrangements, and pay for their meals eaten in the Hospital. Nor were they permitted to wear the Hospital Nurse's Badge, that sign of professional qualification designed by Miss Carpenter Turner. The Hospital, too, were not dealing only with enthusiastic volunteers; other important authorities, like the War Office, began to have a say in its affairs. The War Office was explaining that it might need some of the services of the Honorary Medical Officers. The Head Porter, Gamble, was called back as a Naval Reservist, and Mrs Gamble was told she might stay on in the Lodge, and her husband's service pay was made up to his usual wage, 25 shillings a week. The temporary House Physician went off to India, and the House Surgeon offered to do his work as well as his own. Perhaps with the advent of soldiers in mind, smoking was now allowed in the male surgical ward. There were, as yet, no casualties from the Front, but H.Q. at Salisbury wrote to enquire how much the Hospital would require per man, per day, offering three shillings. The Committee settled for three shillings and eight pence, and 'other classes' of military patients cost six shillings, under an existing agreement with the War Office. There were occasional false alarms, telegrams sent by military hospitals (Netley and Queen Alexandra) announcing the arrival of casualties who did not appear. The Hospital's only ambulance (horse-drawn) was borrowed by the Hampshire Automobile Club, whose members were acting as voluntary drivers for the moving of wounded soldiers. Whilst these early weeks were hurrying by, the new balconies on the south side of the main building were being completed. Miss Nightingale would not have approved, but the hitherto anonymous donors, Mr and Mrs Cholmondeley of Preshaw Park, eventually allowed their names to be commemorated by a suitable plaque.

Then, at last, the first military patients began to arrive. Offers of beds and bedding had already begun to come in and the Emergency Committee agreed, without hesitation, to provide 15 beds for French and Belgian soldiers. Military hospitals needed to pass on some of their cases, though it was difficult for everyone when a warning telegram arrived, and not the expected ambulances.

Different aspects of the story of these difficult years appear not only in the Minutes of the War Emergency Committee, but also in the records of the Building Committee and of the Special Staff Committee, as well as in the small committees set up *ad hoc*, for specific purposes, like the Hut Committee of 1917, consisting of Lady Portal, L. Keyser, Charles Warner, C.W. Oddie, Doctor Bodington, Doctor England and Mr H.I. Godwin. It was usually this Committee which first heard of some of the problems which arose from the large number of service patients, and from the difficulties of running a Hospital staff which included professional nurses and an increasing number of eager, inexperienced and sometimes undisciplined volunteers. In April 1917, Lady Portal made 'various suggestions' about the nurses working in the huts, and the matter was referred to the Nursing Committee, who were asked to define the duties of the V.A.D.s. Women had become very important indeed, and there was even a woman R.M.O., Miss Madin.

It was L.B. Keyser, as Treasurer, who was able to report, on 2 September 1916, that the Hospital was actually free from debt. Next month, when Canon Vaughan preached the Sermon for the St Luke's Day Festival, he said 'It would be interesting

14. Miss Mocatta and her nurses, 1895-1905.

15. Emily Carpenter Turner, Matron 1904-24.

and it would not be uninstructive to trace the history of our Hospital ... Hospitals today are one bright spot in the colossal and overwhelming warfare'. He was talking to a congregation who understood personal loss on a horrific scale, not just to people whose understanding of death was limited to their varied experiences in the County Hospital. The Hospital's reputation stood deservedly high, and there were many and widespread efforts to improve its finances, and above all, to help care for the soldiers who made up such a large proportion of its patients. On Military Hospital Pound Day, on 9 June 1917, there were some 150 military patients being cared for in three temporary huts on the lawn; the Burrell Hut, given by Miss Burrell, was furnished and decorated in pink, the Bluebell Hut's decorations do not need describing, but the Blighty Hut's colour scheme was green. Each patient had his own cupboard, there was a separate Mess or Dining Hut, and the Board Room in the main building had been turned into a Recreation Hall for convalescent patients, where there was a piano, and bagatelle and billiard tables. Everything was under the control of the Hospital, with the assistance of Lady Portal, who was the Resident Commandant of the V.A.D. nurses.

In the same year, 1917, there was an August Bank Holiday Fête in the grounds of Winchester College; a great success. About two hundred visitors were taken round the buildings by Herbert Chitty (the College Steward and Archivist), and J.C. Warner. The indefatigable Mr Keyser was selling 'Artistic buttons' at sixpence each, all of them decorated with a view of the Hospital, and the enormous success of the day's activities brought in £1,785.

The volume which contains the Minutes of the War Emergency Committee for 1917 and of the various Sub-Committees is thin, in comparison with others; and it seems certain that some pages have been torn out.[2] Early in April, a Sub-Committee of four, including Lady Portal, was set up to consider the work of the Laverstoke Red Cross Section, though, at the end of the month, the hours of service of V.A.D.s was left to Matron, Doctor England and Doctor Godwin. Lady Portal's suggestions about those nursing staff in the huts were referred to the Nursing Sub-Committee. Apart from the V.A.D.s and their problems, almost the only other thing discussed was the addition to the mortuary, which Norman Nisbitt, then Architect to the Dean and Chapter, was asked to reduce in area.[3] In July the difficulties concerning the V.A.D.s came to a head at a War Emergency Committee meeting, when Lady Portal produced her list of complaints. The food was insufficient and unvaried; nurses and the Sister in charge went on leave without Lady Portal being told, and Matron should remove nurses who were not satisfactory.

There is only a hint of the discussion which followed. Doctor Godwin said there was too much rice pudding, and the Secretary pointed out that Sister Ireland was greatly overworked; amongst other duties, she was carving the meat each day for some 240 patients' dinners, and then for the Second Dinner for the Staff. The only resolution agreed was that all messages from and to the military authorities must be sent through the Secretary's Office but, in the next month, the Building Committee ordered urgent improvements to lavatories and bathrooms and, in late July, after more complaints about food, the Medical Committee was asked to draw up a diet for military patients. What the Minute Book calls 'A Meeting' was held in the Hampshire County Club on 2 August 1917, attended by the County Director of the

Red Cross and Messrs. Warner, Keyser, Godwin, and Colonel Corkery, and this meeting decided that Lady Portal be asked to report any complaints brought to her to the Matron; 'it was not considered desirable that she should herself inquire into them', and those present expressed the most friendly feelings towards Lady Portal 'in her arduous work for the Military Patients'. When the Special Staff Committee met in October, Miss Carpenter Turner was asked her opinion about those suggested new appointments of an Assistant Matron, a Cook Housekeeper, and a Super-intendent of Staff of the Laundry and Domestic Servants, and she was asked to short-list three suitable applicants for the job of Cook-Housekeeper. The behaviour of the V.A.D.s living in the Golf House was a worry to her.[4] Lady Portal, to quote the Minutes, now 'admitted her reponsibility of the good behaviour and welfare of V.A.D. Nurses living in the Golf House'. The Matron was now told that she alone was to choose the Assistant Matron and the Superintendent of Laundry, and that the posts would be reconsidered once the war was over. It was not the end of her difficulties; it was very hard to get Probationers, the Committee knew that the nurses' hours were far too long, and food was a problem. Miss Carpenter Turner asked for definite instructions 'as to meat and bread', and civilian rations were fixed at 10 ounces of meat per day for males, three ounces for females, with 12 ounces of bread for all patients. The scale was almost immediately revised; men civilians were allowed eight ounces of meat daily, all women were to have five ounces, all rations 'inclusive of bone', and with no allowance for waste.

In the autumn of 1917, convalescent soldiers took on gardening work, and put the paths around the Hospital into order. A large new mess room was erected on the site of an older building, and Lady Portal was complaining that she could not find billets for her ladies. 'Matron said she had done all she could to help', but some further accommodation was offered by Mrs Pearce, and Lady Portal went to view it. There were now even more serious problems. When the W.E.C. met on 20 November 1917, Doctor Godwin revealed that he had been asked by Colonel Corkery to take in 60 extra wounded soldiers, making a total of 210 beds in occupation, and he added that Matron, to do this, would need two more trained Day Nurses, one extra Night Nurse, one extra Theatre Nurse, one extra Masseuse, four V.A.D. Day Nurses, and two V.A.D. Night Nurses. He ended by asking if the kitchen and the laundry could cope with all the additional work. With the instant generosity that was typical of her, Lady Portal offered to provide an extra hut or huts and, by 30 November, Miss Burrell had sent a cheque for £800, and Lady Portal guaranteed another £1,000, but these were voices of caution raised in December. 'Mr Keyser could not support the scheme', and Lord Northbrook had sent a letter, the contents of which were not recorded in the Minutes.

On 1 March 1918, Lady Portal wrote an unselfish letter of resignation. The immediate cause of this was that the War Office was now offering all Hospitals 4s. 9d. a day for every bed used by a service patient, as well as six pence for every empty bed. The rate would secure an income of £3,000 annually for the Hospital, twice the worth of the work of Lady Portal and her V.A.D.s. The Committee was very reluctant to accept this resignation, but it wanted to claim the full grant from the War Office. Some measure of compromise was reached between the Committee and Doctor Lockhart Stevens, who wantd nothing to do with the V.A.D. nurses. There were to be 163 Red Cross beds, for which he was not to be responsible, and 176 Hospital beds, including those for military cases. West Hill Lodge was to be placed at the disposal of the Matron, for the use of the Hospital staff, and £200 was to be spent on it with the assistance of Mrs Barrow Simonds. Matron was to carry out Army Regulation No. 159 as to the diet of her military patients.

The Emergency Committee Minutes do not continue until after the end of the war, and the next entry is for 5 June 1919, a meeting attended by Matron, at the request of the Committee, and by Noel Hanbury, the County Director of the Red Cross. It was announced that Lady Portal and Miss Burrell intended to present their Huts to the Hospital, 'with the wish that they should be used for the treatment of Discharged Disabled Sailors and Soldiers'. There were unanimous votes of thanks all round, particularly warm for the personal services of Lady Portal and the members of her family, and to Sisters Torry and Docherty, and all the V.A.D. nurses.

The Committee of Management had met on 18 December 1918, when the total balance at the Hospital's two banks amounted to £2,170 8s. 7d.; the immediate bills which had to be paid came to £2,599 16s. 2d. The cost of administering the Hospital over the war years appears to have risen by some 348 per cent, but the state of the Hospital's finances was not the only standard of change. There was peace, but not perhaps general forgiveness, and a request that interned enemy aliens from Portsmouth might be admitted as in-patients was briskly refused. The war was over, and when the Special Staff Committee met on 14 January 1919, Miss Carpenter Turner was present and the Hospital was beginning to return to its civilian role; 160 beds were available for civilian patients, and Matron needed a total of 56 nurses for their care, irrespective of the patients still in huts, and 12 private nurses working in the Hospital. Accommodation for nurses was the problem. Four rooms previously used by Sisters in the main building had been given to the Hospital's domestic staff, and an offer (from Miss Sunderland Lewis) of a house in West End Terrace was gratefully accepted.

There were other acts of great personal generosity; the particular connection between the Hospital and the owners of the Hursley estate and its great house had begun in the days of the Founder when the first Baronet, Sir William Heathcote, had persuaded Clarke to sit for that portrait which still adorns the Hospital's Board Room. It was a connection which became close in the days of the fifth Baronet, another Sir William, and was strengthened still further in the years of the First World War. After Sir William died in 1881, the Dowager sold the estate, and eventually, in 1902, Hursley passed to George Cooper, who had been a solicitor in Scotland and who had a wealthy American wife. Their generosity was tremendous, as was the welcome which they offered to vast numbers of serving soldiers of the 8th and 28th Divisions who camped in the Park. The entire second floor of the house was 'offered for use as a Hospital'; the top floor became a hospital for wounded officers, and in 1917, an American Military Hospital was erected near Standen Farm; it could take 450 patients and at the end of the war, the Coopers gave their Hursley X-Ray plant to the Hospital. In turn, the old plant was to be given to the Basingstoke General Hospital.[5] Much later, in 1940, Hursley's owner, by this time Sir George, died; he was succeeded by his son, Captain Sir George Cooper, who soon became the Chairman of the Board of Governors, and whose service to the Royal Hampshire County

Hospital was to last for more than 20 years. Hursley was once more offered as a Hospital, but almost at once it was requisitioned for Vickers Aviation Ltd, who had lost their premises in Woolston through enemy action.

Mrs Preston Joy, of 10 The Close, gave £500 to endow a bed in memory of her late husband and as a 'thank-offering for peace', and Miss Burrell of Fairthorne Manor, near Botley, sent £1000 as a 'thank-offering for victory'. There were problems of personnel. One of the first resignations was that of the Chaplain, Mr Slater, who was really working in London, unavoidably, and with Hospital permission at St Mary Abbots. Another devoted servant, the Hospital's engineer, Mr R. Riquier, died, and the need to raise the salaries of probationers, at least to the same standard as those of the staff of the 'Royal Berks' in Reading, had to be considered. In any case, there was still a serious lack of accommodation for nurses and, as an emergency step, the house offered in nearby West End Terrace had been accepted. The real problem, as usual, was money.

By the end of March 1919, the Hospital had dealt with 1,394 civilian patients and 1,395 military cases. In May, J.C. Warner retired, and was presented with a French marble clock, and in July, the long-delayed new Maternity Department was opened, on the second floor; it faced south and was called Florence Portal Ward. Thre was no doubt that the Hospital's reputation had been greatly enhanced by its war-time record, and in particular by the varied activities of Leonard Keyser, J.C. Warner, and Emily Carpenter Turner. Keyser, the Treasurer, was particularly far-sighted; a preparatory school master by profession, working at West Downs, in Romsey Road, it was he who produced the Hospital's Contributory Scheme and, from the very first, he understood the need to explain his ideas to the Winchester Labour Party and to the Winchester and District Trades Council. *The Hospital: the Workers' Newspaper of Administrative Medicine* had been successfully established as a small magazine selling at two pence a time, and in No. 1780, Volume LXVIII for 13 July 1920, it put forward Keyser's scheme, printing his address to the Winchester and District Trades and Labour Council. His audience were unanimous in their enthusiasm for the idea, and a Committee was formed to assist the Hospital Authorities. Keyser had suggested that, for every £1 earned, a penny should be given to the Hospital, or a general flat rate of two pence a week, which he had calculated would bring the Hospital in £2,000 a year. 'If you will support us when you are well, we will care for you when you are sick.'

In effect, this is what eventually happened, and the income from contributions proved to be a blessing indeed. In 1920 and 1921, the Bank were getting very alarmed at the size of the Hospital's overdraft, beyond its limit of £2,500, and something simply had to be done besides the depositing of Hospital title deeds and share certificates as additional collateral. Wards had to be closed. Keyser wrote to *The Times* in a letter of 31 May 1921, pointing out how disastrous things were for the voluntary hospitals; some London hospitals had had to shut wards and he felt that a Contributory Scheme was the only solution. Eventually, it was adopted in Winchester. Free treatment for every workman and his family was offered in return for a contribution of sixpence a week, and there were appropriate scale charges for small traders, beginning with as litle as £1 11s. 0d. a year. By 1937, the scheme was producing half the Hospital's annual income but, by 1944, receipts had fallen and only paid for almost half the cost of administration. By the time that the fund was wound up, in 1948, no less a sum than £400,000 had been contributed.

In May 1921, Doctor Fuller England retired; he had been Physician for 24 years at the Hospital and in his farewell speech he paid a handsome tribute to his medical colleagues. He had seen the rise in a new era of surgery, for which 'full credit must go to Mr Wace', whose skills were now being carried on by Mr Godwin, Doctor Child and Mr Roberts. The medical work of the Hospital had been extended in many more directions. There were excellent Ophthalmic Departments, X-Ray Departments, a Pathological Department and provision for maternity patients, partly maintained by the Hampshire County Council. He was retiring from a 'self-contained Hospital', with an excellent and efficient Secretary, Herbert Maslen. Soon there were other changes on the staff, most notably the arrival of a new young surgeon, who was to become one of Winchester's most distinguished servants; a master of his craft and eventual Chairman of the County Magistrates. The late Mr James Troup most kindly sent the writer his personal recollections of what the Hospital was like when he joined the staff in September 1924:

'The staff of the hospital at that date consisted of three Surgeons, three Physicians, a Radiologist and a Pathologist. Two of the Surgeons and the three Physicians were all in general practice and their appointment to the hospital was honorary.

'The resident medical staff consisted of a Resident Medical Officer at £200 a year, one House Physician and one House Surgeon each paid at the rate of £100 a year. The appointments were for six months when there were no paid holidays, but after six months they were entitled to a fortnight's holiday to be taken when convenient to the Hospital Management Committee.

'The administrative staff consisted of a Secretary, Finance Officer and a Shorthand/Typist Secretary.

'The accommodation was five Wards, all in the main building, the Children's Ward being on the top floor which also contained the Chapel, the Operating Theatre and the Pathological Laboratory. There was a small Maternity Ward of six beds and a Labour Ward. The physician on duty for the week was responsible for the maternity work if the Resident Medical Officer required any help.

'The porter's lodge at that time was used for puerperal sepsis. It was always staffed with agency nurses and was under the control of the Medical Officer of Health for the County, but the patient care was the responsibility of the Resident Medical Officer, the Medical Officer of Health taking no part in the clinical care of the patient.

'There was an X-Ray and massage department housed in what were the stables of the honorary staffs' carriages with slight modifications. There was a hospital ambulance driven by the head porter.

'The out-patients were housed in the basement of one room which was divided by sliding doors. There were two clinics held per week, one for surgical patients and one for medical patients, and a V.D. clinic on a Saturday afternoon run by the Health Authorities.

'Children's tonsils and adenoids were dealt with as out-patients in the same accommodation. The children were brought to the hospital at 8 o'clock, they were then operated on and carried across the garden to a corrugated iron hut which was a relic of the 1914-18 war. There they waited until about 4 o'clock in the afternoon when the parents came and fetched them home by taxi.

'There was a second hut of the same vintage which was used for storage of anything not affected greatly by water as the roof leaked and the floor was non existent.

'The Residents had another corrugated iron hut also in the garden with no heating in it. The Residents also had a sitting-room which overlooked the front courtyard.

'Dangerous drugs were kept in a cupboard in the Resident's sitting-room and were issued each morning at 9 a.m. by the Resident Medical Officer.

'Miss Carpenter Turner was then the Matron and on the evening of my arrival I was sent for and told I would read the Lesson in the Chapel the following Sunday. That I never did.'

When the General Nursing Council was formed in 1916, it had been Emily Carpenter Turner who was asked to draw up the first syllabus for nurse training, accepted with little alteration, and she also encouraged her nurses to become State Registered. As soon as the war was over, a Preliminary Training School for Nurses was set up at Winchester; the first Sister Tutor was Miss Thornton Down. In 1925, the year of the first State Examination, all the Winchester candidates were successful, but there was more to nursing than the passing of examinations. A good nurse was self-disciplined, according scrupulous procedure to her seniors (opening doors, standing aside in corridors, etc.) and always dressed in an impeccably clean uniform. After three months' trial, and an interview with Matron, the successful candidate was given her dress material, and strict instructions for making it up. 'Skirts gathered to the waist to clear the instep, a four-inch hem, and three half-inch tucks. Bodices fitting and lined with calico, long plain sleeves to the wrist, fastened with four white bone buttons, upstanding collar at the neck, and stiff linen collar about three inches deep; also stiff linen cuffs about four inches deep. Big white aprons almost covering the skirts all round,with bib fastened with straps crossing at the back. First year, a stiff belt of navy cotton; second year, striped belts of same material as dress; third year, white belt, and strings to new caps.'

The layout of the Hospital was still basically what it had been in Butterfield's time, that is to say all the wards were in the main building, with the one operating theatre, a small dispensary, and a Pathological Laboratory. Next to Victoria Ward, on the first floor, was the Gordon Room, with two beds, used for sick nurses. In the main building, two small rooms (the Lavender and the Vyne) were available for private, paying patients. The three war-time huts, Bluebell, Burrell and Blighty, were still in use, on the 'lawn', and the Probationer nurses slept in Beatrice Hut, near the Preliminary Training School. Work began at 7:00am and continued till 8:30pm (four hours off duty). Compulsory Chapel at 9:00pm, after supper, meant a walk of 103 stone steps from the Dining Room. In the first year of training, nurses received £20, rising to £40 in the fourth year, and the staff had to buy their own uniform and text book, and pay their own fees for the State Examinations. Much time had to be spent on cleaning the wards and one ... nurse has recalled the 'time consuming treatments', four-hourly formentations, anti-phlogistine poultices, tepid sponging, hot packs, and 'the filling of water beds, etc.'.[6] On night duty, the nurses slept on the top floor of

Ashley. A graphic account has survived of what it was like to be a nurse in the Hospital in the 1920s, under Miss Carpenter Turner.[7]

'Each ward had four nurses, as well as Sister (who came on duty at 8:00am); Staff, 'assistant' (a second year nurse) and a junior and senior probationer or 'pro'. Beds were made by the staff and assistant, who also saw to other special jobs. Each 'pro' did the actual work of keeping the side of the ward neat and clean. The ward was swept just before we went on duty by the ward maid. After bedmaking, each side was swept again by the 'pro' in charge.

'The Staff Nurse gave medicines, etc., and attended to other responsible duties, working of course with Ward Sister. The 'assistant' took charge of the centre of the ward, and all its furniture.

'At the end of the ward on one side was the bathroom, looked after by the 'pro' in charge; on the other side, the lavatories, etc. In the bathroom was a slate slab several feet long, in which was sunk a row of four white earthenware basins, with hot and cold taps, for the use of patients who could get up to wash. In the floor just inside the bathroom door was a kind of sink about two feet square, with an upstanding rim about four to six inches high, and half or three quarters of an inch thickness. The centre of this box affair sloped gradually to a strainer, and the whole was covered in zinc or lead. This was for throwing down waste water, and that, and the slate slab with basins had to be cleaned and dried and polished with turps and linseed oil every morning, as well as the basin taps polished. All these things had to be finished in good time, as well as drinks of hot milk taken round to the patients. Sister, nurses and junior and senior pros were each allowed a very few minutes, taken in that order, to get lunch, make their own beds (in the case of nurses), put on a clean apron and get back to the ward for the full business of the day. Our lunch was bread and cheese and milk, in the Dining Room.

'Butter was not set on the table for nurses' meals. A certain small allowance was made to each weekly, and we each kept our ration in some sort of small dish in a cupboard in the Dining Room, and these dishes had to be fished out and replaced for and after meals. We were considered very well fed, only one quality all through – Matron, Doctors, Patients. We were always told by visiting nurses how lucky we were. Also, off-duty on Sundays was the same for all, either from ten am to two pm, or two pm to ten pm. Night nurses got one night off monthly. Every Sunday we each had a good big slice of excellent fruit cake for tea, and on Wednesdays a currant bun, the bun the gift of a kind old lady touched by our spartan fare, who left money to provide this. First year nurses got a half day once a month from two pm to ten pm, when we had to hand in a 'Permit' at the office in the hall on our return. We were then allowed supper in bed, brought to us by a friend.

'Second year nurses got off monthly from eleven am to ten pm, and Third Year meant a whole day. If you could fit that in with evening leave the night before, you could sleep out. Each ward had two coal fires placed in the north wall, made up by the nurses. I cannot remember cleaning away ashes, which was probably done by the ward maid before we came on duty. There were also big clumsy hot water pipes near the floor all round the ward. There was also a very old fashioned fireplace in each ward kitchen, where a fire was kept in night and day, as there was no gas ring or any easy way of getting hot water. Every ward had a piano and each patient's locker contained a bible and hymn book. When Sister came on at eight am, prayers were read and a hymn sung – the hymn generally the choice of a patient. They loved this.

'Each week, one half of the ward was polished, the beds drawn across from one side to the other directly after first dinner. The ward maid was off duty in the afternoon, so the junior nurse quickly swept the floor to be polished, and then, starting at the far end, applied the polish from an enamelled bowl, with a lump of old flannel or blanket. The polish was a soft sticky mess of bees wax and turpentine, and the nurse kneeling, wriggled vigorously backwards the whole way to the door. Gambel (The Porter) started as she had done, to work from the far end – polishing/working with what appeared utter casualness, he swung to and fro rhythmically a large square pivoted polisher, very heavily weighted and looking rather like a very stiff scrubbing brush. First he used this thing as it was, and then with a big pad of old flannel or blanket to polish. This frantic and exhausting job could be just managed and the beds back in place in time for the patients' tea. We had twenty minutes for our own tea.

'Night nurses came in at eight pm, but our out of sight jobs were not quite done till supper at eight-thirty pm. Whenever possible, prayers were held at eight pm. After that, the ward was quiet. At nine pm, the gong called us to prayers in the Chapel, said by Matron, and with a hymn. The very good American organ was set at concert pitch. The Chapel was at the top of the building and the sound of the singing, heard downstairs, was lovely. Once a week, the Chaplain came and took a short service at nine pm, and also our male organist. I don't think any of us much enjoyed it because the Chaplain, a shy, elderly single man, was rather given to telling us that we sang as if we were all going to sleep – which was exactly what we were doing. Night nurses had prayers, but no hymn, in Chapel, and taken by Matron before going off duty.

'There was only one night nurse to each ward with an extra, a junior, known as the 'Emergency', who worked each night giving help where it was most wanted. This was a hard job – but usually popular – because you learnt so much. There was not time for a set meal or rest for the night nurse. The last thing the kitchen staff did before going off duty was to go round to each ward kitchen and leave a meal for the night nurse, to be warmed up if she could manage it. Fairly often there might be a rush of work all night, leaving no time for more than a cup of tea.

'All the ward crockery and cutlery was kept in the ward kitchen and washed up by the ward maid. The night nurse had a certain place for her own things. All night nurses kept soft silent slippers for the ward. The kitchen fireplaces were odd, old fashioned things, rather high above the floor, with horizontal bars and hobs forming a kind of oven or hot place underneath. This was shut by an iron door which dropped forward, hinged at the bottom. Tea was made in a large and terribly heavy urn. Patients' meals were served from this kitchen on square, white-painted trays, with white cloths. Plates were piled in front of the fire to get hot for dinner, which sister served from the table. Each patient's fruit was kept in a numbered compartment of a cupboard at the end of the ward, and handed out after dinner.

'The ward kitchen was the only place where patients' friends – staying to be at hand for serious call – could sit and wait. One kitchen was plagued with cockroaches, which performed if and when all was quiet, sometimes sampling the midnight meal if left unguarded on the table, especially if it happened to be a bowl of soup.

'One winter night a very nice elderly vicar of a village a few miles out had brought in a young farm labourer for immediate operation. While this was going on and this good gentleman was waiting, the kitchen chimney took fire and a very big mass of soot rolled down and out on the floor. We were told in the morning how very helpful the visitor had been in dealing with the awful mess. The patient made a good recovery.'

When Miss Carpenter Turner retired from the Hospital in 1924, the occasion was marked by a great presentation party, which followed a Chapel Service. The Chairman of the Governors (the Earl of Northbrook) presided and the platform party included the Mayor of Winchester, Councillor H.P. Vacher, and Charles Warner, who had come out of his retirement to be present on this special occasion. It was he who spoke of Emily Carpenter Turner and her long years of service; never once had the Governors' choice of 1904 been a matter of regret. What he proceeded to point out was the wisdom with which she had controlled both the nursing and domestic staff; 'she possessed the admirable gift of sometimes putting the telescope to the blind eye', and sympathy for others was one of her main characteristics. He spoke particularly of the way in which she managed the young ladies of the Red Cross during the war years, went on to mention her award of the Royal Red Cross at the end of the War. A sum had been collected sufficient to augment her pension for the rest of her life, and then the capital could become available for some other purpose, to be called the Carpenter Turner Fund. Lord Northbrook then presented the retiring Matron with an illuminated book, containing the names of all the subscribers. The speech which she made was typically brief, and simple. On someone who knew her well, and some of her nurses, the impression she made was of an old lady of great courage and with a wicked sense of humour. The stories about her are innumerable. As a young probationer, her father had insisted that she had her own room, for which he paid. Not until she was a Theatre Sister did she tell him that as she got out of bed at 6 a.m. each morning, a night nurse got in. Some of the best of her own stories concerned the arrival of important visitors at her Hospital, the then Prince of Wales giving out violets to patients and kitchen maids, and asking her 'who are these dear little things' when some unexpected faces appeared at the lift entrance in order to see H.R.H. At well over eighty, she could still carry on marvellously interesting conversations, not just about the past, with all kinds of people. She was a really professional person, and someone for whom the so-called generation gap never existed.

It is not possible to chronicle all the modern changes in staff, an ever-increasing number after the end of the First War, but a surgeon who joined a few years before the outbreak of the Second World War has kindly provided his recollections. Mr Cuthbert Roberts writes:

'I was appointed House Surgeon to the Royal Hampshire County Hospital in the spring of 1935, at a salary of £50 a year plus board and lodging.

'*The Honorary Medical Staff* at that time comprised three surgeons and one assistant surgeon, three physicians, one pathologist, one radiologist and one anaesthetist.

'*The Resident Medical Staff* comprised one Resident Surgical Officer, two House Surgeons and one House Physician.

'Most of the anaesthetics at that time were given by the resident medical staff who also had to cover the Casualty Department in addition to their duties in the wards. The Resident Surgical Officer carried out such operations (emergency or otherwise) as were delegated to him by the Honorary Staff, and organised the duties of his fellow

16. Nina, Countess of Northbrook (portrait in the R.H.C.H. after the original by J. S. Sargent).

Residents, but had also to be prepared to lend a hand in the operating theatre (as assistant or anaesthetist) or in Casualty, if the need arose. He was responsible for arranging the admission of patients from the waiting list.

'None of the resident medical staff were allotted any formal off-duty time during their period of office but it was usually possible to go out one afternoon or evening (or both) a week and an occasional weekend by arrangement with one's colleagues.

'There were about 150 beds in the Hospital at that time, all housed in the main block except for the comparatively new Children's Ward, which had been built adjacent to the eastern end of the main block.

'The administration of the Hospital was in the hands of the Matron and the Secretary, of whom the former was the more important; in fact the status of the Hospital was largely dependent upon her. Ward Sisters were also very important people.

'There were six private rooms in the Hospital for which the charge was £4 a week, in startling contrast to the £600 to £800 a week they now cost.'

In 1928, the Governors had elected their first woman Chairman, the Countess of Northbrook, who succeeded her husband, and whose charm and energy made her leadership in 1936 of great importance, for in that year the Hospital celebrated 200 years of its existence. Most of the events were to take place in the summer of 1936 in order to raise money. The appeal was for a total sum of £50,000, a special Appeal Director had been appointed (Mr Harold Gibson) and money came in from all sides. The Winchester Rotary Club organised a car competition, which produced £850, and there was a Winchester Carnival which lasted for four days, despite dreadful weather, and the damping of all the many decorations. There were many distinguished visitors, and the Hospital and the City was graced by the presence of the Duke of Gloucester, who stayed at the *George Hotel*, and the Duchess, who stayed with a member of her family at Shroner Wood. Crowds turned out to see her, despite the awful weather; the Winchester Red Triangle Club playing field was opened at Weeke, and there was an official luncheon at the Guildhall, with the usual plethora of speeches and toasts. Later on in the day – and it was still raining – the Carnival Queen, Doris Frampton, had to be crowned inside the Guildhall, instead of outdoors in the Recreation Ground, and various cheques and vouchers for the Appeal Fund were presented; Winchester citizens had donated, so far, £1,336 16s. 6½d. Miss Grace Treble, that senior member of the R.H.C.H. staff, offered £500 from the Hospital, Sister Thomas represented the Maternity Department (£200), Peter Symonds' School (£100) and the Carnival Queens of the surrounding towns and villages then gave in their districts' donations, totalling £4,633 6s. 10½d.

When the afternoon's proceedings at the Guildhall were finished, the distinguished visitors moved on to the Hospital itself; the Duchess was taken round some of the wards, and amongst those presented were the Matron, Miss C. Parker, the Hospital Secretary, Hubert Maslen, Doctor Wainwright and Doctor Fuller, and Admiral Waistell, whom the Countess of Northbrook had asked to welcome the Duchess, an act of thoughtful kindness on the Chairman's part. The other presentations included that of Reginald J. Harris, the Winchester solicitor who had only recently resigned the post of Honorary Treasurer, through ill health, and Emily Carpenter Turner. Thursday's weather also meant that the Health and Beauty Display and the Carnival Dance had to be held in the Guildhall, and a huge display by Winchester children was postponed until Friday, including dancing and flag waving of semaphore messages. The weather could have ruined everything, and the traffic problems were considerable for, needless to say, in the words of the local press, the difficulties of Winchester's narrow roads were accentuated by road excavations. The Carnival finished with a drumhead service in the Park, at which Canon R.B. Jolly from St Mary's, Southampton, was the preacher, but the Cathedral service itself was the climax of all the activities. Bishop Garbett preached, and the Mayors of Winchester and Andover were present. There was a massed choir, the Dean had written a special hymn, and the Countess of Northbrook and the Lord Lieutenant, Lord Templemore (Chairman of the Bi-Centenary Committee), were amongst the distinguished congregation. After it was over, Canon A.W. Goodman, the Cathedral Librarian, showed a small party, including Lady Northbrook and Admiral Waistell, the List of Subscribers of 1736, kept in the Cathedral Archives and displayed in the Chapter House on this particular afternoon. The same press report which described Winchester's great celebration week also gave the current Hospital statistics. Two hundred years after Opening Day, there were 159 patients in Alured Clarke's Hospital.

 Though the total of the Appeal money took some time to reach, the celebrations of 1936 were an interesting social contrast to those of 1836. Hundreds of people were involved; it was a true celebration of two hundred years of history, by Hampshire people, of their Hospital.

17. Aerial view of the Hospital, 1934.

18. Nightingale Nurses' Home, opened by H.R.H. Duchess of Kent in 1939.

XII The Second World War

1939-1945

The outbreak of war on 3 September 1939 did not find the Royal Hampshire County Hospital unprepared, but it could not hope to escape the uncertainties of the situation.[1] No-one knew what was going to happen, though even that curious person, the man in the street, understood that this was not going to be a war which was likely to be fought in trenches on the other side of the English Channel; there was widespread belief that attack from the air was certain, that it would occur almost at once, and that the effect would probably be devastating. The Hospital had to be prepared to take in large numbers of casualties, for Southampton and Portsmouth were deemed to be at great risk. Even before the Declaration, the Hospital was cleared of every patient except those who were too ill to be moved, and only emergency cases were admitted; the city itself began to fill with evacuees. This preliminary emptying of the Hospital beds was made possible only by much voluntary help, organised by Miss Urmston, and it was that kind of help which was to be of immense value as the war went on and innumerable problems made their inevitable appearance. The whole building had to be sand-bagged, and a rather incomplete black-out attempted. When the Committee of Management met on 6 September 1939, its members were told by the Chairman, still Admiral Sir Arthur Waistell, that only urgent cases were being admitted, that the Hospital had been lent an emergency lighting unit, and that 20,000 sand-bags, out of a total of 75,000, had already been filled under the direction of Brigadier Kemp Welch. They were also told that the auxiliary nurses being drafted in by the Government were going to get more money than the ordinary nurses, and it was decided without discussion that all nurses should get the same rates. Five huts were to be put up without delay 'in the garden, late the lawn', and the Committee agreed to meet only once a month, and to allow the weekly visiting to lapse. The simple fact was that no-one really knew what was going to happen; there might be an invasion or wide-spread attack from the air. In the event, a special meeting had to be called on 10 November 1939 to hear the news that the Matron had had to resign through ill-health; the post was advertised at £300 per annum, and with very little delay Miss Mackay from Glasgow was appointed and took up her duties on 7 February 1940. She was to prove a splendid choice. There were other additions to the female staff, including three telephonists who worked in shifts of eight hours each, thereby releasing the porters for other duties. An early sign of the times was the decision, in December 1939, to issue the Annual Report for 1938 in an abridged form, but it was a curious moment to give up the old tradition of keeping Hospital pigs; no new pig sties could be built for lack of a suitable site, but the rigours of food rationing were not yet apparent.

In fact, the country was still in the period of what has been called the 'phoney war', but a pattern of what were to be recurring problems had begun to emerge; shortage

19. Preparations for war, 3 September 1939.

of staff, shortage of supplies, and the calling up of those who were already in the Hospital's service, not to mention rising prices and what had been for many years a persistent problem, the need to adapt the building to changing situations. Above all, and as usual, there was a shortage of money and, looming dreadfully in the background, the possibility of enemy attack from the air or by invasion.

In April 1940, Doctor Fuller had to report that additional resident doctors were not to be had at a mere £100 p.a., and the posts were readvertised at £175.[2] There was some discussion, too, on the proposed Federated Superannuation Scheme for nurses and hospital staff, and the limit of annual earnings was fixed at £600. The idea, correct in its way, that to serve the Hospital was such an honour that money was a mere secondary consideration, was still current in some circles, and the Committee of Management continued to look for an Honorary Engineer, who was to be made a Governor. There were also problems with catering and domestic staff. None were in what eventually came to be called reserved occupations, and chronic shortages soon developed despite offers of voluntary help. In May 1940, catering was put into the hands of a private commercial company, Mecca Ltd, for a trial period of six months, a decision which proved to be excellent and very successful. Paper was beginning to be in short supply; the April Minutes of the Committee of Management could not be circulated. Some building work went on throughout the War; the building licensing system had not yet been introduced and eventually the Hospital gained some exemptions from that particular restriction. At this stage, there were alterations in the Children's Ward but it was decided that no more private wards were to be provided until the end of hostilities. Directions were beginning to come in fairly fast from the Ministry of Health, and very often meant sudden and unbudgeted expenditure. Large stocks of X-Ray films had to be bought in case of emergency. The X-Ray and massage staff were given a higher rate of pay, £90 p.a., and the scale for resident domestic helpers was also put up – £25 p.a. for under-sixteens, increased to £30 after six months' satisfactory service; over-sixteens got £30 p.a., with an annual increment of three pounds.

In the high summer of 1940, Mr J. Rubin was appointed as the full-time Resident Surgeon and attempts made to find a Surgical Registrar and five House Surgeons 'who need not live in'. At the end of the staff list, two messenger boys were to be engaged, one for the Administration's Office, one for the Out-Patients Department; two were obtained apparently quite easily, and at a rate of 10 shillings per week. All these various rates of pay may seem shockingly low to a modern reader unable to remember the cost of living before 1939, but the gift of £10 from the Mayor's Fund 'for Comforts for Service Patients' was in fact a generous sum; most of the service patients who had been admitted were convalescent soldiers with special privileges, and whose occasional robust behaviour sometimes proved to be what the Minutes called 'distressing' to the civilian patients who were only in this particular Hospital because they were critically ill.

On 14 May 1940, a famous radio broadcast produced what came to be known as the Home Guard. The war was at a critical state, and plans were drawn up to defend central Winchester ('Tank Island'), with the Barracks area as the Citadel, the area of ultimate resistance.[3] The Hospital lay beyond the Citadel and outside Tank Island. By August 1940, it seemed very unlikely that it could escape air attack, though there were as yet no air-raid shelters, until the main basement store was hastily turned into a shelter by the former members of St Paul's Girls Club, working under the direction of a well-known artist, Margaret Niven, and her sister. Winchester College provided volunteers who dug an air-raid shelter near the Nightingale Home, but the work was held up because of the difficulty in getting timber. King Alfred's College was closed down.[4] Its beds and bedding were hastily purchased, and the already over-worked Hospital Porters began their nightly patrols of the Hospital rooves. The unimaginable might be about to happen, and the Hospital might be bombed. Not surprisingly, the Committee of Management accepted with grateful thanks Doctor Mary Capes' offer to assist with psychological cases amongst service patients, though they had to refuse, very reluctantly, Lady Northbrook's generous offer to provide a children's playroom 'because of the needs of the Almoner's Office'. In comparison with the fall of France and the evacuation of the British Army through Dunkirk, and the siege of Calais, matters which were not unimportant in the history of the Hospital must nevertheless have seemed sometimes almost trivial. The Superintendent had had to report that the catering cost, per head per patient, had risen by over 25 per cent since 31 December 1939, when it was one shilling a day, and attempts to give the nurses a 48-hour week proved impossible; they were working 56 to 59 hours per week, and even longer once the nearby bombing of Southampton and Portsmouth produced its horrific results. The work load on nurses, from its very nature, can never be deemed to be light, but the situation was improved when a regular ward routine was established.

On 12 August 1940, Bonchurch Convalescent Home had been damaged in an air-raid and, by the early autumn, a Hospital investment property in Southampton had suffered the same fate. By the first week of September 1940, invasion seemed likely. Soon the Auxiliary Hospital in Hursley Park had to be cleared with less than 24 hours' notice. The main black-out in Winchester was not yet complete and blue lamp bulbs were hastily fitted in the Nurses' Home. The Ministry of Health ordered the medical staff to begin the collection and distribution of blood plasma; two new wards were made available, making the total number of beds 331, of which half might be used for civilian patients, and a second Assistant Matron had to be found because of the extra work. The Hospital garage was cleared of cars for use as a Gas Decontamination Centre, and Doctor Fuller and Doctor Wrigley were directed to make suitable arrangements for the reception of air-raid casualties. On 4 December 1940, the Committee heard that the Royal South Hampshire and Southampton Hospital was 'out of action'. Winchester had suddenly received 102 casualties from this neighbour, which, despite severe damage, had managed to re-open in part after only two days. There were all kinds of rumours about what was happening, and Sir Arthur Waistell found it necessary to write to all the Hampshire newspapers to repudiate one of these rumours, the suggestion that the Royal Hampshire County Hospital had been taken over by the Ministry of Health. It was still a voluntary Hospital, and adapting itself marvellously to the changing situation.

Early in the new year of 1941, it was apparently decided to duplicate the Hospital's archives, in view of the destruction wrought at Southampton, but little progress appears to have been made with that project. Nurses from the Royal South Hants were continuing their training in Winchester whilst repair work was going ahead on their own building. Costs of all kinds were rising rapidly; private patients were soon paying more, and Matron's salary was increased from £300 to £400. The Ministry of Health was getting anxious about the water supply, but the cost of boring for a new independent well was deemed prohibitive.

There were attempts to return to normality; the Committee of Management determined to meet weekly again, and to re-introduce weekly visitors, but these decisions were taken against the knowledge that the main Hospital at Portsmouth had been so devastated that there would be no attempt to rebuild above ground floor level, and that Portsmouth nurses would be trained in Winchester 'for the duration', and that dangerously ill children in Winchester would only be moved from their ward if Mr Rubin himself judged the danger from enemy aircraft to be imminent. By March 1941, the Hospital had agreed to take in the serious casualties from the American Hospital occupying St Swithun's School[5] and, in April, the Ministry of Health gave permission for minor repair work to be done to the wards; all the usual Sub-Committees were re-formed and Sir Arthur Waistell re-elected as Chairman, but the background was more sinister than the short April meeting suggested.

Invasion seemed certain and the alternative possibility had to be considered of moving the Hospital inland, or setting up an emergency Hospital within Tank Island, if, to quote the Minutes of 7 May, 'the enemy were outside the walls'. The Minutes were getting shorter and shorter, very largely because the Emergency Committee, which met once a week, usually on Saturday mornings, was having to take so many *ad hoc* decisions. The situation fluctuated from month to month. June saw the arrival of a 5000-gallon emergency water-tank, a mobile X-Ray unit presented by 'Hampshire U.S.A.', and permission from the Ministry to spend £2,380 on textiles of various kinds. Thre were still some members of the Committee with what might be called old-fashioned ways, and it was necessary to minute a resolution that 'no criticism be made (for the duration) of clerical staff who did not wear stockings', but even the Minutes themselves still bore occasional traces of the distant past, as when it was agreed to take on financial responsibility for the provision of surgical appliances for 'the necessitous poor', or when, later still, the Hospital was discussing with the civic authorities the purchase or erection of what they were still calling a Pest House.

By the end of August 1941, life seemed sufficiently secure for the Committee of Management to resume its twice-monthly meetings and for weekly visiting to begin again. An Executive Committee had been set up, consisting of all Chairmen, that is of the Committee of Management, of the Court of Governors, of the Medical Sub-Committee, and Special Purposes Committee, with the Hospital Treasurer, but in fact there was no real lull in the war. Air-raid casualties were continuing to arrive, in September one of the hard-working Porters fell down the lift shaft and was seriously injured, and Doctor Penny and Mr Everett were expressing their concern about the Hospital's own arrangements in case of air-raids. A difference of opinion arose with Admiral Waistell, and Doctor Penny resigned as 'Gas Officer', though his suggestions for improving the Hospital's A.R.P. were eventually accepted and, of course, he remained on the Hospital staff. Finance was still the nagging problem that it had been since the days of the Founder. Supporters of the Hospital in the surrounding villages were asked to organise Whist Drives, and Eastleigh held a 'Potato Show' and sent in £30. There were arguments with the Winchester Rural District Council about the Ambulance Service; the Ministry of Health never appears to have reimbursed the Hospital promptly for duly incurred expenditure, and civilian patients (never a good financial prospect) were being admitted at an alarming rate. By the end of the year, Admiral Waistell felt it necessary to draw attention to the financial situation.

Few of the Hospital's problems have ever proved to be non-recurrent. The Contributory Scheme was of considerable help with finances, but it was not sufficient to cover real costs; the number of civilian beds was reduced from 210 to 180, and patients who were in the scheme were henceforth to be admitted in the proportion of three contributors to one non-contributor. There were still not enough beds for nurses. Mrs Murray of Twyford House eventually took in 10 nurses, and 43 were sent out to Lainston; both arrangements had to be approved by the Ministry. They were, but for fewer numbers than the Committee had been offered by the respective owners of these two Hampshire houses. The number of Probationers coming into Preliminary Training School had to be limited to 12 or 14; a significant statistic this, since it was based on the supposition that the Hospital was going to survive the War, and contain a total number of 250 beds.

One of the most irritating and surprising small deficiencies was that there was still only one locker to every two patients, and for this the Mayor promised money from his War Fund, and Matron opened her usual Christmas Fund Subscription List. There was some cheerfulness around; Lady Northbrook presented medals to nurses and, in January 1942, the student probationers put on 'Hay Fever'. Mr Rubin's request for an increase in salary could not be met, however, and the Committee was considering selling off some of its War Stock. It was not altogether surprising that even Matron had to have a month's sick-leave.

As soon as problems were solved or partly solved, others appeared. Early in 1941, the Government enforced strict building controls; not more than £100 was to be spent on any one building, but in the event, hospitals were exempted from this requirement which eventually produced so much general hardship. Wards were changed around; Ward 3 took in only military cases. Jubilee was reserved for women surgical cases. Private patients were not to be allowed to use private patients' china, or to have different food, or extra meals, or extra visitors. The Ministry of Health decreed that 10 per cent of all nurses must be available at any time for immediate transfer anywhere if the need arose, and Mr Rubin was given £100-worth of Savings Certificates in lieu of his hoped-for rise, and as a 'Token of Esteem', a not ungenerous gesture in view of the fact that the Management Committee was now proposing to increase the Hospital's overdraft to £50,000 and to place all its marketable securities in Lloyds Bank; at the same time, all the Endowment Fund investments were placed with the Charity Commissioners.

There were increasing signs of Government interest – or what some felt to be interference – in the affairs of the Hospital. In mid-February 1942, it was decreed that, in future, the accounts would be regularly submitted to Government Audit. The number of civilian patients was then 215, instead of the 180 permitted, soap was being rationed (3 oz. a month of toilet soap for each member of staff), and rubber gloves and cat-gut were in very short supply. Soon there were fresh alarms about possible air-raids; convalescent soldiers were required to act as stretcher bearers in the military wards, medical orderlies from the Barracks were ordered to report to the Hospital at once when the alert was sounded. Three new fire pumps were ordered, each of which could be worked by only one person, instead of two using the more conventional stirrup pump. Looking back on these days of war, when so many people were working such long hours, it still seems surprising that there was time and energy to consider the future. At the end of April 1942, the Hospital appointed its first Speech Therapist, Arthur Tolfree, who held a clinic on Thursday afternoons, and a National Committee was beginning to meet to discuss the future suggestions for nurses' salaries. One other small region of change needs to be noted: from 15 April 1942, all Hospital Minutes are in typescript.

In May 1942, the Ministry agreed to release the Hospital from its obligation to take in military patients for one month only from 1 June, and the Committee also discussed the possibility of converting what was then called Ashley House into rooms for private patients, a change which would help financially, but produced problems of where the nurses thus dispossessed might sleep. Maternity patients in 1941 had been paid for by either the County or City Councils. The hardcore, in terms of the Hospital's economic problem, was probably the non-contributory patient admitted as an emergency, unable to pay much – or anything – himself, and not supported by Councils, or the Ministry; the very large waiting list must surely in itself have increased the number of emergencies. The situation was doubly ironical; in April 1942, there was an average of 120 empty beds, but there were widespread rumours that the place was full of air-raid casualties, sleeping two to a bed. Within the building, on the staff, there was clearly an overall sense of determination and an ability to improvise and to survive the endless series of large and small crises which was such a feature of war-time England. In the middle of 1942, the Children's Ward Sister was called up for the Army Nursing Service, and there was a warning that either Doctor Penny or Doctor Robertson would also be called away, though this did not happen. The hydrants and hoses in the Nightingale Home were found to be different from those in the main building, and water leaking into one of the A.R.P. shelters was contaminated with sewage. Yet by the end of June, 265 patients had been taken in from the waiting list, and the 'double banking' of rooms in Nightingale was going ahead, to replace lost rooms for nurses in Ashley.

In early autumn 1942, it was possible for the first time to assess the value of the work of the Hospital Almoner, who produced a Report for the first six months of the year, and was working closely with the Superintendent, Mr H. Ewart Mitchell. Despite the great feeling for voluntary effort, more and more of the Hospital's work was inevitably being handed over to paid administration. The Superintendent had taken over the administration of the Contributory Scheme and the Almoner's Report showed that 572 contributors had been admitted, as compared with 183 non-member patients. Additional payments were usually required from all in-patients. In 1942, the sum was 3s. 7d. per day, compared with 2s. 1d. in 1941. This apparently dull collection of statistics must have been of great value to the Committee, if only to emphasise the rise in costs, and, despite the relative smoothness of the administration, there was still the occasional crisis. By 24 August 1942, the Hospital had been left with only one stoker; all the others had been called up and, though replacements were found, the whole Hospital could well have come to a standstill. Just how much the Hospital owed to the Superintendent and the Matron cannot be calculated. The latter had agreed to take in six to ten young nurses each year from the West Cornwall Hospital in Penzance, and the Superintendent was trying to hasten the very slow progress on the new Operating Theatre, being built by the Ministry of Health, by discussing the affair with Winchester's Member of Parliament.[6] There had been frequent delays. Rigorous attempts were being made to conserve supplies of other kinds, and to cut down costs, but the £30 per annum now agreed to be spent on the new internal telephone system was a welcome improvement, a saving of that perpetual walking which seems to be a feature of life in any hospital. The shortage of manpower was making itself felt in many ways; women were now liable to fire watch, and the Superintendent asked for 15 heavy coats for them, for they would be expected to serve long spells of duty on cold rooves. The waiting list was growing longer, the Superintendent reported on Trafalgar Day 1942; he himself had won a considerable victory – the medical staff had met delegates from the Ministry of Health and from the Ministry of Works and Planning, and work was to recommence immediately on the new Operating theatre. All these 'political' matters had to be considered, as did the news that all nurses and girls wishing to nurse would have to be given intelligence tests and that a Nurses' Council was going to be formed with direct access to the Governing Body. In November, 12 members of the staff were sent off at the Governor's expense to take an A.R.P. course at Reading. The days were simply not long enough to do everything required of civilians at this time in the Hospital's history, when it was also becoming increasingly necessary for much thought to be given to the future. The British Hospitals' Association were inquiring about facilities for undergraduate and graduate teaching. There were already a few final year medical students who had been taken in to gain clinical experience, 'and this could be continued'. It is not clear how this arrangement was to be financed; the overdraft stood at £24,743, and the Telephone Account was 'too high'. Though presumably one particular impending change had been known for some time at least to Sir George Cooper, the resignation of the Superintendent, H.E.T. Mitchell, presented to the Committee on 16 December 1942, appears to have come as a surprise to most members. He continued to attend meetings for the next three months and, on 3 February 1943, a long letter from Sir George paid tribute to this man who had done so much for the Hospital under such difficult circumstances. 'He brought a knowledge of modern requirements which together with an alert brain and a keen grasp of the financial needs of the situation has been proved of the utmost assistance in the many and varied negotiations with the Ministry of Health. He instituted many medical reforms in the Administration and running of the Hospital', and he had 'enhanced the reputation of the Hospital'.

His successor, R.M. Reeves, took over on 1 March 1943, and the process of change continued. A Nurses' Council of 10 members was set up, which matrons might attend, and this meant more administration of a different kind, and the Committee of Management agreed to meet once a month on the first Wednesday for the duration of the war. The administration still had to deal with the Committee of Management, the war-time Executive Committee (now concerned with the Rushcliffe Report), the Finance Sub-Committee, the Nursing Sub-Committee, and the Medical Sub-Committee. From April 1943, there was also a non-medical Staff Council, which met every three months. The newly appointed Mr Reeves was called up almost at once (he had to leave by 7 July 1943) and was replaced by an Acting Superintendent and Secretary, Miss D.M. Stanbury.

The matters which had to be discussed by the Committee of Management in the second half of the war were of an extraordinary variety, a curious mixture of small detail and very important business. One result of the war and the shortage of labour was that the Committee became more realistically interested in labour-saving ideas. In May 1943, it was decided that white cuffs for nurses might be discontinued for the duration, 'except for S.R.N.s'. In the next month, the Hospital bought what was probably its first automatic bed-pan washer, for Florence Portal Ward; it cost £95, £15 above the estimate. A bacon-slicing machine was another purchase, and a mechanical bottle washer for the Pathological Laboratory, both expensive items. There were problems in the new Operating Theatre, where the Ministry had not provided all the equipment deemed necessary. A transformer and a theatre trolley had to be bought, and there were not enough operating instruments; soon the floor surface became unsatisfactory, and it had to be replaced with terrazzo. Floors were becoming a problem everywhere; the surface of the ramp constructed to the new wards on the south side of the Hospital was giving trouble and, in some of the old wards, linoleum was wearing out, and there were dangerous patches. A new boiler was badly needed, and a redundant Lancaster boiler was available from Southampton Water-Works at a cost of only £200; it was bought, but could not be fitted, because the Ministry would not grant a licence for the necessary building work.

It was on that negative note that 1943 ended, but 1943 in reality was far from being a negative year. The Hospital's finances were in a poor state, and in April, the Committee therefore decided to lift the restrictions on the numbers of civilian patients; no special appeal was to be made 'as the time was not opportune'. The waiting list was very long, and patients did not always arrive when expected. Patients who did not intend to come in had their names removed, after two letters of warning. An attempt was made to improve the Hospital's investments, and certain holdings, large and small, were re-invested, largely in three per cent Savings Bonds (1950-70) and H.C.C. three per cent Stock (1956-61). Money was indeed needed, for it was a year of considerable change and of exciting and interesting new medical developments.

A 'Cancer Follow-up Clinic' was established, largely as the result of pressure from the Hampshire County Council, which was prepared to pay the Hospital one guinea per person per session and, almost simultaneously, a proposal was made to set up a Mass-Radiography unit for the detection of tuberculosis 'if Doctor Jagger can do it in his Department'. He had to reply that the proposal could not yet go ahead because of the shortage of staff.[7] The apparatus for a Dental Radiography unit was bought, at a cost of £203. The increase in the number and type of patients meant that it was reasonable to get extra part-time administrative staff who had to be paid, and a gratuity was offered to some of the medical staff, including Mr J. Rubin, the Surgeon, for all his extra work because of the inevitable absence of some members of the Honorary Staff. Temporary staff of all kinds came and went and the senior Honorary Surgeons and Physicians had a changing supply of young House Surgeons and Physicians. It was necessary to install an Indicator Board in the main hall which medical and surgical staff could consult to find out who was in the building. Despite the decision not to have a general appeal, there was a considerable local effort for the Christmas Fund, a concert at the Odeon cinema, a dance at the Guildhall, organised by Doctor T. Freeman, and the Eastleigh Carriage Works had a show which raised the very considerable sum of £540 'for the two Hospitals'.

The need to win the War in as short a time as possible was the underlying reason for so many of the new regulations and orders which originated with central Government, and which began to flow over the Hospital in increasing numbers. There were undoubtedly those men and women who found these demands and comments irritating and even unfair to an Institution which had always placed so much emphasis on voluntary effort and on public support. Yet against the background of continual crisis and its attendant English characteristic of perpetual improvisation, there was emerging a school of thought which had begun to wonder how much longer a large Hospital could survive on a voluntary basis once the War was over. As early as July and August 1942, the Contributory Scheme Committee, under its Chairman, Mr R. Knox, presented a highly important Report to the

Committee of Management. There were six items in this Report, and they are so important in the Hospital's story that they need to be recorded here in full:

1. It is absolutely essential that a Hospital service be provided for everyone regardless of income.
2. That the voluntary principle must be maintained in the interests of the patients, the medical profession, and the staffs of Hospitals.
3. That this Committee is of opinion that with proper organization the Contributory Scheme throughout the County can be made to maintain fully the voluntary Hospitals.
4. That this Committee therefore empowers the delegates to the British Hospitals Contributory Scheme Association to vote as they think fit in the interests of the contributory scheme of the county at the special General Meeting of the Association to be held to consider the adoption of the Interim Report of the Joint Sub-Committee.
5. That this Committee hereby resolves to accept the findings of the National Association and to put into operation any recommendations they may make.
6. That the Committee of Management is recommended to give its whole-hearted support to the British Hospitals Association in any action to be taken in connection with the Interim Report.

The Minutes never record the length of its discussions, but the eventual resolution was as follows:

'To refer the matter to the Board of Governors with an expression that this Committee, whilst realising the important nature of the recommendations contained in the Report, hereby resolves to support the proposals, preferring a form of Hospital management in which the voluntary principle is preserved, rather than a wholly state-run Hospital Service.'

When the Rushcliffe Report on nurses was considered early in 1943 by the Hospital's Executive Committee, the estimated extra cost was £1,450 a year. More change was already envisaged. A Staff Sub-Committee was set up in April which did not include members of the medical profession; its 16 members were to meet every three months, and its particular form of democracy is interesting; its members were to be elected by secret ballot, but only those who had worked for at least 12 months in the Hospital could serve, and the Committee's powers were restricted to providing recommendations to the Committee of Management or the Hospital Superintendent. Carpenters, caterers, the dispensers, the Sewing Room, the telephonists, engineers, gardeners, the laboratory technicians, 'massage and X-Ray'; each provided one member. Those long-established groups of Hospital servant, the administration, the porters, and the domestic staff were all represented by two members. There was still no complete pension system for the staff, but attempts were made to deal with this difficult problem soon after the setting up of the Staff Council, when staff with at least 15 years' service and who had reached the age of 65 could expect a pension of three-tenths their average weekly pay for their last five years' work, subject to a maximum payment of £1 7s. 6d. a week. Paid leave for resident maids soon included 15s. a week board wages. The National Health Service already being considered was certainly going to include a wide variety of men and women with skills of all kinds. The Annual Report, from 1 January to 31 December 1944, provides a much broader view of the work of the Hospital during this year of the Allied Invasion of Europe, but Sir George Cooper, as Chairman of the Committee of Management, was critical of the recently issued White Paper on the National Health Service which had been briefly discussed at the Annual Court of Governors of 10 March 1944, a meeting which could be attended by all Subscribers. It was on this occasion that he spoke with regret 'of the apparent death knell of the Voluntary Hospitals and the Contributory Schemes'. The Government should have offered a grant of £200,000 to each of the large Hospitals to set them free from debt and enable them to carry on with the monies received from the Contributory Schemes; Major G.G. Petherick reported that this year's expenditure was already up by £4,000 because of the greatly increased cost of salaries, provisions, surgery and the Dispensary.

One of the reasons for all this increased expenditure was that, early in the year (1944), the Hospital had received a rather vague indication that something of importance was going to happen, and then orders began to arrive, to reduce the number of occupied surgical beds, to increase the stock of drugs and dressings. At length came the news that the Hospital was to be a Transit Hospital for the occupation and transfer of wounded from the Continent. Two days before D-Day, the preparations were complete. There was an additional staff of nearly one hundred persons who made up six surgical teams, general duty medical officers, medical students, orderlies, sisters and radiographers; there were 30 R.A.M.C. orderlies, 14 guards, and 10 ambulance drivers. The non-medical staff were put on to 12-hour shifts of duty, all the wards were reorganised and reallocated. Householders nearby gladly took in many members of this enormously increased Hospital household. The guards and the R.A.M.C. orderlies lived in tents in the Hospital grounds. Sir George described the Hampshire Red Cross as a veritable Fairy Godmother, producing all kinds of extra comforts, and local civilians and local members of the Armed Forces did all kinds of voluntary work. A total of 2300 war casualties passed through the wards, including a number of prisoners of war. The out-patients department had to be closed for just over six weeks but, surprisingly, the number of civilian in-patients remained high, almost 430 men, women and children being admitted each month. As one who was a civilian patient for a short period just before the invasion of Normandy began, the writer can testify personally to the 'skill and refreshing cheerfulness', in the words of the Committee of Management later on, which was a hallmark of the Hospital at this difficult time,not to mention the excellent food.

The work of the Hospital after D-Day had been reported to the Quarterly Court of Governors at the end of September, but it was recognised at once by a visit from H.M. The Queen on 23 June, and later visits from the Deputy Prime Minister, C.R. Attlee, and from several distinguished serving general officers. All the usual problems continued. Nightingale was already too small, and plans were prepared to enlarge it. A large room for the Almoner's Department was added near the Out-Patients Department. More provision was made for paying patients; Victoria Ward was no longer kept empty for emergency resuscitation cases, but filled with over 25 beds, and Jubilee Ward could therefore be devoted to paying patients. By the end of 1944, the number of nursing staff was 198, though all the nurses from Portsmouth had been able to return to that battered city. The total bill for salaries at the end of the year showed an increase of £6,000, the Contributory Scheme had produced £3,000, less than it had in 1943, but a very large legacy enabled the Treasurer to show a surplus of £1,656, and the Contributory Scheme money still provided the agreed rate of 11s. 0d. per day per in-patient, and the full costs of out-patients. Nevertheless, only eight per cent of the Hospital's income came from voluntary sources but, in the words of the Chairman, 'we look forward to the future, knowing that whatever changes are in store, the voluntary spirit of our hospitals will not be defeated'. He had already formed a special committee to consider the extensions and future development of the Hospital.

The Annual Report for 1944-5, ending on 31 December, was presented as a Report from the Committee of Management, 'By order of the Court of Governors'; Sir George Cooper was still the 'senior officer of the Institution', but it was not his signature which appeared at the end of the document; instead it was signed by Brigadier General M. Kemp Welch, in the absence through illness of the Chairman, Admiral Sir Arthur Kipling Waistell. His opening paragraph explained explicitly the situation of the Hospital at the end of 1945. '... it has been necessary to take into account the undoubtable changes of the near, but so far unknown, future. The calls made upon the Hospital continued to increase; every department ... demands more room, more staff, and new equipment which cannot be provided under present conditions.' Chernocke House, in St Thomas Street, Doctor Combes' old home, had been rented as a Nurses' Home, and the staff no longer had to go out to Lainston, five miles away. Though the number of service patients had decreased, the number of civilian cases had gone up, from 4152 (in 1944) to 4855, including a small number of repatriated civilian internees from the Far East, after the end of the war with Japan. There was no convalescent Home, for that at Bonchurch had not been re-opened, and the house had had to be returned to the heirs of its former owner. Plans for improving and enlarging the Radiological Department proceeded slowly, but one of the main needs was for more maternity accommodation. The whole of the first floor of Butterfield's Hospital became a maternity unit of 40 beds (which meant a loss of 40 general beds), and became, under Doctor Penny, one of the most famous and modern departments of its kind.

The staff had changed, inevitably, and this Annual Report paid a special tribute to Doctor C.B.S. Fuller, Chairman of the Medical Sub-Committee during the war years. One Anaesthetist had been killed in autumn 1943, Doctor Jagger had retired, Doctor J.R. Bodington rejoined the Hospital after his absence on active service since 1941, but the need for increased medical staff was so great that four entirely new appointments had to be made.[8] By the end of the year, the list of Honorary Staff consisted of two Consulting Physicians, four Surgeons, a Radiologist, two Dental Surgeons, two Physicians, two Surgeons, an Ear, Nose and Throat Surgeon, an Ophthalmic Surgeon, an Obstetrician, a medical officer in charge of the X-Ray Department, a Dental Surgeon, a Clinical Pathologist, an Anaesthetist with an Assistant, an Orthopaedic Surgeon, a Speech Therapist, an Assistant Surgeon, and seven resident Medical Officers. Administering the Hospital in many differing ways required a much larger number of men and women who served on the various committees, and there was still a Chaplain, the Rev. J.A. Stiff, a Free Church Chaplain (Honorary), the Rev. A.G. Edgerton, and the Chief Pharmacist was a woman, Mrs G.E. Mewburn. The task of coping with all these volunteers, administrators and advisers, some of whom served in a personal capacity and others represented various bodies, must have fallen heavily on the Superintendent and

Secretary, Mr R. Morrison Smith, who still had the invaluable Miss D.N. Stanbury as his assistant.

The most gloomy feature in the Honorary Treasurer's Report for this year, when the end of the war had brought so much rejoicing and so great a feeling that the Hospital has good cause to be proud of its war-time service, was the miserable fact that the Hospital's finances were in a very poor state. A smaller number of service patients had meant a reduction in grant income from the Ministry of Health and, though money from voluntary sources had arrived and the Contributory Scheme was working splendidly, the deficit on the year was £3,134 8s. 6d. The future for voluntary hospitals was indeed uncertain. The Annual General Court of Governors met on 27 March 1946, and Sir George Cooper reported on the National Health Service Bill in no uncertain terms. He condemned it, utterly, as a ruthless sacrifice to a political ideal, and spoke in favour of the British Hospitals' Association Scheme, which would have allowed voluntary hospitals to survive and to manage their own internal affairs. He did say, however, that he accepted the need for a National Health Service for everyone and a long discussion followed, which resulted in a rather general resolution, proposed by Sir George, welcoming the desire of the Government to provide a comprehensive Health Service, but stating that the proposals would not provide the best hospital services, and deploring the discouragement of voluntary effort.

Yet it must have been obvious to any close observer of the Hospital as it emerged from the end of the Second World War that, even without the prospect of a National Health Service and without its own particular financial problems, the Hospital's future was going to be dominated by one single word, change. Much has been written about the society of 1945 as if it was a society dominated by the disillusioned and the aggrieved. In fact, England seemed full of idealists, men and women who believed in democracy, who believed that the technological advances which had helped to win a war could have peace-time uses which could give everyone a better life. There were also those who believed that part of the success of this new life would be found in logistics; planning became the key word. In the new world of civilians, there would have to be better, not necessarily more, organisation, and this would obviously include a very well-administered National Health Service, financed by central government, and available to all.

What the local press called 'the end of voluntary status' came effectively on Tuesday, 29 June 1948, with the last meeting of that Court of Governors whose predecessors had first met so many years ago.[9] It was preceded by a short and sad ceremony at the front entrance of the Hospital, when an oaken plaque, designed by that great Hampshire craftsman, Eric Sharpe, was unveiled in honour of the Hospital's only woman Chairman. 'We remember with gratitude the life and work of Florence Anita, Countess of Northbrook, Governor of this Hospital, 1911-1946; Chairman of the Court of Governors, 1929-1939.' It was dedicated by Dean Selwyn who spoke briefly of Lady Northbrook's other memorials, the Children's Ward and the new nursing block. This Act of Remembrance was followed by the business meeting, and Sir George spoke bitterly of the imminent changes; it was 'a sad thing that everything was coming to an end, and in such an arbitrary manner'. Yet the work of the place, at that very moment, was still going on, and Brigadier Kemp Welch reported the appointment of Doctor J. Dawson as full-time Radiologist, in charge of the X-Ray Department, and of Mr J.A. Robertson as Second Ophthalmic Surgeon. It was a matter, too, of great pride that the famous Plastic Surgeon, Sir Harold Gillies, had agreed to act as Consultant. There was a new Secretary for a new Management Committee to welcome, Mr Morrison Smith, and an old friend back from the R.A.F., Mr J. Rubin. In a moving final vote of thanks to Sir George Cooper, W.H. Carpenter also reminded the Committee that it had not been until 1921 that some responsibility for managing the Hospital had been entrusted to those who had the most to benefit from it, with the introduction of the Contributory Scheme. Mr Carpenter's praise of Sir George was probably the last official word spoken in the last Court of Governors.

XIII After The Appointed Day

Alured Clarke had not imagined that his Hospital would always be maintained by voluntary contributions. 'Whenever a better provision is made for the poor sick by Parliament this Hospital will either cease or may become part of that provision.'[1] He could envisage a time when Parliament might place the responsibility for a hospital service on the nation as a whole, but he would not have been surprised to learn of the long years when his foundation was maintained by generous donations and the unselfish service of successive generations of enthusiastic voluntary workers. He was a man needed in his time; in his Hospital's story, the right person frequently appeared at the proper moment; Richard Taunton, John Hoadly, Sir William Heathcote are the obvious examples. Yet, long before 1736, the care of the sick and the poor had become increasingly a care based on the community, and not the responsibility of some worthy individual. The whole idea of community care, community obligation, became increasingly effective, increasingly influential, when 19th-century legislation placed more and more responsibility on local government, the Corporation of the city of Winchester and, after 1889, the Hampshire County Council.

In 1888, the Governors refused to allow the Hospital's private nurses to take part in a scheme for nursing the sick poor in their own homes within the city of Winchester, but they eventually agreed that two-thirds of the money collected in the next street collection should be passed on to the Corporation for that purpose. There was another refusal in 1908, when the medical staff was not allowed to take part in the new arrangements for the medical inspection of school children. It was not so much an objection to the work, as an objection to the idea that Hospital doctors should be paid for the work – 'it would be a departure from the lines on which the Hospital had worked since 1736'. The Court of Governors was resolute against what many of its members considered undue interference in people's lives, and some of this resolute opposition was certainly political. The proposals for National Insurance in 1911 were criticised through the British Hospitals Association, and through the calling of a public meeting to protest. In 1917, Winchester's Medical Officer of Health suggested the setting up of a Maternity and Child Welfare Unit; other proposals for special clinics for tonsil and adenoid patients, for venereal diseases, and for eye problems were all opposed at first, though all eventually came into existence.

It was finance which eventually proved the determining factor which ended the long years of voluntary effort in this voluntary Hospital, for a majority of the Governors were sternly opposed to what they regarded not as welcome help, but as unnecessary interference. In 1922, they regarded the setting up of Hospital Committees by the Ministry of Health as a dreadful example of what could happen, and seven years later, when the Local Government Act of 1929 gave the responsibility of all Poor Law Union Institutions to local government, they were horrified that medical men and nurses were going to be paid by local government. The Sankey Report went even further; it envisaged a regional hospital scheme for the whole of the country, but all the Governors could really do was to publish a statement urging all voluntary hospitals to band themselves together to avoid absorption and nationalisation. Above all, the War which began in 1939 was the factor which determined the Hospital's future. The multiplicity of orders and requirements from central government *via* the Ministry of Health forced the Hospital to accept government money for what it had to do, to provide, in the cause of national necessity. Hand in hand with this government control went a vast increase in the Hospital's staff, of the medical care offered, and these changes were in their turn accompanied by what can perhaps be called the organisation of that staff, whether it was domestic workers, surgeons, doctors, or nurses, staff of all kinds, who all had to be paid at a rate which must have seemed to be absurdly high for those who remembered 1939 prices and incomes.

By the National Health Act of 1946, 'the appointed day' when the voluntary hospitals would be taken over was 5 July 1948, and from that day onwards the Royal Hampshire County Hospital has seen many changes. What sometimes seems so remarkable is that, faced with tremendous upheaval, its own particular spirit, a feeling which is modern and yet embodies all that is best in the traditions of this historical household, remains unharmed and undisturbed.

Not everyone welcomed the prospect of a new kind of Hospital, and many people found the new arrangements very difficult to understand, especially since the administration was apparently going to be directed from London. The local press did what it could to illuminate the confused and confusing situation. Hampshire was now under the South Western Region Hospital Board, and its Chairman was a Surrey County Councillor, F.H. Eliott, D.L., J.P., with an office in London. At once it was realised that some sort of more local administration was essential, and a Western Area Committee was set up from Hampshire, the Isle of Wight, Dorset, Somerset and Wiltshire; its Chairman was G.E. Coke of Bentley, and it had 21 members, of whom three were medical men and one was a dentist; amongst the 21 were Sir Alan Lubbock, Chairman of the Hampshire County Council and Doctor G.B.S Fuller. Sir George Cooper's work in the past, of course, had to be recognised and he was co-opted to the Committee with Mr H.H. Langston of Winchester. There were other tiers of administration. Within Hampshire, practically the whole county was covered by four Management Groups from Portsmouth, Southampton, Bournemouth and Winchester; the Winchester Group Hospital Management Committee had an old friend as Chairman, Brigadier M. Kemp Welch, and took an early decision in February 1949 to admit the press to its meetings. Kemp Welch had succeeded Sir Arthur Waistell, who had retired through ill health in 1947. It controlled 17 Hospitals, with a total of about 1,500 beds, and soon acquired the unenviable reputation of being the most expensively administered group within its county.[2] Its administration made up 9.9 per cent of its outgoings, compared with 7 per cent for all the other groups. One of the other criticisms soon made was admirably explained in a local newspaper: 'Its weakness lies in the fact that membership of each tier is appointed by the tier above'. Moreover, it was a group which had been hard hit by the War; some of its buildings had been bombed, and all were run-down; the various claims of the differing institutions produced much rivalry. There were also problems of increasing numbers of old, ageing, and geriatric patients, and also of a rising birthrate.

Not surprisingly, there were cries of astonishment at the cost of the changes which followed the Appointed Day. The estimated expenditure for the Winchester Group for 1949-50 was £14,285, which included £2,000 on capital works. One local evening paper suggested that people were now being paid for what they had done previously as volunteers. Savings had to be discussed, but the problem was national; the National Health Estimates for the country as a whole were far too low, probably by as much as £5,015,000. 'Nursing standards will suffer' said Brigadier Kemp Welch, and many people blamed the general rush for free bandages and quantities of aspirin.

In the meantime, H. Ewart-Mitchell was writing a series of articles on 'The Welfare of the Hospital Patient' in *The Hospital and Social Services Journal*, read with much interest in his old Winchester Hospital. In 1948, Sister Treble, the last of the Senior Sisters, retired. She had been Sister in charge of the X-Ray Department since 1923, and was greatly loved, the only nurse in the Hospital's history to have had a road named after her.[3] She was a near contemporary of her friend, Emily Carpenter Turner, who died in 1949. Nursing had changed indeed since those days when Miss Carpenter Turner, at Leicester, had to take 'her' Surgeon's old jackets for use in his operating theatre after he had worn them out in his garden. A battle was being fought by Doctor Fuller and Mr Langston against the spectre of central buying and huge and extravagant bulk purchases, and Sir George Cooper was enjoying himself at the Hursley Flower Show, and still working hard for his Hospital. The end of a number of old 'Winchester' arrangements was in sight. In April 1949, the Linen Guild finished its work; it had been founded by Miss Beatrice Heathcote in 1907, and had been absolutely invaluable by the way in which it had helped to keep down costs, and encouraged interest in the work of the 'Royal Hampshire'; Miss Urmston had been its devoted Secretary for many years.

The 'new' Hospital was going to have 118 beds, and a 15-bed maternity unit, according to an advertisement in *The Times*. It still seemed to be remotely controlled, for when Doctor Wilfrid Brinton came as a part-time Consultant Physician his appointment had to be approved by the South West Regional Hospital Board in London. Nevertheless the St Luke's Day service of 1949 was quite in the old tradition; the Chaplain, Mr Stiff, took the service in the Chapel at which Bishop Neville Lovett preached, and Sir George Cooper read the Lesson. Later, in the Nightingale Nurses' Home, there followed the Annual Prize Giving, the presentations being made by Miss M.P. Browne, the new Headmistress of the County Girls' School.[4] In fact, nurses, or rather the lack of them, were a problem and hospital beds were kept empty. In July 1950, as part of a recruitment campaign, a travelling historical procession of *Tableaux vivants* went around Winchester. Twelve additional full-time nurses, 13 part-timers and five full- or part-time ward orderlies were recruited, and then there was a great Open Day in Romsey Road. The historical exhibits included a medical text book of 1699, and the many aspects of present-day care exemplified by a variety of practical demonstrations, including the making of false eyes from plastic, presumably cheaper than glass. There was still not enough

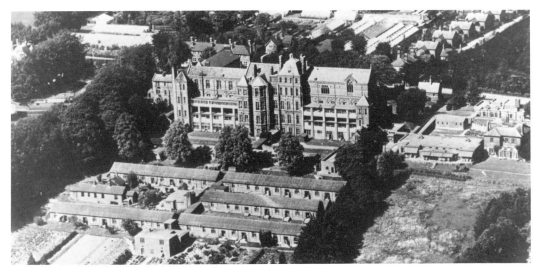

20. Aerial view: the Hospital in 1953.

21. Nurses' prizegiving, 1953.

money, though Sir George Cooper was able to report that the whole Hospital had been rewired, that the Hut wards had been redecorated, and the old beds were being replaced with ones with interior sprung mattresses. The little Isolation Hospital in Crabwood had also been redecorated, but the charge for a private room in The Royal Hampshire County Hospital had risen to £2 17s. 0d. a day; 'Absurdly high', said one of the Consultants.

In December 1950, Doctor G.B. Wainwright died; he had joined the Hospital's Honorary staff in 1921, and from 1926 till he resigned in 1936 was its Senior Physician. He was also one of the long series of Hospital doctors whose practice included Winchester College, and he did not finally retire until 1945, greatly loved and known for his gentle manner. He must surely have been the only Hospital Physician who had gained a First in the Theological Tripos before qualifying as a Doctor. In 1953, Mr Peter Smithers M.P. raised the problems of Winchester in the House; there was a 19-month delay for ear, nose and throat patients. The basic problem was money for salaries – but the Chapel was redecorated 'as a matter of urgency'. By this time, the Hospital had lost other valued servants; G.C. Hamlyn, who had been Clerk of Works since 1924, died in July 1951, as did Leonard Keyser's brother-in-law, Brigadier Kemp Welch; Doctor Penny retired after 25 years' service at the end of 1952, and Admiral Waistell himself died in 1953, at the age of 80 after a long and distinguished career which began with his service with the submarine flotilla in the North Sea, during the first World War, and ended with his work as Chairman of the Management Committee from 1938-47.

Even before the end of the War, some members of the Governing Body, and certainly Sir George Cooper himself, had begun to think that a measure of new building was needed at Romsey Road, and no-one envisaged that the huts on the Hospital's lawn were anything else but temporary expedients. The coming in of the National Health Service focused attention on the architecture and the structural condition of the existing building. Victorian buildings were not held in general esteem in 1948. The argument for a *tabula rasa*, complete demolition, was deemed to be strong; Butterfield's beautiful Chapel seemed to be in the wrong place (in fact, it was soon dismantled and turned into a store) and another site appeared desirable. The writer of this *History*, in another capacity, was present at a great many discussions about the physical future of the Romsey Road building; the arguments on all sides were always lucidly put, and seemed convincing. Small wards, or larger wards, multi-storey or not, new site *versus* old site, were all discussed, and usually against a changing pattern of Health Service Administration. Sir George Cooper's Committee were reported as 'displeased' in 1954 when the Wessex Area Committee refused them permission to engage an architect to draw up a Block Plan for a new Hospital on the site of Butterfield's building. The Chairman's practical approach was that such a plan was essential in order to know where to site the new buildings already needed, but he was more than reconciled in general terms to most of the changes brought about by the Act of 1946. At a meeting in Basingstoke in May 1954, held to review the situation after six years of the National Health Service, he said 'I do claim that we have a much better lot of hospitals than when we took over six years ago ... six years of hard work and progress'. One of the smaller improvements in Romsey Road had been the use to which the balance of money in the Contributory

Scheme Account, amounting to nearly £8,000, had been put, a canopy to shelter arrivals in the front courtyard and some limited accommodation for the families of seriously ill patients.[5] Change was still very much part of the order of the day, not only in administration, but in medicine itself and in the social changes which produced new kinds of patients. Doctor C.B.S. Fuller, President of the Southern Branch of the British Medical Association and Doctor Wainwright's successor as Senior Hospital Physician, warned a large audience in the Guildhall in 1954 of the dangers of the indiscriminate use of some of the new remedies, including penicillin and streptomycin, which he considered needed to be used only in cases of real necessity.[6] This was the year, too, when the full significance of what the motor car had come to mean in terms of Hospital treatment was first realised. Between 31 December 1952 and April 1954, 717 road accident cases had been received, of whom the greatest number were motor cyclists with head injuries, passengers were more vulnerable than drivers, men more than women, and four per cent of the casualties had died, and a further two per cent were completely disabled.

By the autumn of 1954, the Hospital had a new Chaplain, Canon H.C. Carden, a familiar and greatly loved figure in Winchester society, as indeed his predecessor, Mr Stiff, had been. It was he who invited Bishop Lang to preach at the St Luke's Day Service that year, a man who understood the problem of suffering, who had been badly wounded in the First World War, and who used the occasion to speak particularly to the nurses, with an apt quotation from a former Matron of Guy's Hospital; 'When you have passed all your examinations, don't imagine you will be good nurses – you will only be good nurses when all the people in your ward feel better because you have come in'. Though nurses were still in short supply, the reputation of the Hospital's work was attracting many talented people. In the same year, R.G. Bromfield of the Pathological Department was awarded the Sims Woodhead Medal, the highest possible honour of the Institute of Medical Laboratory Technology. In the 30 years of its existence, the medal had only been awarded on 11 previous occasions. Reg Bromfield was a much admired member of the Hospital's new household and, after he retired, became an excellent and hard working member of the City Council. Voluntary work was indeed once again beginning to be attractive. The words 'Voluntary Help in Hospitals - Reawakening welcomed by Winchester Hospital Group', headed the local paper's account of the Annual Report of 1955. There was talk also of 'Frustration and delay over buildings', but the paper could announce a new Hydrotherapy Department and a Department of Daily Living to show the disabled and handicapped how to adapt themselves to the problems of everyday life.[7] Moreover, new offices for the Winchester Group were going ahead in Romsey Road, but not the new Hospital kitchen. This particular Report had some unusual statistics. Pace Doctor Fuller, 22,000,000,000 units of penicillin had been used, and 90 miles of surgical gauze. The administrative costs had been broken down – the 'admin' itself cost 7d. in every £1 spent, the nurses 3s. 6d. in every £1, and the provisions 3s. 7d. Between April 1953 and March 1954, 12,689 patients had been discharged. There had been a great improvement in the number of nurses in the National Hospital Services Reserve (the Nurses' 'Bank'); it had a membership of 340, compared with a mere 175 in the previous year. At the end of March 1955, the proposed formation of the League of Friends took a further step forward with a 'meeting sponsored by the Winchester Rotary Club and held in what was then Fuller's Restaurant over W.H. Smith and Son in the High Street.[8] It did something to relieve the disappointment of the news which arrived in February that the £40 million scheme announced for the new Hospitals contained nothing for Winchester; the first priority was, and probably rightly, a new Hospital for Basingstoke. By 1960, the future of Butterfield's Hospital was a matter of much discussion; it was decided to pull it down, replacing it by a new building constructed on nearly the same site, so that the work of the Hospital might continue without interruption; the event of the year was probably the completion of the new Dining Room Block, opened on 5 August 1959.

All these years of uncertainty about the buildings were accompanied by changes in administration, in nursing techniques and in the variety of professional opportunities offered to doctors and surgeons, and changes in the treatment of patients. Butterfield's building had continually to be adapted; small improvements were made, temporary buildings added. The objects were always the same, to improve patient care, and to improve the conditions in which the staff worked. In 1953, a new staff canteen was opened, and Chernocke House was purchased as a Nurses' Home. Twelve months later, one of the temporary huts had been turned, with the utmost economy, into a rehabilitation centre by the genius of Doctor Russell Grant, and with some help from the Nuffield Provident Hospitals Trust; Doctor Grant's Department of Daily Living and Hydrotherapy became famous. By the time of the Tenth Report of the Winchester Group Hospital Management Committee (April 1958 - March 1959), the Committee had decided to describe its own work in some detail. For once, they had not been 'unduly hampered by lack of money', the staff situation had taken a turn for the better, and the League of Friends had held a very successful Caledonian Market. The newly-formed Wessex Regional Hospital Board held its own first meeting at the Hospital. More provision had to be made for the increased number of nurses, by the purchase of a former private Nursing Home, Enniskerry on Sleepers' Hill, and Kirtling House in Chilbolton Avenue, for many years the home of one of Winchester's best known physicians, Doctor H.V. Hensley. Another event of the year was the re-naming of all the ward huts.

When Sir George Cooper died on 5 January 1961 in Winchester 'in Hospital', the *Hampshire Chronicle*, in an admirable obituary notice, recalled his long years of service to the community and to the Royal Hampshire County Hospital in particular. He had become a Trustee for its lands and buildings in 1934, a member of the Management Committee in 1936, and then Honorary Treasurer, and Chairman of the Governors, and after 1948, Vice-Chairman and then Chairman of the Winchester Group Hospital Management Committee. For 17 years, this public-spirited man had also been a Governor of Guy's Hospital in London, and Chairman of the Health Committee of the Winchester Rural District Council, all this in addition to his work for farming, his years as a Magistrate, as a Deputy Lieutenant, and as High Sheriff of Hampshire in 1937. He had lived long enough to see the Government's Ten Year Plan provide for the expansion and eventual complete rebuilding of the Royal Hampshire County Hospital. It was the Hospital's good fortune that one of his neighbours at Hursley agreed to carry on his work as Chairman.

22.   Sir George Cooper, Bart.

By 1968, the Winchester Group Hospital Management Committee had a substantial number of medical men serving on it under the Chairmanship of Lord Northbrook. Since 1966 they had also administered the Lord Treloar Hospital Group in Alton, and in 1969 the Winchester Group was amalgamated with the Park Prewett Hospital, Basingstoke, under the name of The North Hampshire Group. The following year, the Group offices moved to Basingstoke from the County Hospital where they had been based since 1948, a step which caused some misgivings. The 1960s saw definite progress in the plans for the redevelopment of the Hospital, eventually dispelling the fears that the County Hospital and its workload could find itself split in some way between the growing hospitals in Southampton and Basingstoke. The Government Ten Year Plan of 1960 provided (*inter alia*) for the expansion and, eventually, the complete rebuilding of the Royal Hampshire County Hospital, Winchester. Meanwhile the old Ministry Theatre was improved in various ways, but the alterations resulted in the closing of Butterfield's beautiful Chapel. A small temporary Chapel was created on the east side of the ramp which leads *inter alia* to the new twin-theatres.

Inflation revealed itself in every section of Hospital life. In 1968-9, nurses' salaries cost £234,579, the administration £48,804, and the total gross expenditure was £995,795. These statistics were published in the Biennial Review for 1967-9, when the average cost of treating an acute patient was £54 8s. 6d. a week. There had been no extravagances; as the Report said 'The Committee had been hard put to keep its expenditure within the estimates (because of) an increase in the volume of work, rising prices and new methods of treatment'. One interesting sign of the times was that the Biennial Review was commercially printed, and included commercial advertisements, presumably to keep down the costs.

A major reorganisation of the Health Service occurred in 1974; the new administrative structure now consisted of Regional Health Authorities, Area Health Authorities, and Health Districts, and the Hospital became the principal acute Hospital of a large area, predominantly rural, serving approximately 200,000 people. In 1982, a further reorganisation took place; Area Health Authorities disappeared, leaving Regional Health Authorities, with Health Authorities covering the former districts. The County Hospital was administered within the Winchester Health Authority, yet senior management remained comparatively undisturbed over a period of about 30 years, and offered what has been called 'first-rate service in third-rate conditions'.

Date	Beds	Patients Discharged
1949	326	6,952
1951	311	7,234
1961	362	9,397
1968	362 (approx)	11,000
1974	362 (approx)	13,181
1977	425	15,058
1984	434	17,344

Butterfield's building simply had to change; out-patient facilities were poor, the hutted wards were unsatisfactory, operatng theatres inadequate, and all the time the techniques of nursing, and of treatment whether medical or surgical, were rapidly changing.

After years of discussion about the development of the Hospital, detailed planning of the 'Nucleus' building started in 1976. Previous proposals had included ward blocks that were six storeys at the Romsey Road side, and nine storeys at the back, much to the disapproval of the City Council. By the end of 1978 the specification for the new building was virtually complete, and redevelopment became a reality with the completion of the Education Centre and Library in 1979.

The period from 1979 to 1981 was taken up with clearing the site for the new Hospital. Houses in Queen's Road were acquired to make way for the new stores, office, and transport complex. Purchases also included a public house (*The Battery*), a petrol station, and houses in Romsey Road. One of the most contentious issues was the junction of Queen's Road and Romsey Road, the Local Authority insisting that it should be realigned at a cost of £¼ million before any major redevelopment of the site could take place. Finally, the new residential development at 45 Romsey Road was completed in 1982. The way was now clear for signing the £14 million contract for the new building and the demolition of the Nightingale Nurses' Home.

Developments in Nursing

The years which have passed since the appointed day in 1948 have seen some tremendous changes in the scope and variety of treatment offered to patients through the enormous advances of post-war medicine and surgery. Moreover, since the average patient spends the greater part of the 24 hours of each day in the direct care of the nursing staff, changing attitudes within the nursing profession, changes in nurses' training, and in their working conditions, are always of vital importance to patients,and indeed to every aspect of the Hospital's development.

There have been a multitude of reports on the training of nurses including, to mention only a few, the Hospital's own reports of 1956-69, the Salmon Committee of 1966 on Senior Nursing Staff Structure, the Briggs Report of 1972, and the Halsbury Report into the pay and conditions of nursing in 1974. A mere list makes dull reading, but the changes that were carefully considered in so many ways become at once alive when considered in terms of what has actually happened in the Hospital. The Salmon Report led to the disappearance of 'Matron'; the first Nurses Education Committee was set up under Doctor Wilfrid Brinton in 1956. Attempts were always being made to reduce working hours and Extra Duty payments made for working unsociable hours. Student nurses' experience was widened to include some work in St Paul's Hospital with elderly and geriatric patients. Lectures were given by Ward Sisters; Mrs Suckling would have approved of the opportunities which provided as wide a nursing experience as possible. In 1969, the Winchester and Basingstoke Schools of Nursing were combined and the Director of Nurse Education located at Basingstoke. This arrangement continues, and the training and development of nurses has developed apace. Doctor Clarke would have been proud of the 100 per cent pass rate achieved by student nurses in 1986 for the second successive year.

By 1973, serious consideration was being given to the amount of time nurses had to spend on non-nursing duties, and Ward Clerks were introduced to remove some of these functions, and this at a period when there was some serious overcrowding in the Hospital. The general problem of how to provide additional nurses when they were needed had usually been answered by the employment of Agency staff, but a nurses' 'bank' had been set up, to augment staff as the need arose. Another particularly welcome development at this time was the decision to keep a bed in Blakeway Ward, in the Victoria Hospital, for 'continuing care', to enable families with particularly heavy problems of home nursing to have some rest from their anxieties.

From 1979, the normal nursing week was reduced to 37½ hours. By this time, uniform dress had changed from cotton to man-made fibre, because of the problems and expense of laundry, but black shoes and stockings have remained; they have always been popular. The last few years (1978-85) have seen the old qualification of S.R.N. giving way to that of R.G.N., Registered General Nurse, and the creation of a new United Kingdom Central Council for Nursing, Midwifery, and Health Visiting, the U.K.C.C. It is an age of abbreviations and initials, and nursing could not be exempt from the prevalent fashion. Today, a nurse in the Royal Hampshire County Hospital will need to have all the attributes of her predecessors in the past; she must be physically strong, endlessly patient and kind. She will be well-educated, will not be sentimental but will need to see her patients as an individual, and probably as an anxious individual separated from family and home. The words of a Staff Nurse describing her working day in 1986, explain it all:

'My day starts at 6:30am with breakfast in Marlfield House, one of the nurses' residences.[9] One advantage of this is that I only have to walk across the main car park to the Butterfield Block of the Hospital where I work as a Staff Nurse on an acute medical ward. I have lived in Marlfield House for several months now, but I am looking for a rented flat to share with some friends, as I can only have Hospital accommodation for a temporary period.

'I join my colleagues on the ward at 7:15am to receive a report from the night nurse in charge. Sister then discusses with us how we will work for the morning. I am a team leader and work with a Student Nurse and a Nursing Auxiliary to care for a specific group of patients. We are responsible for all aspects of their care and the first thing we do is to give them their breakfast.

'We then plan our morning's work by looking at each patient's individual care plan. Some care will mean two of us working together and it is important to decide priorities and to co-ordinate the work that needs to be done. It would be easy to break down the care of each patient into a series of tasks, but this is what we try to avoid. The emphasis is on giving total and personalised care to all our patients.

'Some tasks do exist of course, and one of these is administering drugs. Two nurses will do this, but even then, if possible, each team of nurses will administer drugs to their own patients. Unfortunately, this is not often possible because of the amount of work to be done. However, when the doctors do their rounds, I do join them as leader of the team. This is important as I can share with them the most up-to-date information about my patients and implement promptly any changes in treatment which they decide upon.

'Once the most important aspects of care have been undertaken, I sit with my team colleagues to discuss any changes to care plans which should be considered. This means evaluating the progress of each patient in our care and modifying nursing care instructions, as well as those related to specific medical treatment. We discuss the care plans with the patients when their condition allows and when they wish to be involved. This often provides an opportunity for patients to ask questions or offer additional information about themselves which may be valuable. The establishing of this type of relationship with my patients is very rewarding.

'During the course of the morning we have each had a coffee break. The patients' lunchtime comes very quickly and, when they have eaten, we help our patients to choose their meals for tomorrow from the individual menu cards. Soon, patients will be able to order each meal separately, lunch at breakfast time, supper at lunchtime, and so on. This will be much better for many patients who order and then change their mind, or just forget what they have selected.

'The last thing I am responsible for this morning is updating the information on the dependency categories of all our patients, which is held on computer. This provides us with daily workload information, which is useful in planning the way in which we work. Not all the wards use computers yet, but we will all be using them more and more in the coming months and years. It is planned to include all kinds of information, such as admission, transfer and discharge of patients, ordering stores and eventually receiving clinical information from departments, such as pathology and radiology.

'The nurses who will work through the afternoon and evening arrive at 1:30pm and I report to them on the progress of my patients. They also have the care plans to give them details of the special care needed by each patient, so my report concentrates on any new or important aspects of care. We can work together for the last 30 minutes or so of my period of duty. This is an opportunity to meet our patients together. The morning shift nurses go off duty at 2:30pm since we have now elected to work through without a lunch break, a change which is proving very popular.

'Tomorrow I shall be one of the nurses coming on duty at lunchtime, but much of the care will be very similar to that which I have given today, since most of my patients are quite ill and need a consistently high level of nursing care throughout the day.'

The current emphasis on allocating nurses individually to each patient so that they can look after all aspects of their care continuously is something which Alured Clarke would have applauded, even if he would not have recognised it as 'the Nursing Process'. He too expected his nurses to be literate and today's nurses face the realities of computer technology; by 1990, all wards will have a visual display unit, and nurses will have a basic computer training. It will all be part of what the Founder intended when, 250 years ago, his nurses offered their patients their 'tender care'.

23. The Consultants, 1980.

24. The Caring Team, 1986: from *Link* (Wessex Health Staff Journal), April 1986.

Developments in Clinical Care

Perhaps the two questions, put in their simplest form, to which most patients want answers (whether the questions be asked or not) are, 'Can I be cured?' and 'Is it going to hurt?' Some will not ask the questions, some will not want to hear the answers, but the second question can now often be answered optimistically, thanks to the development of pain killing drugs, and to the great changes in anaesthesia. Human, physical, suffering is far from over; today's surgery still calls for heroism, though perhaps not in the way in which it was demanded from Lord Nelson, or from Fanny Burney.[10]

The most recent changes have been described by Doctor D.J. Bowen.[11] 'Two major changes laid the foundations of modern anaesthesia.' Firstly, the introduction in 1935 of an ultra-short acting barbiturate meant that the disliked anaesthetic mask was replaced by an injection. Secondly, in 1942, a muscle relaxant drug, curare, was used in anaesthesia and this enabled the anaesthetist to control the patient's breathing. Longer and more complicated operations could now be performed safely, particularly for the very ill and elderly.

In 1948, the Hospital had two Honorary Anaesthetists, Doctor H.Mallinson and Doctor J.R. Bodington, together with a supernumerary anaesthetist, Doctor K.O. Harrison (who was appointed under the scheme to place doctors returning from the War), and a Registrar Anaesthetist. A total of seven surgeons in two operating theatres undertook about 3,000 operations per year.

In 1967, two new operating theatres (off the ramp) were opened and, five years later, the workload reached 7,000 operations per year, but anaesthetists were now extending their work outside the operating theatres; they were becoming involved in the emerging field of Intensive Care. The careful monitoring of the patient no longer stopped at the end of surgery but extended into the post-operative period and beyond. In 1967, a Consultant Anaesthetist was appointed with a special interest in Intensive Care. Life support machines were primitive and the first patient to be placed on one in Winchester was nursed in a screened off area at the end of one of the surgical wards. The machine itself had to be hired and the firm requested its return before the patient was fully recovered. A side room of the same surgical ward was then designated as the Intensive Care Unit and, despite cramped conditions, high standards of skill and care became commonplace and the machines became more and more sophisticated. Their use, together with careful control of fluid balance and blood transfusion, and the introduction of many new drugs, saved lives which would previously have been lost. Increasingly complicated surgery became possible, and the Intensive Care Unit, run by anaesthetic staff, will expand considerably with the opening of a purpose-built eight-bedded area in the Nightingale Block in 1986.

In the field of obstetrics, it became apparent that pain relief in labour was far from satisfactory. In order to improve the standard of care for pregnant women, anaesthetists began to specialise in obstetric anaesthesia and analgesia. The obstetric epidural service started in the year that Florence Portal House opened and a Consultant Anaesthetist with a special interest in Obstetrics was appointed. The demand for this form of analgesia in labour was increasing steadily and currently

25. Aerial view, 1985.

26. The Nucleus Development, 1986: the Nightingale Block.

about one third of all the mothers in labour choose this form of pain relief. With the increase in anaesthetic staff, it has been possible in certain circumstances to offer epidural anaesthesia for the operation of Caesarean section. About a quarter of these operations are done using this type of anaesthesia.

Just as the sixties had seen the advent of the Intensive Care Unit and the seventies the development of obstetric anaesthetic services, so the eighties have witnessed the emergence of the Pain Clinic, and of techniques for the relief of chronic pain. In 1981, a Consultant with a special interest in Pain Relief work was appointed and a most valuable service has been built up. The demand for this service has grown so rapidly that a second Consultant with an interest in this field has now been appointed. Techniques used by these doctors range from the non-invasive, such as transcutaneous nerve stimulation, to highly sophisticated chemical nerve blocks under X-Ray control.

Since 1939, two of the most important developments in the story of the Hospital's concern for its patients has been in the realm of diagnostic medicine. Something has already been said of the value and high reputation of the work of the Hospital pathologists. The provision of an X-Ray Department began when the Hospital stables were converted into an X-Ray and Electro-medical Department. The writer is grateful to Doctor John Dawson for a brief account of developments which have occurred since Doctor Jagger's work during the Second World War. 'Under Doctor F.F.C. Jagger and later Doctor R.I. Roberts, diagnostic radiology, radiotherapy, diathermy and ultra-violet light treatment was available to Hospital patients until 1948. At the coming of the National Health Service, the X-Ray Department services were confined to diagnostic radiology, but the Department was re-equipped with up-to-date X-Ray apparatus. The work rapidly expanded from 8,000 X-Ray examinations in 1947, to 20,000 in 1952, and has steadily increased to 48,000 per annum in the 1980s. In addition to the increase of routine X-Ray examinations, more and more complicated techniques, such as arteriography, have been introduced over the years. Ultrasonography is now well established at 5,500 examinations per annum. The original Hospital stables have served as an X-Ray Department for 65 years, and are due for demolition with the opening of the new Hospital and its X-Ray Department in 1986.'

Alured Clarke's Hospital was not a Lying-in Hospital, and women found to be pregnant were sent home, but the introduction of a National Health Service has had a profound effect on the development of maternity and gynaecological services. Not least, it created the means whereby each major town or city could establish a Consultant-led professional team to meet the special needs of obstetric and gynaecological patients. The spread of the post-war blood transfusion services and the introduction of antibiotic treatments were much to the benefit of maternity and gynaecological patients. At first, there were only two Obstetricians, Doctor C. Penny who was a General Practitioner and Obstetrician, and Mr Philip Mitchell who was a professionally trained Obstetrician and who had been appointed in 1945. Before Mr Mitchell's appointment, gynaecological surgery and Caesarean sections had been carried out by that very well known Winchester Surgeon, Mr James Troup.[12]

Doctor Penny was succeeded by Mr Geoffrey Hammond in 1953 and from that time the service was led by two fully trained Consultants and a comprehensive range of gynaecological operations could be performed. The Hospital's midwifery training school was opened in 1948, and in 1953, following a visit by the great Frederick Gibberd, the Unit was recognised by the Royal College of Obstetricians and Gynaecologists for training for the D.R.C.O.G. and M.R.C.O.G. examinations.

All advances in obstetric practice are too numerous to mention, but the development of ultrasound investigation has been of major importance and revolutionised the management of many obstetric difficulties. These advances are reflected in the dramatic fall in maternal and perinatal mortality rates since the NHS was created. One mother in a thousand died in childbirth in 1948; today it is less than one in ten thousand.

The high birth rate of post-war years and an improving perception of what constituted high risk, soon led to a shortage of hospital beds. The building of obstetric units became a National Health Service priority, and so Phase I of the rebuilding of the Royal Hampshire County Hospital was the construction of a new Maternity and Gynaecology Block of 90 beds, later named Florence Portal House after the Lady Portal of First World War fame, and opened in 1973. In obstetrics as in other specialities, links with local General Practitioners became stronger in the '60s and '70s. Florence Portal House provided for those G.P.s and Community Midwives who wished to deliver obstetric patients themselves. Gynaecological services have likewise prospered. *In Vitro* fertilisation and artificial insemination are rightly considered to be regional services, but so far as district services are concerned, the department offers a fully comprehensive and expert service and is proud to boast that in 1986 it functions without long out-patient or in-patient waiting lists.

There have also been many changes in the Orthopaedic Department, which had been founded in the small brick building (the Porter's Lodge), Romsey Road, at the entrance to the Hospital. The secretaries worked upstairs, Sister Nobes and Peter the Plasterer[13] (still a well-known member of the staff) on the ground floor. Orthopaedic in-patients were nursed in the Taunton (women) and Clarke (men) wards, and the Accident Department was housed in the first two rooms on the left in the present day Out-Patients Department. There were two part-time Consultants, Mr (now Professor) Ellis and Mr Langstone, both of whom worked additionally at Southampton, and in the care of Mr Langstone at Lord Mayor Treloar Hospital, Alton, where the R.H.C.H. had a small bed complement.

In 1965 equipment was limited. 'Power tools were very restricted. We had an air-drill which had as an accessory a circular saw which had been designated for cutting bone grafts through long bones. It was of course impossible to use this on the neck of a femur and, when doing joint replacements, then a hand saw was used, and in fact, I used a hack-saw, which had been bought in an ironmonger's shop in Winchester.' The Orthopaedic Theatre, for some time, was moved to the Twin Theatre (off the ramp) but later returned to the present main Theatre, after the Chapel had been closed. One of the biggest medical advances was the establishment of the Intensive Care Unit, and the opening of the new Accident and Emergency Unit.'The first knee replacement was carried out in 1967 ... the patient still walks on it well.' Further developments have been the use of the AO Internal Fixation system for fractures (i.e. the using of screws, etc.) and more recently the establishment of arthoroscopy for diagnosis and treatment of knee derangements.

There have been other significant changes, amongst them the treatment of diabetics. 'It is appropriate to record that, at the time of writing, the first patient known to be treated with insulin for Diabetes Mellitus at the Royal Hampshire County Hospital in 1924 is still alive. The original records, with her present Physicians in Dorchester, gave handwritten details of diet and insulin dosage. Over those 62 years, she would have witnessed many developments in diabetic care, both nationally and in Winchester. The County Hospital now has its own Diabetic Clinic in line with most other Hospitals throughout the country, providing comprehensive care in all aspects for patients with diabetes and their families, largely as out-patients. We are now moving confidently away from long periods of in-patient treatment to 'stabilise' new patients or, for instance, pregnant diabetic women, to community out-patient care. The service will remain firmly based on the County Hospital with renewed emphasis on communication with patients and their doctors, and on education.'

A glance at the list of Consultants in 1986 indicates how much change there has been in the last few years, in the variety of treatment now available to present day patients. Things have certainly changed since Matthew Combe could be consulted only about those patients he felt like attending. 'In 1948, the medical staff consisted of twelve resident doctors and twenty-two non-resident consultant staff. The resident staff were young doctors gaining experience before taking up a more permanent career in whichever branch of medicine they had elected to follow. They were employed on a full-time basis to the Hospital on salaries ranging between £70 - £200 per annum, according to their seniority and position on the staff. The Consultant staff, a number of whom were also in general practice, were part-time officers to the Hospital, who gave their services to the Hospital on a voluntary basis. With the coming of the National Health Service, radical changes were to take place in the medical sector, as they did in other parts of the Service. A Consultant could no longer be engaged in both general practice and consultant hospital practice; those who were already on the staff, and a number had already given many hours of valuable service, were invited to remain, provided they withdrew from general practice. In future, a Consultant must be someone who has received an accepted training and gained a higher qualification recommended by the Royal College, in his chosen speciality, and they would be appointed by a Statutory Committee, as laid down by the Ministry of Health. The appointment was to be remunerated on either a full or part-time contract. The former meant that the Consultant was on a full-time commitment to the Hospital and unable to partake in any form of private practice; the latter would be on a sessional basis, up to a maximum of nine and a half notional half days, and they were permitted to engage in Private Consultant Practice at other times.'[14]

Now in 1986 the Hospital is undergoing its most fundamental organisational change since 1948 with the introduction of 'General Management'. This follows recommendations by the Managing Director of Sainsbury's, Mr Roy Griffiths, who was asked by the Secretary of State to examine the management of the N.H.S. In 1985 the Hospital's first General Manager, Mr F.J. Moynihan, Consultant

27. Lord Northbrook receives the first cheque for the Scanner Appeal. From left to right: The Right Worshipful The Mayor of Winchester, Councillor J. Freeman, Mrs. J. Richardson (Chairman of the League of Friends) and Lord Northbrook.

Orthopaedic Surgeon, was appointed for a two year period. His appointment was quickly followed by the establishment of a Board including eight Directors of Clinical Services. Thus has started a brave attempt to introduce a different kind of management in the Hospital designed to meet the challenge of providing increasingly sophisticated and expensive hospital care within tight financial constraints to a rapidly ageing population.

It is fitting that 1986 should see the largest ever appeal to the local community for financial assistance towards the purchase of a body scanner. The Appeal for £250,000 was launched on 28 January by Lord Northbrook, as Chairman of the Winchester District Health Authority, who pointed out that the area covered by his Authority stretched from Andover to Eastleigh. It is a smaller area than that nominally served by Alured Clarke's Hospital in 1736, but the total number of potential patients is now something like 200,000 people. Doctor Clarke would surely have approved of this combination of voluntary and National Health Service effort.

It is also fitting that the year of the celebration of the 250th Anniversary of the Hospital should culminate in the opening of the Nightingale Wing. The first patients will be admitted in October, followed shortly afterwards on 27 November by the official opening by Her Majesty The Queen. The new Wing will cost more than two million pounds a year to run, and will require more than 100 additional staff, most of them nurses.

Current medical descriptions and terms may have changed, from Colebrook Street to Parchment Street, and on to Romsey Road, but the work that the Hospital has always done goes on, with the high standards that have been associated with the household since its formation 250 years ago.

Appendix I

CHAIRMEN OF THE COURT OF GOVERNORS

The County Hospital, Winchester

1736-1741	The Rev. Alured Clarke D.D.
1741	The Rev. John Burton D.D.
1742	Edward Hooker Esq.
1743	The Rev. John Burton D.D.
1744	The Rev. John Coxed
1745	The Ven. Robert Eden
1746-1748	The Rev. John Hoadly
1749	John Merrill Esq.
1750-1774	The Rev. John Hoadly
1775	The Rev. Harry Lee D.D.
1776-1778	The Rev. Charles Blackstone
1779-1804	John Jenkinson Esq. M.P.
1805-1837	The Rev. Harry Lee D.D.
1838-1840	The Rev. David Williams
1841-1860	The Rev. R.S. Barter
1861-1862	The Ven. Philip Jacob
1863-1867	The Rev. E. Stewart

The Royal Hampshire County Hospital

1868-1877	Sir William Heathcote, Bart.
1787-1882	The Ven. Philip Jacob
1883-1890	Rowland Jones Bateman Esq.
1891-1897	William W. Portal Esq.
1905-1907	The Right Honourable Evelyn Ashley
1908-1912	The Duke of Wellington
1913-1927	The Earl of Northbrook
1928-1939	The Countess of Northbrook
1940-1947	Captain Sir George Cooper, Bart.

CHAIRMEN OF WINCHESTER GROUP HOSPITAL MANAGEMENT COMMITTEE

1948-1951   Brigadier General M. Kemp Welch
1951-1961   Captain Sir George Cooper, Bart., D.L., J.P.
1961-1974   The Lord Northbrook J.P.

CHAIRMAN OF WINCHESTER HEALTH AUTHORITY

Lord Northbrook, Bart., D.L., J.P.

Appendix II

THE SURGEON: G. K. Lyford at the County Gaol and Bridewell

(From *Report of the Committee ... [on] the State of the Hampshire County Gaol and Bridewells*, Hatchard J, London, 1817.)

The Surgeon of the Gaol is Mr Giles King Lyford, who is likewise Surgeon of the Bridewell. He appears to have held this situation for nearly twenty years: his salary upon his first appointment was £100, for which he engaged to attend the prisoners in both Gaols, and to provide the necessary medicines; he continues now to receive the same salary without any additional emolument. Mr Lyford has not applied for an increase of allowance, nor do your Committee conceive that any is called for, the salary being as large as is generally given at this time to professional men for the same services in other counties; but it appears that he has never hitherto received any payment of attending persons on the Master's side of the debtors' Prison, which, under the terms of his appointment, he was entitled to have demanded; and there exists no impediment, if he pleases, for the future to require payment from them. The Surgeon has received no written or verbal instructions from the Magistrates respecting his attendance at the Gaol, or any rule to guide and direct his conduct in the performance of his professional duties, but has been governed entirely by his own discretion. This defect has not been found to have occasioned any relaxation on the part of Mr Lyford of what he considered to be his duty; for, from the representation of the Gaoler of both Prisons, he appears to have been regular in visiting the prisoners when sick, assiduously attentive to their bodily complaints, and faithfully to have discharged the functions of his office. But there remains an important service connected with the department of a Surgeon which Mr Lyford might have performed, and which, from his not being aware that it constituted any part of his duty, has hitherto been neglected, viz. visiting the wards, ascertaining and regulating the number to be confined in each room, examining the state of the walls, the bedding, clothing, and persons of the prisoners, with reference to health and cleanliness. This seems an obvious duty for the Surgeon to perform, and would materially tend to keep the Prison in a constant state of health. Your Committee look to the importance of this inspection on the part of the Surgeon, as well as to the interference of the Magistrates, as a means of preventing the different parts of the Gaol from again getting into the very foul and filthy state in which they were discovered to be at the time of the inquiry. Mr Lyford, moreover, has no regular days for visiting the Gaol, but attends only when called upon by the Gaoler.

He keeps for his private information a book in which he enters his observations upon the cases of the patients in the Gaol, but keeps no book or record at the Gaol for the inspection of the Magistrates, and has for some years past discontinued to make any report to the Quarter Sessions, the return contained in the Calendar at each Quarter Sessions having been inserted, as he states, entirely without his knowledge or authority. It is of the utmost importance that the Surgeon and all the officers of the Gaol should have the duties of their respective stations defined. It must be left to the visiting Magistrates to frame and submit for the approbation of the Magistrates at their Quarter Sessions a complete code of regulations for the government of every part of the Prison, as well as of all the officers connected with it; and your Committee strongly recommend to their attention the several regulations already stated, and likewise that the Surgeon should be required to examine every Prisoner upon admission into the Gaol, and before any intercourse is had with the other prisoners, taking care that their bodies have previously undergone a complete cleansing in the bath; that he also be required to keep a journal of his proceedings and observations, which should be left in the Prison for the inspection of the visiting Magistrates.

Surgeon to the Bridewell

Mr Lyford, as before stated, is the Surgeon also of this Prison; and, from the Keeper's account, is regular and frequent in visiting the prisoners. He either attends himself, or sends his son, or assistant. Thre is no want, therefore, of medical assistance for the sick. The Surgeon keeps no book of observations, which it would be desirable he should do, for the information of the visiting Magistrates' and in which, observations on the personal cleanliness of the prisoners, and the state of the Prison, should be inserted; and any suggestion for securing, in this respect, the health of the prisoners mentioned, which it will hereafter, it is to be hoped, constitute part of the duty of the Surgeon to examine into.

Appendix III

THE SALE OF PARCHMENT STREET

LARGE and IMPORTANT PROPERTY

HANTS COUNTY HOSPITAL
PARCHMENT STREET AND UPPER BROOK STREET
WINCHESTER

T.S. MORRIS is honoured by instructions from
the Building Committee to SELL by AUCTION, in
ONE LOT, at *The George Hotel*, Winchester, on Thursday
the 15th of October 1868, at three o'clock in the afternoon
THAT VERY DESIRABLE PROPERTY
Comprising
All that extensive Range of Buildings, formerly
the COUNTY HOSPITAL
The Centre Building was originally a large Family
Mansion, and the wings on either side were erected by
the Hospital Governors as the requirements of the insti-
tution demanded, and the Chapel wing, with its superior
stone staircase, was built about forty years ago in the
most substantial manner. There will also be included in
the purchase –
A comfortable DWELLING HOUSE and
Garden in Upper Brook Street,
As well as the OLD WINCHESTER ASSEMBLY
ROOMS.

The Block of Buildings forming Laundry and Brewhouse, and another Block of Buildings, with frontage to
Upper Brook Street, easily convertible into good Tenements, are shown upon a plan.

The Freehold Land and the Leasehold portion comprised in this sale is la. Or. 30p. or thereabouts, in extent,
offering eligible sites for the erection of good Dwelling
Houses in Parchment Street, with a frontage of 290ft.
9in. and sites for Tenements in Brook Street of 225ft.

6in. frontage, with good depths for gardens, offering a
rare opportunity for an enterprising investment.

The Valuable BUILDING MATERIALS
consist of about 350 rods of brick work, 100,000 plain
tiles, three three-story stone staircases, double-winding
stone staircase to entrance, about 150 squares of sound
oak and deal flooring, all the beams, rafters, roofs, and
quarterings. 120 panelled and other doors and frames,
180 pairs of sashes and frames and skylights, several
force pumps, jack pumps, sinks, dressers, cupboards,
and shelving. 14 lead-lined cisterns, 10 water closet apparatus, 13 lead-lined sinks, nine lead mop wringers, all the
lead pipes from wells and cisterns in about the entire
building, lead pipes from closets and drains to cesspools,
the water and gas piping and burners, all the heavy stack
pipes and guttering, lead flats on roofs, house bells, and
the substantial iron railing in front, with two pairs of
iron gates to Parchment Street.

The Auctioneer particularly invites the attention of
builders and capitalists to this property, offering as it
does an unusual opportunity for good investment, either
as a convertible property, whereby several large and
commodious Dwelling Houses may be made at a comparatively small outlay, or, if taken down, the valuable
Materials would more than suffice to erect a double
Terrace of Houses, of moderate dimensions, with
an outlay only of the requisite labour.

Printed particulars, with conditions of sale and plans,
may be obtained of Messrs. C. and F.I. Warner, solicitors,
Jewry Street; Mr. J.G. Comely, Surveyor, Southgate
Street; Messrs. Thring and Gale, Surveyors, St Peter
Street, Winchester; or of the Auctioneer, St Peter's
Street, Winchester

Appendix IV

In June 1870, the in-patients Diet was revised:

Allowance	*No. 1 Diet*	*No. 2 Diet*	*No. 3 Diet*

Allowance Daily	Bread 12 oz.
	Broth 1 pt.
	Milk 1 pt.
		Meat 6 oz.
		Potatoes or other
		  vegetables 6 oz.
		Bread – for men 16oz.
		Bread – for
		  women 12 oz.
		Milk ¼ pt.
			Meat 8 oz.
			Potatoes or other
			  vegetables 6 oz.
			Bread – for men 18 oz.
			Bread – for
			  women 14 oz.
			Milk ¼ pt.

		Supper Cocoa with milk ½ pt. or Vegetable soup ½ pt. or Cheese 1 oz.	*Supper* Same as No. 2

Dietary Rules
1. The meat is to be of the weight specified after cooking including bone.
2. Cold meat is to be supplied on Sundays; on three of the other six days the meat to be roasted, on the other three boiled.
3. All patients on their admission will be on No 1 diet till otherwise ordered by the Medical Officer in charge.
4. All children under 14 years of age will receive as much of the diet on which they are placed as the Medical Officer shall direct.
5. Milk diet where required is to be specially ordered.
6. Nothing special will be delivered out unless the Physician Surgeon or House Surgeon shall have stated on the book or paper the actual articel to be added.
7. Extras – Beef tea, fish, fowl, bacon, eggs, beer, portes wine, and spirits will be considered special, and be delivered only under such daily directions as aforesaid.
8. Barley water, rice water, and lemonade, when specially ordered as aforesaid, will be made as follows:-
1. Barley Water – Barley, 2oz. Sugar, 2oz for 5pts.
2. Rice Water – Rice, 2oz. Sugar, 2oz for 5pts.
3. Lemonade – 1 large lemon. Sugar, 2oz for 5pts.

9. Under no circumstances is a patient to be allowed to retain any Liquor or food in the ward, and only under very special circumstances is a nurse to be allowed to retain in the ward any liquor or food for future use by the patients.

10. The meals are to be at the following hours:-

Breakfast, 7.30 a.m.; Dinner, 1; Tea, 4.30; Supper, 7.30. All the Officers of the Hospital are expected to co-operate in the carrying out of the above rules.

Appendix V

MEDICAL MEN IN WINCHESTER IN 1784
(*The Hampshire Directory*, printed by J. Sadler, Winchester, 1784.) (Original spelling)

ANDERSON, George. Chymist and Apothecary; Pesthouse.
BRERETON, John. Apothecary; Upper Brook.
CHARLES, Richard. Surgeon, Apothecary and man-midwife; St Thomas Street.
EARLE, George. Druggist and Chymist; High Street.
KENTISH, Nathaniel. Surgeon, Apothecary and man-midwife; Penthouse.
KIMBER, Richard. Surgeon and Apothecary; Back Lane [St George's Street].
LIPSCOMBE, Thomas. Apothecary; High Street.
LITTLEHALES, John. Physician; Southgate Street.
LYFORD, Charles. Surgeon; Peter Street.
McITTRICK, John. M.D.; Kingsgate Street.
SMITH, John. Surgeon; Giles Hill House [the inoculating Doctor].
SMITH, John. Surgeon and Apothecary; High Street.
THOMAS and CAUT. Apothecaries; Kingsgate Street.

Appendix VI

HONORARY MEDICAL STAFF INVITED, WITH THEIR WIVES, IN JULY 1939 TO ATTEND THE OPENING OF THE NIGHTINGALE HOME BY H.R.H. THE DUCHESS OF KENT

R. H. Balfour Barrow, Esq.
Doctor J. R. Bodington
Doctor H. N. Davis
W. Everett, Esq. F.R.C.S.
Doctor C. B. S. Fuller
Doctor M. H. Gleeson White
Doctor F. F. Jagger
Doctor H. Mallinson
I. Mann, Esq.
Doctor C. J. Penny
B. H. Pidcock, Esq. F.R.C.S.
Doctor R. I. Roberts
Doctor K. M. Robertson
Doctor Ross
J. Troup, Esq.
Doctor Wrigley

Appendix VII

MEDICAL AND SURGICAL STAFF, JANUARY-JUNE 1948

Hon. Physicians: C.B.S. Fuller, M.C., M.A., M.D., M.R.C.P.; K.M. Robertson, M.D., F.R.C.P.

Hon. Surgeons: B.H. Pidcock, M.B., B.S., F.R.C.S. (on Sick Leave); J. Troup, M.B., Ch.B., F.R.C.S.E.

Hon. Assistant Surgeons: J. Rubin, B.A., M.B., B.S., F.R.C.S.E. (On Service with H.M. Forces); P.W. Ingram, M.A., M.B., Ch.B., F.R.C.S.E.

Hon. Ophthalmic Surgeon: R.H. Balfour Barrow, M.DM., D.O.M.S.

Hon. Clinical Assistant to Ophthalmic Department: J.A. Robertson, M.B., B.S., D.O.M.S.

Hon. Surgeon in charge Ear,Nose and Throat Department: B.H. Pidcock, M.B., B.S., F.R.C.S. (On Sick Leave)

Hon. Assistant Surgeon, Ear, Nose and Throat Department: G.S. Midgley, D.L.O., M.R.C.S.

Hon. Obstetrician: C.J. Penny, O.B.E., M.A., M.D., B.Ch.

Hon. Assistant Obstetrician: P.R. Mitchell, O.B.E., T.D., M.B., Ch.B., M.R.C.O.G.

Hon. Surgeon to Obstetrical and Gyneacological Department: James Troup, M.B., ChB., F.R.C.S.E.

Hon. Assistant Gynaecologist: P.R. Mitchell, O.B.E., T.D., M.B., Ch.B., M.R.C.O.G.

Hon. Radiologist: R.I. Roberts, M.R.C.S., L.R.C.P., A.D.M.R.

Hon. Clinical Pathologist: C.H. Wrigley, M.A., M.D.

Hon. Anaesthetist: Hugh Mallinson, M.B., B.Ch.

Hon. Assistant Anaesthetist: J.R. Bodington, M.A., M.B., B.Ch., M.R.C.S., L.R.C.P., D.A.

Hon. Orthopaedic Surgeon: G.N. Golden, F.R.C.S.

Hon. Psychiatrist: W. Lindesay Neustatter, M.D., B.Sc., M.R.C.P.

Hon. Dermatologist: A.S. Hall, B.Sc., M.D.

Paediatrician: G. Ormiston, M.D., M.R.C.P.

Physician in charge of Physical Medicine: W. Russell Grant, M.R.C.S., L.R.C.P., D.Phys.Med.

Hon. Dental Surgeon: I. Mann, L.D.S., R.C.S.

Hon. Speech Therapist: A.P. Tolfree, F.C.S.T.

RESIDENT MEDICAL STAFF

R.SO.
Assistant Pathologist
Anaesthetist
Orthopaedic Registrar and Senior Casualty Officer
Junior Casualty Officer
Two House Physicians
H.P. to Maternity Department
H.P. to Paediatric Department
Two House Surgeons
House Surgeon to Ophthalmic and E.N.T. Departments

Appendix VIII

CONSULTANTS AS AT APRIL 1986

Anaesthetics: Dr. R. W. Buckland, F.F.A.R.C.S.; Dr. D. J. Bowen, F.F.A.R.C.S.; Dr. R. W. D. Clunie, F.F.A.R.C.S.; Dr. K. J. Davies, F.F.A.R.C.S.; Dr. M. L. Nancekievill, F.F.A.R.C.S.; Dr. W. D. White, F.F.A.R.C.S.; Dr. P. M. H. Duboulay, F.F.A.R.C.S.; Dr. E. D. Spark, (Associate Specialist); Dr. R. J. Summerfield, F.F.A.R.C.S.

Chest Medicine: Dr. D. C. Lillie, (Honorary Appointment).

Dermatology: Dr. P. R. Montgomery, M.D., M.B.B.S., F.R.C.S.; Dr. M. K. Martin, (Associate Specialist).

Ear, Nose & Throat: Mr. T. H. Guerrier, L.R.C.P., M.B.B.S., F.R.C.S.; Mr. P. B. Ashcroft, L.R.C.P., M.B.B.S., F.R.C.S.

General Medicine: Dr. D. A. F. McGill, F.R.C.P.; Dr. J. D. Powell-Jackson, F.R.C.P.; Dr. A. P. Brooks, M.R.C.P.

General Surgery: Mr. J. S. Mousley, F.R.C.S.; Mr. A. P. Ross, M.S., F.R.C.S.; Mr. R. H. S. Lane, M.S., F.R.C.S.

Geriatrics: Dr. K. K. Nayyar, M.R.C.P.; Dr. G. I. Carpenter, M.R.C.P.; Dr. P. G. Gaffikin, (Associate Specialist).

Neurology: Dr. P. Kennedy, M.R.C.P.

Obstetrics & Gynaecology: Mr. A. D. Noble, F.R.C.S., F.R.C.O.G.; Mr. A. T. Letchworth, M.D., F.R.C.O.G.; Mr. M. S. Buckingham, D.M., M.R.C.O.G.

Ophthalmology: Mr. J. C. McGrand, F.R.C.S.; Mr. M. J. Absolon, F.R.C.S.

Oral Surgery: Mr. T. H. Redpath, L.P.C.P., M.R.C.S., F.D.S.; Mr. R. A. J. Mayhew, B.D., F.F.D.

Orthodontics: Mr. R. T. Broadway, M.D.S.(Lond.), F.D.S., D. Orth., R.C.S.(Eng.).

Orthopaedics: Mr. K. T. Hesketh, F.R.C.S.; Mr. F. J. Moynihan, F.R.C.S.; Mr. A. W. Samuel, M.D., F.R.C.S., F.R.C.S.(Ed.); Mr. W. E. Hook, M.B.chB., F.R.C.S., M.ch.Orth.

Pathology

Chemical Pathology: Dr. C. S. Shaw, M.B., F.R.C.P., F.R.C.Path.

Haematology: Dr. W. O. Mavor, M.A., M.B., B. Chir., F.R.C.P.(Ed.), F.R.C.Path.

Histopathology: Dr. M. J. Sworn, M.R.C.S., L.R.C.P., M.B., B.S., F.R.C.Path.

Histopathology: Dr. A. C. Vincenti, M.D., M.R.C.Path.

Microbiology: Dr. J. M. Graham, M.B., B.S., Dip.Bact., F.R.C.Path.

Paediatrics: Dr. T. F. Mackintosh, M.D., F.R.C.P.(E)., D.C.H.; Dr. P. R. Betts, M.D., F.R.C.P.; Dr. A. G. Antoniou, M.B., ch.B., M.R.C.P., D.G.H.

Psychiatry

Child: Dr. A. J. Burnfield, (Associate Specialist); Dr. S. W. Hettiaratchy, M.B., B.S., M.R.C.Psych., D.P.M.; Dr. R. I. Stewart, M.B., Ch.B.

Adolescent: Dr. W. A. Saunders, M.A., M.B., B.Chir., M.R.C.Psych., D.P.M.; Dr. P. M. White, M.B., B.Chir., M.R.C.Psych., D.P.M.

Adult: Dr. M. Norman-Nott, D.R.S.med., M.R.C.Psych., D.P.M.; Dr. P. D. Bartlett, M.B., Ch.B.; Dr. E. E. Blackstock, M.B., B.ch., B.A.O., M.R.C.Psych., D.P.M.; Dr. N. Wright, M.B., B.S., M.R.C.Psych.

Psychogeriatrics: Dr. P. D. Hettiaratchy, M.B., B.S., M.R.C.Psych., D.P.M.; Dr. S. Olivieri, D.M.S., M.D., M.R.C.Psych.

Radiology: Dr. R. C. Michell, M.B., B.S., D.M.R.D., F.R.C.R., F.R.C.P.; Dr. O. J. C. Wethered, M.B., B.S., M.R.C.P., F.R.C.R.; Dr. J. M. Laidlow, M.B., B.S., M.R.C.P., F.R.C.R.

Radiotherapy: Dr. P. Bodkin, M.B. B.Chir.

Rheumatology & Rehabilitation: Dr. J. B. Morrison, M.D., D.Phys.Med.; Dr. N. L. Cox, B.M.R.C.P., B.A., B.M., B.Ch., M.R.C.P.

Urology Surgery: Mr. G. S. M. Harrison, F.R.C.S.

Notes And References

Abbreviations

Ann.Rep.	*Annual Reports of The Royal Hampshire County Hospital*
Cath.Monuments	Vaughan, John, *Winchester Cathedral: Its Monuments and Memorials*, Selwyn and Blount, 1919
D.N.B.	*Dictionary of National Biography*
Foster	Foster, Joseph, *Alumni Oxonienses*, 4 vols., Oxford 1891.
H.C.	*Hampshire Chronicle*, 1772 continuing
H.O.	*Hampshire Observer*, 1886-1957 [formerly *Winchester Observer* from 1877
K.A.C.	Rose, Martial, *King Alfred's College*, Phillimore, 1981
Mayo	Mayo, C.H., *A Genealogical Account of the Mayo and Elton Families*, 2nd edn, pp 1908
Scholars	Kirby, T.F., *Winchester Scholars*, Henry Froude, 1888
Statutes	*Statutes of the Hampshire County Hospital* (as amended and published at various dates), e.g. Wilkes, Winchester, 1772
V.C.H.	*Victoria County History of Hampshire*, vols.1-5, 1910
Venn	Venn, J.A., *Alumni Cantabrigiensis*, (v.d.)
W.C.A.	*Winchester City Archives*, C. Bailey, 1856
W.Q.R.	*Winchester Quarterly Record*, [c.1841-c.1855]
Winchester	Carpenter Turner, Barbara, *Winchester*, Cave, 1980

INTRODUCTION

1. *Winchester*: 48, 49. B.C.T.
2. *V.C.H.*: T. Round's Account of the 'Winchester Domesday', 532,533.
3. Milner's *History*, 231.
4. The builder was William Kernott, a supporter of the County Hospital.
5. *Winchester*: 48.
6. According to T.W. Shore, the Hospital belonging to Hyde was so popular and so costly to sustain that in the reign of Edward II the Abbey was permitted to appropriate the great tithes of Micheldever Church for the relief of the sick, infirm and poor. Shore, T.W., *A History of Hampshire*, Eliott Stock, London (1892), 143.
7. *Winchester*: 148.
8. *Wykehamica*, 463-5; *Obedientary Rolls*, various years (Dean and Chapter archives).
9. *W.C.M.*
10. *An Ancient Manuscript*, ed. by W.De Gray Birch, H.R.S. (1889)and Item 162, *The Golden Age of Anglo-Saxon Art*, British Museum Publications, for a herbal written in Winchester in the mid 12th century.
11. *Winchester Cathedral Chartulary*, item 301, ed. A.W. Goodman, Wykeham Press, (1927)
12. *Ibid*, item 225.
13. *Winchester*: 73.
14. *D.N.B.*
15. H.C.R.O. Inventory, *Winchester*: 87.

16. Inventory, *Winchester*: 87.
17. I am grateful to Doctor John Harvey for much information about Wykehamist doctors.
18. See the interesting selections of plague references in Charles Bailey's small book *Winchester Archives* (1856).
19. Spaul, J. *Andover.*
20. Published in *Hampshire Churchwardens Accounts*, ed. J.F. Williams, Wykeham Press (1913).
21. B.C.T. *H.C.*
22. Inventory, H.C.R.O.
23. Inventory, H.C.R.O., St Cross Ledger (St Cross Hospital Archives)
24. Deeds in private ownership; *Winchester Cathedral Register.*
25. Their inn was called the *Fleur de Lis* until the beginning of the 19th century.
26. Willis, A.J. (ed.), *Hampshire Miscellany*. Vol.II. Laymen's licences in the Diocese of Winchester, 1675-1834. Hambledon, Lyminge, Kent.

CHAPTER I

1. Leach, A.F., *Winchester College*, (Duckworth, 1899), 370; an additional factor was a notorious quarrel between Warden Nicolas and the Fellows.
2. B.C.T. *Winchester*, Chapter XI.
3. *Ibid*, 149.
4. See St Maurice's Parish Overseers Accounts. H.R.C.O.
5. Fox, Robert, *The History of Godmanchester*, (1831).
6. *D.N.B.*
7. Another Trimmell uncle, Hugh, was Apothecary to the King's Household from 1719 until 1723.
8. Clarke's Trimmell (Deanery) cousins also died young. The Dean's eldest son had been buried on 22 October 1726, William died in August 1729, and the third, another Edward, died in May 1735. Cathedral Burial Register.
9. For Charlotte Clayton, see *D.N.B.* under Sundon.
10. Defoe's words.
11. *A proposal for erecting a Publick Hospital for Sick and Lame etc.* was published and circulated from Winchester on 22 May 1736: it included *The Form of the Preamble to the first Subscription Paper according to the manner of the Infirmary at Westminster*, dated 6 August 1736. Next came *Some farther (sic) Considerations in Behalf of a Proposal for erecting a Publick Hospital etc.*, dated 14 August 1736, again from Winchester.
12. Including Clarke himself.
13. Robert Waldron the Elder (d.1719). Robert the Younger, Mayor 1728-9 and 1732-3; he died in 1741. These Waldrons lived in a substantial house in Kingsgate Street which had once belonged to the Countess of Exeter, but their cousins, William and Thomas Waldron, worked as carriers from Upper Brook Street.
14. D. and C. Archives.
15. First Minute Books of both bodies.
16. London, 1737. Printed for J. and J. Pemberton at the Golden Buck in Fleet Street.
17. The Corporation bought 'The Abbey' in 1890 and turned the principle house into the Mayor's official residence. Its purchase price was £5,500; Thomas Stopher's Manuscript Notebook, Winchester City Library.
18. A substantial medieval door survived the demolition of 1959 and is now in the Winchester Museum.
19. Which survives only amongst the family papers of Jervoise of Herriard in the Hampshire County Record Office.
20. Both timbers now in the City Museum.
21. B.C.T. *Winchester*: A pew in St Maurice's Church belonged by right to the occupant of the Hospital building (Pescod lease).
22. *Winchester Sixty Generations*, (1955), Catalogue Item No.93.
23. Though according to Doctor Trail Henry Hoare was operated on in the Hospital, and presumably in a private ward.

24. *Sun Fire Office Policy No. 72784*. The arrangements were made through the Company's Winchester agent, Alderman Samuel Smith. The same Company insured Clarke's own house in The Close, as well as the Deanery and the other Close houses. Smith, a Yorkshire man from Saltby, died in 1757, and was buried inside the Hospital's church, St Maurice. His memorial tablet disappeared when the church was pulled down. Clarke's canonical residence was insured for more than the Hospital, £550 and £50 for his coach house and stable. Sun Fire Policy No. 84723.

CHAPTER II

1. He was Samuel Ogden, son of a Vicar of Wherwell, and a graduate of Brasenose.
2. Twelve copies of Alphabet books were bought early on, and a volunteer, 'Miss Smith', taught the patients to read.
3. Lady Lymington had been Bridget Bennett, the eldest daughter of the first Earl of Tankerville, and died in 1738. Shortly after her death, her husband, John Wallop, became a Governor of the Foundling Hospital; his second wife, Elizabeth, was the widow of Henry Grey. The Wallops were an ancient Hampshire family; John, Clarke's friend, had been created Baron Wallop and Lord Lymington in 1720, and became Earl of Portsmouth in 1743.

CHAPTER III

1. Joyce was St Thomas' Treasurer.
2. Moody, H., *Notes and Essays*, (1851), 'Statistics of Crime in Hampshire'.
3. H.C.R.O.
4. H.C.R.O.
5. He was a Londoner, from the Parish of St Dunstan-in-the-West, but his family lived in Worcester. The Apothecaries were allowed to purchase their supplies only from one or two approved 'druggists' or 'chymists'. It looks as if Pratt was taken ill at the Committee of 5 October 1758; his list of patients breaks off with the death of Ann Crossingham, and is continued in another hand. He was 'the late Mr Pratt' by 21 November.
6. 6 November 1736 (Committee). 'Mr Wavell having declined offering himself as a candidate.'
7. W/B1/8/ Ordinances, VIII, 112 (c). 'New Built' at this time could mean over 100 years old.
8. P.C.C. Wills, PRO.
9. King's disputed appointment probably reflected the political disputes in the College and in the Corporation. He was Mayor of Winchester in 1758 and 1764.
10. *winchester Scholars; s.a. 1715*. Deeds of 13 Kingsgate Street. (Winchester College Archives; ECC 1540942/2. 21 August 1799. H.C.R.O.
11. *Ibid*, W.C. Deeds.
12. His will, H.C.R.O. His continued involvement with the Oglanders. I.O.W. C.R.O.
13. Furley, J.S., *Chernocke House*.
14. Willis, *Calendar of Deeds relating to Episcopal Deeds (before 1850)*, 1958.
15. He was Sole Physician in January 1744.
16. His will, H.C.R.O.
17. He was an early supporter of the Hospital.
18. His next leave was ten years later.
19. He lent £250 at 4 per cent on 3 December 1755; it was repaid, with interest, on 8 September 1756.
20. Wills, H.C.R.O.
21. Cathedral *Registers*
22. Burton's opinion of Coxhead's tenure of the Warden's office. (1740-57) 'We sank to nothing'. Leach, *Op cit*, 380.
23. For Lady Sundon. *D.N.B.*, the article corrects the mistakes made in a Victorian biography. See also *Lord Hervey's Memoirs* edited by Romney Sedgewick, Kimber, 2nd edn. 1952.
24. cf. 30 September 1767. Martha Craddick discharged 'Improper object (consumptive)'; a hundred years later the Hospital was still refusing to accept this kind of patient.
25. Insurance Policy No. 84723; Chapter Act Book, s.a.

26. Russell, P.M.G., *A History of the Exeter Hospitals, 1170-1948*, James Townsend and Sons Limited, Exeter (1976)
27. Hoadly had to pay Clarke's executor a considerable sum for the fittings there.
28. *G.M.* Vol.XII. Deaths, 1742.
29. Sedgewick,*op cit*, Chapter 9.

CHAPTER IV

1. 'I'll go tomorrow to the painter to hasten down the picture' wrote Peter Dobree to the Governors (19 May 1752).
2. Taunton was buried in St John's Church on 7 April 1752; his memorial survived its demolition. Davies, *Southampton*, 180, 181, 372.
3. *D.N.B.* and 'Sir John Clobury', *Wessex Life*, 19 , B.C.T.
4. W/E3/5, W.C.R.O.
5. Unfortunately, Abree Senior's will (1749) has been lost; the family lived in the Soke, and Clobury House had presumably been acquired as an investment property, or even as a workshop or store. The Abrees were not natives of Winchester.
6. His will, P.C.C., P.R.O.
7. This decision was eventually published in the *Salisbury and Winchester Journal*, under the date of 8 February 1755, presumably to encourage further subscribers.
8. A decision taken by only five Governors, who gave a mere five days' notice by advertisement in the London, Salisbury and Reading newspapers 'that all the gentlemen and well-wishers to the charity in or near Winchester be requested to meet at the Board Room and go together from thence to attend the laying of the foundation stone'.
9. The Trustees for the Hospital capital fund were Cheyney, Burton and Chancellor Hoadly.
10. The matter was very embarrassing; for Cheyney, see Blore, G.H.,*Thomas Cheyney, Wykehamist*, Wykeham Press 1950. Henley, the famous lawyer and Lord Chancellor, *D.N.B.*
11. *The correspondence of Edmund Pyle, Chaplain in Ordinary to George II, with Samuel Kerrick, D.D.*, edited by Albert Hartshorne; Bodley Head (1905), 1729-1763.
12. Trail *op cit*.
13. See *Winchester 100 Years Ago*, B.C.T. (Cave 1980).
14. Below, pp for its effect on the Hospital.
15. By Hunt's, now of Silver Hill; Earle's house is now the National Westminster Bank.
16. Below.
17. See the answer to Clarke's letter from the Treasurer of St Thomas' Hospital.
18. The future Lord Chancellor; *D.N.B.*
19. The next year, Keziah Butt was also discharged quickly; 'improper object, lunatick'. (17 June 1767).
20. In October 1766, John Ford and his wife offered to nurse any smallpox patients in the smallpox hospital at the rate of ten shillings per week per person.
21. The price suggests perhaps just a peg leg.
22. Willis, A.J., *Winchester Settlement Papers, 1667-1742*, Lyminge, Folkestone (1967). 28, 30.

CHAPTER V

1. Swanton came from a family of famous lawyers; Pratt went because a member of his family was dying.
2. Edward Pyott, 'A Person called a Quaker'. 143 *Hampshire Allegations for Marriage Licences*, Vol. II, Harleian Society 1893.
3. 44m/69/42/7; H.C.R.O.
4. It was an arrangement which did not last.
5. Now Trafalgar Street.
6. See p 31
7. Pulled down in 1844; George III visited the Pentons in 1778.
8. The Founder's brother, Charles Clarke, so successful at the Bar that he had been able to rebuild the family home at Godmanchester, and had become a Judge, himself died of gaol-fever caught

at the Old Bailey in 1756, where he was presiding over the trial of a duellist who had killed his opponent.

9. *Report of the Committee appointed to enquire into the state of the Health of Prisoners confined in the King's House, at Winchester and the Preceedings of the House therefrom: 1780.*

10. John Smith had a widespread clientele. In 1771, he was advertising his skills in the Andover area. 'Doctor Smith innoculates the smallpox at a very convenient house by Weyhill in Hampshire on the usual terms; servants at two guineas; coffee, tea and sugar excepted. Patients are taken in at any notice without preparation.'

11. Which of the Winchester doctors or surgeons Sarah was referring to in this way remains a mystery.

12. The Williams Correspondence (MSS) kindly lent to this writer by the late Mrs Edwin Jervoise, and now in the Archives of Winchester College.

13. Robert Scott, who died intestate in 1798, much in debt,his principal creditor being William Gover, the land surveyor and builder.

14. Howard, John, *An Account of the Principal Lazarettoes in Europe ... and additional remarks on the present state of those in Great Britain and Ireland*, 2nd edn., London, (1791). p.179.

15. Undertakers' Records. Father and daughters all buried near each other in the Cemetery on·the Western Hill. He is commemorated by a window in St Michael's church; his son, the Reverend John Charles, died aged 24, and was buried in College Cloister on 11 November 1843, when mourning scarves were sent to Doctor Harris, Doctor Crawford, Doctor Phillips, Mr Wickham, Mr W. Wickham, Mr Lyford and Mr Mayo.

16. Though his brother Charles fell out with the Tory Dean and Chapter over who owned the end of his garden (Chapter Minutes, November 1830).

17. When the Reverend H.J. Wickham died in June 1914, the *Hampshire Chronicle* devoted nearly a column to the genealogy of his family which had so many connections with the Hospital and Winchester College. Most of the information had probably been provided by J.S. Furley, H.J. Wickham's successor as Housemaster in Chernocke House, and the note records H.J.'s grandfather, William Nicolas Wickham, as the first to practise medicine in Winchester. In fact, a William Wickham subscribed to the Hospital in October 1766. The young man Wickham to whom 'Doctor Mak' left £100 in 1784, whom Sarah /bib/called 'the son of an Apothecary from Sutton' – (who seems to have been Jacob Wickham of Sutton Scotney) – was buried in St Michael's churchyard in 1798, aged 47. He had clearly had some warning before his final illness – 'Many a threatening stroke was gave, before that I, (with patience could submit) and prepare myself to die'. There is evidence too, that the Wickhams also served St Cross Hospital: (St Cross Stewards' Accounts, 1810 'Mr Wickham Apothecary's bill, £7 12s. 6d.')

18. *The Letters to Gilbert White of Selborne ... From the Rev. John Mulso: passim.* Ed. Rashleigh Holt-White. R.H. Porter, London·(i906).

CHAPTER VI

1. The Rector of Weeke, near Winchester, the Rev. Daniel Mayo, appointed 1734, resigned 1759 when he moved to Michelmersh.

2. Sir Charles Blicke, 1745-1815: *D.N.B.* John Abernethy, later to be Mayo's adviser, was his apprentice.

3. Both men were Governors.

4. Avebury House, called so because of family connections with that village.

5. Mayo, C.H., *The Mayo and Elton Families*. 2nd edn, 1908 (privately printed).

6. Mayo was also Registrar of Births and Deaths in Winchester and so registered the death certificates of his own patients.

7. See Zachery Cope 'Jane Austen's Last Illness' in *British Medical Journal*, 18 July 1964, for Lyford's treatment of Jane. Marghanita Laski, for a brief account of Jane's last days in Winchester; 114 in *Jane Austen and Her World*, Thames and Hudson, 1969.

8. See Appendix II

9. Ordinances XVI 3a(a); 135(c); 175(g).

10. See also his memorial in the church.

11. H.G. Lyford seems also to have been interested in the problems of eyesight. As there was no treatment offered in the Hospital at this time, in January 1849 he allowed the *Chronicle* to publish

a testamentory letter which he had written in favour of a visiting optician. 'Mr Alexander ... has excellent knowledge of vision and the use of glasses.'

12. For his political career, see Sir Lewis Namier's biographical note in *The House of Commons, 1784-1790*, vol.II, Members: pp.678-79 (H.M.S.O. 1964)

13. 5M 63/3.

14. Rector of Barton Stacey, Vicar of Collingbourne, Minor Canon of Winchester Cathedral, and Chaplain to the County Gaol and Bridewell.

15. For the later Chaplains, *Cathedral, College and Hospital*, Moxley, C., pp.1986.

16. For Forrest, *Winchester 100 Years Ago*, B.C.T., Cave, 1980.

17. A stipulation which did not last.

18. Mrs Shenton had been appointed on 12 March 1806.

19. The revised Statutes of 1772 required a Winchester majority.

20. Though see below for the cholera epidemic in Southampton.

CHAPTER VII

1. 44M 69/H2/12. Kane had only been appointed Physician and Governor in April 1824.

2. Richard Littlehales, John's younger son, was thus the third member of the family to serve the Hospital. The *Hampshire Chronicle* of Saturday, 18 September 1847 noted his death. 'This city sustained a severe loss in the valuable services of Richard Littlehales, Esq.' He had died after a lingering illness, been three times Mayor before the Reform Act, and since then a magistrate and Town Councillor. 'In private life, his friends and neighbours duly appreciated his /bib/work.' He had represented St John's Ward, a part of the city most in need of main drainage and better houses, and was commemorated by the re-glazing of the east window in St Laurence's church in The Square, Winchester. He had lived in Great Minster Street, with his sister, Maria, who commissioned the window.

3. Howley was a Hampshire Hog, born at Ropley in 1766, and educated at Winchester College. *D.N.B.*

4. Of all the speeches made during the Festival, the most characteristic is that of Palmerston, with its insistence on the value of English voluntary institutions, uncontrolled by the State.

5. The Festival is described at length in *H.C.* beginning with Monday, 20 September 1836, and subsequent issues.

6. The first victim is said to have been a sailor who collapsed in Sunderland on 23 October 1831.

7. Undertaker's book, privately owned.

8. Founded in 1850.

9. Patterson, A.T., *Southampton*, McMillan (1979), Chapter VII.

10. One Councillor fought his election campaign with the slogan that he was 'positively against sewerage'.

11. Faraghk's death certificate shows that the cause of death was 'diseased lungs'.

CHAPTER VIII

1. The first military hospital in Hampshire was a large three-gabled manor house of c.1629, which had belonged to the Tichborne family, standing at the town end of what became known as Hospital Hill in Aldershot. Taken over as the Poor Law Union in 1835, it was acquired by the War Department in 1854, and remained the military hospital until 1879. An anonymous author of 1859 describes the army patients of this time in Aldershot, living in Hospital Huts, each distinguished by a white painted door, and containing 'some circus like Pierrot convalescents hanging about them'. (Cole, Howard N.:*The Story of Aldershot*, (2nd edn.), Southern Books Aldershot Limited, 1980) Army patients in Winchester Barracks seem to have had to be content with temporary buildings until the Hospital block, east of the railway bridge, and facing the Romsey Road, was completed in c.1871 (Ordnance Survey Map, XLI 13/13)

2. Robert Barter's affection for the Hospital has been described by one who knew him well, the Reverend H.C. Adams, in his valuable history of the College, *Wykehamica*, written in 1878. 'At the Hospital, of the Committee of which he was Chairman, he was so constant a visitor at the bedsides of the sick and dying, that he might as well have been the chaplain himself. At his death,

the resolution passed by the Committee declared that "all classes within the walls of the hospital – officers, servants and patients – felt his loss as that of a personal friend".' Adams adds that the Warden's hospitality was so unbounded that his house went by the name of *The Wykeham Arms*.

3. Hospital patients were allowed to use the Turkish Baths, and for a short period, Hospital laundry was sent to a local firm with a new kind of washing machine. Thomas Stopher, the future architectural adviser of the Hospital, remembered the Turkish Bath well; it was kept by Henry Butcher, a baker, at what was then 155 High Street, two doors east of the *India Arms* (Warren's *Directory*, 1877). The arrangements were decidedly primitive, quite a test for anyone ill enough to have been in the Hospital. The 'Hot Chamber' was over the baker's oven, and there was no colder bath, just increasingly colder water thrown over the customers, bucket by bucket, and proceeded by a shout 'cooler'! Stopher liked it, and Butcher was also a barber; 'Many a good shampooing have I had at his hands.' (Stopher's notes on houses in Winchester. MSS Winchester City Library.)

4. *Record*, 13 January 1864.

5. *Record*, s.a.

6. South aisle of nave, near south doorway: the marble medallion profile portrait is by a very distinguished Hampshire sculptor, Richard Cockle Lucas. Wickham's house, in St Thomas' Street, called after him, remains one of the best houses in the city.

7. *Record*, s.a.

8. Information from Mr P.N. Dawe, a recent owner of No. 13 Parchment Street.

9. The Pescod estate was sold off after William Pescod's son became a lunatic.

CHAPTER IX

1. *Autograph Letters, R.H.C.H. Library*. The story that Miss Nightingale chose the actual site for the new building seems without foundation. Sir William wrote to her asking her if she would be able to look at the architect's plans. '... and will give us any hints especially as to administration arrangements.' In a second letter, he had sent back the plans showing the alterations 'by which we have endeavoured to meet some at least of your suggestions', and he went on to praise Butterfield and 'his work of love to his fellow-creatures'. He had talked to him of Miss Nightingale's book, and reported to its author the architect's comments, 'I shall value Miss Nightingale's book very much.'

2. By April 1869, the 'Committee of the Infirmary' to give it its formal title, had already been seeking the advice of a local architect, Thomas Stopher, and 'Mr Stopher' was now asked to attend the Committee regularly, and to be present when the plumber, Glover (from Basingstoke), made his quarterly inspections. He had already designed a vault for amputated limbs, but it was his elderly father and namesake who had been appointed as 'Mr Butterfield's subordinate' in December 1868, and who had to attend the Weekly Committees, all for ten pounds a year. John Colson was dismissed – 'it would be unsuitable for him to be asked to serve under Mr Butterfield'. The new building was insured with the Sun Insurance Company for £5,000, its furniture for £1,000, of which £100 was for surgical instruments and the china.

3. Thompson, Paul; *William Butterfield*, Routledge 1971, p.53.

4. The arrangements for a site are recorded in the Chapter Minutes.

5. See Appendix IV.

6. Butler died suddenly in March 1882, and the Dean spoke in moving terms about him at the Weekly Board ... 'valuable services and constant attention for 26 years ... [he will] live in the grateful memory of all who take an interest in the Hospital'.

7. Bishop McDougall on the Committee. *D.N.B.*

8. The meeting of 2 May 1883 was a very troubled occasion. A proposal, of which proper notice had been given to discuss the patient's diet (arising out of a complaint), was not allowed, thanks to the opposition of Dean Bramston, and another sudden suggestion that more information should be asked for from patients before their admission – to help their dietry needs – was defeated by two clerical opponents who proposed that 'no steps be taken in the matter'.

CHAPTER X

1. And therefore Statute No. 30 could not apply to them.
2. Not for the first time. In 1857, the Court had ordered that alcohol could be prescribed but only for one day at a time. Beer had long been regarded as a healthy drink in the days when coffee and tea were expensive and considered harmful by some physicians. Port was bought regularly from 1842, brandy from 1851, champagne from 1875, and claret from 1876. (Doctor Trail's note.)
3. Tea was still coming from Harrods of Winchester; for this grocery shop see the excellent article by Joy Peach in *Hampshire Magazine* August 1985.
4. It has not survived.
5. 5M 63/191
6. The Rev. J.H. Slessor, Rector of Headbourne Worthy.
7. H.J. Godwin, M.B., B.A., F.R.C.S., M.R.C.S., L.R.C.P.
8. Dock, L.L., and Steward, J.M., *A Short History of Nursing*, (1931), 127.
9. Ether was demonstrated in Boston, USA, in 1846; chloroform in Edinburgh in 1847.

CHAPTER XI

1. See below.
2. 5M 66/77.
3. Nisbitt died in 1918 of the so-called Spanish Influenza.
4. Information from Miss Carpenter Turner to the writer.
5. Peach, D.L., *Merdone: The History of Hursley Park*, 1977 edn., published by I.B.M. United Kingdom Laboratories.
6. H.C.R.O., 187/M83/1.
7. H.C.R.O., 187/M85/1.

CHAPTER XII

1. The story of the Hospital during the Second World War is told, in part, in Fair Minute Book No.43 (5M 63/33). The book begins with the meeting of 10 May 1939, twenty-two members present, including the Chairman, Sir Arthur K. Waistell, Dean Selwyn and his Chapter Clerk, A.L. Bowker, and Doctors Fuller and Penny, and the eight absentees included Lady Northbrook. It ends with the meeting of 6 June 1945, when there were 20 members present, but just under half of this massive looking volume is empty; pages 286 to 602 are blank. The uncertainties of the political situation apart, the Committee was naturally concerned in May 1939 with the impending retirement of the Hospital's Chaplain, the suggestion that a new maternity unit could be formed out of what was the Matron's private office, and more immediately with the arrangements for the opening of the new Nurses' Home by the Duchess of Kent on 3 July 1939. The Letter Book of 1896 to 1948 (letters issued) is even less satisfactory. After only one page of letters written in 1896, great sections have been torn out, and a new section begun on 5 October 1946; the last seven letters 'in' were noted on 2 November 1948. Fortunately, other archive sources are more complete, including a series of Visitors' Books, and a collection of Press Cuttings, for what was happening in the Hospital was always of great interest to the local press. The so-called Committee of Management Book of 1944-8 is equally disappointing, since it is nothing else but an attendance register, simple lists of pencil signatures of those present and again more than half empty. It ends with the list for the final Quarterly Court of Governors on 29 June 1948, and the final Committee of Management on the same day, the one chaired by Sir George Cooper, the other by Brigadier Kemp Welch (5M 63/41). After the passing of the National Health Act in 1946, Governors and Committee continued to meet throughout 1947, until midsummer 1948.
2. Doctor C.B.S. Fuller, M.C., M.A. and M.R.C.P., Senior Honorary Physician.
3. Wayman, S.W., *With the Home Guard*, Warren and Son (1945), Chapter VI.
4. Rose, M., *King Alfred's College*, Phillimore (1981), 90-3.
5. For the School as a hospital, see Priscilla Bain's *St Swithun's: A Centenary History*, Phillimore (1984), p.49.

6. This is the theatre on the north front of the Butterfield building.

7. Jagger, due to retire as Honorary Radiologist in 1940, stayed on till he was nearly seventy, after 26 years of service.

7a. For the early history of the Mount as a sanitorium, see Drewitt, Arthur, *Eastleigh's Yesterdays*, Eastleigh Printing Works, 1935.

8. J.H. Bodington, M.A., M.E., M.R.C.S., L.R.C.P., D.A.

9. 5M 63/186.

CHAPTER XIII

1. *Collection.*

2. In contrast to 1985.

3. Treble Close, Oliver's Battery

4. The School was a potential source of supply for nursing staff.

5. The Ronald Knox Hostel, now demolished. A small plaque on the main front commemorates the erection of the canopy.

6. Doctor C.B.S. Fuller, Senior Physician at the Hospital since 1936 and a man who had joined the staff in 1928, retired in February 1962, and died three months later. He had been, in the words used by Doctor C.H. Wrigley at the Memorial Service in the Hospital chapel, 'a great servant of the Hospital ... no-one who had ever been his patient ever forgot him'. He had been particularly interested in the welfare of the nurses, and he and his wife were greatly loved in Winchester; he worked in the true tradition of the Hospital Household.

7. Inspired by the genius of Doctor Russell Grant.

8. The Mayor, Mrs Vera Charles, had called the first meeting in Abbey House.

9. Formerly the home of Admiral Waistell, at the top of St James' Lane.

10. See her *Diary*.

11. Doctor D. J. Bowen.

12. See his note.

13. Mr Peter Broom.

Bibliography

SOME PRINTED SOURCES

Thomson, Miss, *Memories of Viscountess Sundon, Mistress of the Robes to Queen Caroline*, (2 vols), 1847.

Trail, R. R., *The History of the Popular Medicine of England: the Fitz-Patrick Lectures*, 1964-5.

Rance, Adrian, *A Prospect of Winchester: Guide to the City Museum*, 1978.

Perry, Michael, *The Whole Duty of Man, in today's English*, Ark Publishing, 1980.

A Collection of Papers Relating to the County Hospital for Sick and Lame, etc., at Winchester, printed for J. & J. Pemberton at the Golden Buck in Fleet Street, London, 1737.

Russell, P. M. G., *A History of the Exeter Hospitals 1170-1948*, Exeter Post-Graduate Medical Centre, 1976.

Goodman, A. W. (ed.), *Winchester Cathedral Cartulary*, 1927.

Knowles, Dom David, *The Monastic Order in England 943-1216 A.D.*, Cambridge University Press, 1950.

Williams, J. F. (ed.), *Hampshire Church Warden's Accounts*, Wykeham Press, 1913.

Fox, Robert, *History of Godmanchester*, 1831.

Sedgewick, Romney (ed.), *Lord Hervey's Memoirs*, Kimber, (2nd edn.), 1952.

Deverell, John, *St John's Hospital and Other Charities in Winchester*, Davis & Son, Lincoln's Inn, 1870.

Winchester Quarterly Record, 1842-64.

Sadler, John, *Hampshire Directory*, The Square, Winchester, 1784.

Blore, G. H., *Some Wykehamists of the 18th Century*, privately published, 1944.

Boorman, W., *Provincial Hospital Pharmacy in Eighteenth Century England*, a paper read to the *Union Mondiale des Societies d'Histoire Pharmacentique* in Amsterdam, 1964. (See also *The Chemist and Druggist*, 10 October 1964.)

Hartsherne, Albert (ed.), *Memories of a Royal Chaplain, 1729-63; the Correspondence of Edmund Pyle, D.D. ... with Samuel Kerrick, D.D.*, The Bodley Head, 1905.

Holt-White, Rashleigh, *The Letters to Gilbert White of Selborne ... from the Rev. John Mulso*, R. H. Porter, London, 1906.

Laskin, Marganita, *Jane Austen and her World*, Thames and Hudson, 1969.

Garnier, A. E., *The Chronicles of the Garniers of Hampshire*, (includes the Parey family), Jarrold & Son, 1900.

Jenkins, Elizabeth, *Jane Austen*, Victor Gollanz, 1968.

Cope, Zachary, 'Jane Austen's Last Illness', *British Medical Journal*, 18 July 1964.

Coleridge, Christable, *Charlotte Mary Yonge*, Macmillan, 1903.

Gash, N., *Lord Liverpool*, Wiedenfeld and Nicholson, 1984.

Roddis, Louis H., *James Lind*, Schuman, New York, (n.d.).

The House of Commons, 1784-90, (Vol. II), Members, H.M.S.O, 1964.

Willis, A. J., *Winchester Settlement Papers, 1667-1742*, Lyminge, Folkestone, 1967.

Hampshire Allegations for Marriage Licences, (2 vols.), Harleian Society, 1892.

Wilkes, J., *Statutes and Constitutions of the Hampshire County Hospital*, Winchester, 1772.

White, A. (M.D., F.S.A.), 'The Effect of Different Kinds of Effluvia on Air', *Philosophical Transactions*, Vol. LXVII, 1178.

Newman, H. (Sanitary Inspector to the Corporation of Winchester), *Sanitary Reform: A lecture to the Mechanics Institute*, Hugh Barclay, Winchester, 1857.

Report of the Winchester Sewerage Enquiry Committee, Tanner and Son, City Cross, 1866.

Report of the Sub-Committee Investigating the Influence of Sewerage on Public Health

Report of House Visitaton Sub-Committee

Report of Sub-Committee on Sewerage in Other Towns

Letter from Rev. Doctor Ridding on Sewerage in Whichester (in reply to G. H. Pointer, reprint from *Hampshire Chronicle*, 31 May 1873.

Cole, Howard N., *The Story of Aldershot*, Southern Books (Aldershot) Limited, (2nd edn.), 1980.

Adams, H. C., *Wykehamica*, J. Wells, Winchester, 1878.

Lisle, J., 'Witham Close' in *St. Michael's Parish Magazine*, November 1893.

Furley, J. S., *Chernocke House*.

Webb, I.A., M., and C.J., *History of Chernocke Place, No 35 Southgate Street, Winchester*, published privately, 1980.

Vaughan, John, *Winchester Cathedral: Its Monuments and Memorials*, Selwyn and Blount, 1919.

Thompson, Paul, *William Butterfield*, Routledge, 1971.

Slessor, J. H., *Defence of the Matron*, privately printed, 1894.

Report of the Committee appointed to enquire into the state of the Heath of the Prisoners confined in the King's House at Winchester, and the Proceedings of the House (Parliament) therefrom, 1780.

Howard, John, *An Account of the Principal Lazarettoes in Europe and additional remarks made on the present state of those in Great Britain and Ireland*, (2nd edn.), London, 1791.

Lockyer, E. M., *Chilbolton Fragments*, (n.d.).

Mayo, C. H., *A Genealogical Account of the Mayo and Elton Families*, (2nd edn.), privately printed, 1908.

Crockford's Clerical Directory, (various years).

Peech, D. L., *The History of Hursley Park*, I.B.M. U.K. Laboratories, 1976.

Report of the Drainage Committee of the Royal Hampshire County Hospital, Warren & Son, 1879.

Wayman, S. W., *With the Home Guard*, Warren & Son, 1945.

Rose, Martial, *King Alfred's College*, Phillimore, 1981.

Bain, Priscilla, *St Swithun's: A Centenary History*, Phillimore, 1984.

Carpenter-Turner, Barbara, *Winchester 100 Years Ago*, Cave, 1980.

Stopher, Thomas, *St John's Hospital, Winchester: Notes on its history in the last half century*, Warren & Son, 1924.

Dictionary of National Biography.

Venn, J. A., *Alumni Cantabrigienses*.

Foster, Joseph, *Alumni Oxonienses*, (4 vols.), Oxford 1891-2.

Patterson, A. T., *Southampton*, Macmillan, 1979.

Patterson, A. T., *Portsmouth*.

Sylvester Davies, J., *Southampton*, Gilbert & Co., 1883.

Humbert, L. M., *The Hospital of St Cross*, W. Savage, Winchester, 1868.

Pesvner, N., *Hampshire and the Isle of Wight: Buildings of England*, David Lloyd.

Winchester Exhibition Catalogue, City Council, 1951.

Dock, L. L., and Stewart, J. M., *A Short History of Nursing*, 1931.

Carpenter Turner, Barbara, *Hampshire Hogs*, (2 vols.), Cave, 1977-8.

Winchester: Sixty Generations, City Council, 1955.

Willis, A. J., *Episcopal Deeds in the Diocese of Winchester*, (Typescript 19).

Gentleman's Magazine.

Blore, G. H., *Thomas Cheyney*, privately printed.

de Gray Birch, W. (ed.), *An Ancient Manuscript*, H.R.S., 1889.

Winchester Cathedral Records, 1932, (see Indices).

Seymer, L. R., *A General History of Nursing*, Faber & Faber Limited, (4th edn.), 1956.

Clarke-Kennedy, A. E., *The London: A Study in the Voluntary Hospital System, (Vol.I, 1740-1840)*, Pitman Medical Publishing Company Limited, 1962.

Logan Turner, A., *The Royal Infirmary of Edinburgh*, Oliver and Boyd, Edinburgh, 1927.

Woodham-Smith, Cecil, *Florence Nightingale*, Penguin Books, 1955.

O'Hara, Frances, 'Looking Back', *Hampshire*, September 1985.

The Hampshire Chronicle, 1772 – Continuing.

Salisbury and Winchester Journal, established 1729 as *Salisbury Journal* – Continuing.

Hampshire Observor – 1957.

Hampshire Herald, from 1823, later *Hampshire Advertiser*.

The Lancet.

Carpenter Turner, Barbara, *Winchester*, Cave, 1980.

Victoria County History of Hampshire, Vols. I-V, 1910.

The Winchester Guide, Anon, 1829.

Moody, Henry, *Notes and Essays*, 1851.

Notable Documents from Private Archives: an exhibition arranged by the Historic Manuscripts Commission, London, 1951.

Leach, A. F., *Winchester College*, Duckworth, 1899.

Winchester College Muniments, Warden and Fellows of Winchester College, (3 vols.), 1976-84.

Kirby, T. F., *Winchester Scholars*, Henry Froude, 1888.

Kirby, T. F., *Annals of Winchester College*, H & G Wells, Winchester, 1898.

Bailey, Charles, *Winchester City Archives*, 1856.

Spaul, J., *Andover*, BAS Printers Ltd., Over Wallop, Hampshire, 1977.

ORIGINAL SOURCES

The narrative history of the Hospital as outlined in this book is derived from three main sources, (1) the Minute Books of the Court of Governors, (2) the Proceedings of the (Weekly) Committee (sometimes with varied titles) and the printed (3) *Annual Reports* (incomplete). They are not referred to individually in the text; most are in very good condition. Though there are apparent gaps, (1) and (2) supplement each other, except for 1772, missing in both sets, and the Committee Minutes of 1808-12 (5m 63/13) include those of the Court of Governors.

(1) Court of Governors, 1736-1945. Seven volumes. Ends with 1932-45. (5m 63/7)

(2) Proceedings of the Committee, 1736-1948. Includes 9 April 1817 – October 1821, (5m 63/14) in poor condition.

(3) The *Annual Reports* (printed) have not survived as a complete series, probably because of the very fact that they had a wide distribution. The most substantial and complete group covers the years 1804 to 1850 (5m 63/199), a series, including loose reports from 1804-5; 1807-8; 1810; 1851; and one bound volume, 1942-7;the first surviving *Report* is that for the Hospital's second year and exists only because it was kept with the papers of the Jervoise family. N.B. The Hospital's 'year' varied.

Amongst the modern records of the Hospital the following items are particularly valuable:
Register of letters sent, 1896-1948 (5m 63/48)
Visitors' Book, 1895-1939 (5m 63/50)
Visitors' Book, 1920 (5m 63/51)
Visitors' Book, 1920-34 (5m 63/52)
Visitors' Book, 1934-9 (5m 63/53)
Visitors' Book, 1941-52 (5m 63/54)
Suckling paper, 5m 63/191
Dispensary Sub-Committee Book, 1855-99 (5m 63/55)
Matron's Report Book, 1895-1926 (5m 63/70)
Reports of Various Sub-Committees (5m 63/141)(Nightingale Home papers.)
Annual Reports, 1942-7 (5m 63/168), (5m 63/185-8)
Press Cuttings, 1900-26 (particularly reports on Medical Sub-Committee) (5m 63/57)
Press Cuttings, 1933-5 (badly damaged by water), (5m 63/179)
Press Cuttings, 1949-50 (5m 63/186-8)
Small Selection of Notes on Hospital History (5m 63/192)

After 1960, the Hospital ceased to issue an Annual Report. The following Reports are in the Hospital Library:
Winchester Group Hospital Management Committee; *Annual Reports*, 1954-60.
Winchester Group Hospital Management Committee; *Triennial Review*, April 1960-March 1963.
Winchester Group Hospital Management Committee; *Quadrennial Review*, April 1963-March 1967.
Winchester Group Hospital Management Committee; *Biennial Report*, April 1967-March 1969.

Other sources currently in the collection of the H.C.R.O. are referred to individually in the text,
   including:
Parish Registers, This list consists of the original volumes consulted before the Registers were assembled
   in the H.C.R.O.
Winchester, St Laurence: Marriages 1754-1814, Baptisms/Burials 1760-1804, Baptisms/Burials
   1804-12).
Winchester, St Maurice with St Peter Colebrook and St Mary Kalender: A long and virtually complete
   series beginning in 1538 and continuing in ten volumes until 1812.
Winchester, St Bartholomew: 1563-1704; 1704-76; 1777-89; 1789-1812.

For descriptive accounts for each parish, see *Parish and Non-Conformist Registers of Hampshire and the Isle of
   Wight*, Hampshire Archivists Group, 1984.
Probate Records in H.C.R.O. and P.R.O.
Wills, Inventories, and Admons.

Reminiscences, notes, etc. (with H.C.R.O. ref. nos.)
Miscellaneous Papers (187m 85/1)
Mrs V. E. Atchison, 1924-8 (187m 83/1)
Mrs L. Darling, 1910-4 (187m 83/1)
Report on the Hospital, 1820-31 (4m 52/161)
The Hospital First Century, 1836 (25m 617/7/23 and 26)
Miscellaneous Papers concerning the R.H.C.H. (44m 69 H2/6-12) and (44m 69 K2/5-9)
A Sermon preached at the Opening of the County Hospital 1736, and certain papers concerning the
   Hospital's government, published 1769 (169/484/W/19)
Jervoise Papers (4m 69 H2/6-12)

Items in the Winchester City Archives
The City Tarrage (W/E3/5)
Paving Commission (W/J/1/2 and 3)
Ordnance Books, Vols. VIII, IX, XII, XIII, XIV, XVI, XVII (W/B1/8 etc)
Small Pox Papers (E.48)
Trussel MSS
Winchester Census, 1841; 1851; (1881 in City Library); all on microfilm.
Blore, G. H., Biographical Notes (18th Century).
First Minute Book of the Winchester Water Company.
St Cross Hospital Muniments, St Cross Ledger Book.

Isle of Wight County Record Office
Oglander MSS (IOW C.R.O.) OG/2/616; OG/2/64; OG/2/67.

Archives of the Dean and Chapter of Winchester Cathedral.
Subscribers' Lists.
Ledger Books (alias Proceedings under the Common Seal), various dates.
Chapter Act Books, various dates.
Winchester Cathedral: Baptisms/Burials 1599-1812, Marriages 1603-1754. (see also notes of those
   buried in the Cathedral and in the Great Churchyard – D and C Archives.)
Winchester City Library, Thomas Stopher's Note Book, Thomas Stopher's Scrap Books.

Miscellaneous Items
Undertakers' Records (privately owned).
Deeds relating to the title to the site of the R.H.C.H. in Romsey Road.

British Library
Add.MSS 20102-5; 30516; (Sundon letters).
Add.MSS 6251; (Trippes' Letter Book).

Draft Unfinished Histories of the Hospital in Typescript, at R.H.C.H.
(1) Sinclair, A., *Pioneer Hospital*, 110pp. quarto. (Covers 1736-1759), and
(2) Trail, R. R., *The Royal Hampshire County Hospital 1736-1948*, 83pp. foolscap. (1968).

Index of Persons

Note: C.O.G. = Chairman of the Governors

Index of Places and Subjects